BUSINESS AND HUMAN RIGHTS

Beyond the End of the Beginning

The regulation of business in the global economy poses one of the main challenges for governance, as illustrated by the dynamic scholarly and policy debates about the UN Guiding Principles on Business and Human Rights and a possible international treaty on the matter. This book takes on the conceptual and legal underpinnings of global governance approaches to business and human rights, with an emphasis on the Guiding Principles (GPs) and attention to the current treaty process. Analyses of the GPs have tended to focus on their static dimension, such as the standards they include, rather than on their capacity to change, to push the development of new norms and practices that might go beyond the initial content of the GPs and improve corporate compliance with human rights. This book engages both the static and dynamic dimensions of the GPs, and considers the issue through the eyes of scholars and practitioners from different parts of the world.

César Rodríguez-Garavito is Executive Director of the Center for Law, Justice, and Society (Dejusticia), and director of the Global Justice and Human Rights program at the University of the Andes (Colombia). He is the founding director of the Human Rights Lab and codirector of the Global School on Socioeconomic Rights. He writes a weekly op-ed for the Colombian newspaper El Espectador.

Business and Human Rights

BEYOND THE END OF THE BEGINNING

EDITED BY

CÉSAR RODRÍGUEZ-GARAVITO

Dejusticia & University of the Andes

CAMBRIDGE
UNIVERSITY PRESS

University Printing House, Cambridge CB2 8BS, United Kingdom

One Liberty Plaza, 20th Floor, New York, NY 10006, USA

477 Williamstown Road, Port Melbourne, VIC 3207, Australia

4843/24, 2nd Floor, Ansari Road, Daryaganj, Delhi – 110002, India

79 Anson Road, #06–04/06, Singapore 079906

Cambridge University Press is part of the University of Cambridge.

It furthers the University's mission by disseminating knowledge in the pursuit of education, learning, and research at the highest international levels of excellence.

www.cambridge.org
Information on this title: www.cambridge.org/9781107175297
DOI: 10.1017/9781316797990

First published 2017

Printed in the United States of America by Sheridan Books, Inc.

A catalogue record for this publication is available from the British Library.

ISBN 978-1-107-17529-7 Hardback

Contents

Contributors

Larry Catá Backer is the W. Richard and Mary Eshelman Faculty Scholar and professor of law and international affairs at Pennsylvania State University. His research focuses on governance-related issues of globalization and the constitutional theories of public and private governance, with a focus on institutional frameworks for public-private law governance systems. Recent work focuses on issues of corporate social responsibility, mixed regulatory systems and regulatory governance, the emerging problems of polycentricity where multiple systems might be simultaneously applied to a single issue or event, and problems of translation between Western and Marxist-Leninist (especially Chinese) constitutional systems. He teaches courses in corporate law, transnational law, and international organizations. His publications include *Lawyers Making Meaning* (2013) and *Signs in Law, A Source Book* (2014) (both with Jan M. Broekman), casebooks, *Elements of Law and the U.S: Legal System* (2017), *Law and Religion* (2015, with Frank Ravitch), *Comparative Corporate Law* (2002), *Harmonizing Law in an Era of Globalization* (editor, 2007), and a number of articles and contributions to published collections of essays. His work, especially on Chinese constitutional law and corporate social responsibility, has been translated into Chinese.

Louis Bickford is the CEO of MEMRIA, a social enterprise which develops partnerships with organizations to collect, analyze, and circulate narrative accounts of past violence with the aim of strengthening human rights. From 2012–2017, he managed the Global Human Rights program at the Ford Foundation. Before that, he worked at the International Centre for Transitional Justice (ICTJ), where he was among the founding staff members and where he developed work on memory and accountability in countries as diverse as Bosnia, Cambodia, Canada, Ghana, Morocco, and Peru, among others. He later worked at RFK Human Rights as a member of the executive leadership team, and as the director of the European office. He has consulted with various national and international institutions including the United Nations and various philanthropic foundations in every world region. Bickford is also an adjunct professor at Columbia University and NYU, where he teaches regular graduate seminars on human rights. He has a

PhD from McGill University and an MA from the New School, both in Political Science.

Surya Deva is an associate professor at the School of Law of the City University of Hong Kong, and a member of the UN Working Group on Business and Human Rights. Deva's primary research interests lie in business and human rights, India-China constitutional law, and sustainable development. He has published extensively in these areas, and has advised UN bodies, states, multinational corporations, and civil society organizations on issues concerning business and human rights. His books include *Socio-Economic Rights in Emerging Free Markets: Comparative Insights from India and China* (editor) (Routledge, 2015); *Human Rights Obligations of Business: Beyond the Corporate Responsibility to Respect?* (coeditor with David Bilchitz) (CUP, 2013); *Confronting Capital Punishment in Asia: Human Rights, Politics, Public Opinion and Practices* (coeditor with Roger Hood) (OUP, 2013); and *Regulating Corporate Human Rights Violations: Humanizing Business* (Routledge, 2012). He is one of the founding editors-in-chief of the *Business and Human Rights Journal* (CUP), and sits on the editorial/advisory board of the *Netherlands Quarterly of Human Rights*, and the *Vienna Journal on International Constitutional Law*. In 2014, Deva was elected a member of the executive committee of the International Association of Constitutional Law.

Chris Jochnick is president and CEO of Landesa, a global organization dedicated to strengthening land rights for the rural poor. He has worked for three decades on issues of human rights, development, and corporate responsibility, including seven years in Latin America. Prior to Landesa, Jochnick led and built Oxfam America's private sector team, managing both partnerships with, and adversarial campaigns targeting, Fortune 500 companies. He cofounded and led two human rights organizations, the Center for Economic and Social Rights (NY) and the Centro de Derechos Economicos y Sociales (Ecuador). He also worked as an attorney with the Wall Street law firm of Paul, Weiss, Rifkind, Wharton, and Garrison. Jochnick is a former fellow of the MacArthur Foundation and the Echoing Green Foundation. He is a graduate of Harvard Law School, where he teaches a course on business and human rights.

Juana Kweitel is executive director of Conectas Human Rights. She has a master's in international human rights law from the University of Essex, United Kingdom, and in political science from the University of Sao Paulo. She holds a postgraduate degree in human rights and democratic transition from the University of Chile, and a JD from the University of Buenos Aires (UBA). She serves on the board of trustees of Global Witness, the Brazil Human Rights Fund, and the advisory board of Open Global Rights. She is a member of the Assembly of Partners of the Center for Legal and Social Studies (CELS, Argentina) and of the Developments in the Field Panel of the Business and Human Rights Journal, published by the Cambridge University Press.

Bonita Meyersfeld is a human rights lawyer and academic. She is the director of the Centre for Applied Legal Studies and an associate professor at Wits Law School. She is an editor and chair of the board of the South African Journal on Human Rights and the founding member and chair of the board of Lawyers against Abuse. Meyersfeld obtained her LLB (cum laude) from Wits and her masters and doctorate in law from Yale Law School. She teaches and publishes in the areas of international law, business and human rights, women's rights and international criminal law. She is the author of the book, *Domestic Violence and International Law*. Prior to Wits, she worked in human rights law in the House of Lords. She has presented expert statements to various UN fora and was appointed by the Government of Ecuador as part of a five-member expert panel to provide guidance to the Inter-Governmental Working Group on a binding instrument for business and human rights.

Amol Mehra, Esq. is the executive director of the International Corporate Accountability Roundtable, a coalition of leading human rights, development, labor, and environmental organizations working to ensure businesses respect human rights in their global operations.

Tara J. Melish is professor of law at the University of Buffalo School of Law, SUNY, and director of the Buffalo Human Rights Center. A graduate of Brown University and Yale Law School, she has worked in the UN Department of Economic and Social Affairs, as United Nations representative of Disability Rights International, staff attorney at the Center for Justice and International Law, and legal advisor or consultant to a range of national and international human rights organizations. Specializing in strategic rights-based advocacy and litigation, she teaches in the Global School on Socio-Economic Rights, works locally on incorporating human rights principles and methodologies into city policymaking, and writes broadly in the areas of economic, social and cultural rights, human rights enforcement strategies, disability rights, transitional justice, the inter-American human rights system, and participatory approaches to bridging the governance gaps in the business and human rights context. Following graduation, she clerked on the US Court of Appeals for the Ninth Circuit and received professional fellowships from the John D. and Catherine T. MacArthur Foundation, the Fulbright Foundation, and the Orville H. Schell, Jr. Center for International Human Rights.

César Rodríguez-Garavito is executive director and cofounder of the Center for Law, Justice, and Society (Dejusticia), an international action-research human rights center based in Colombia. He is the founding director of the Human Rights Lab and the program on global justice at the University of the Andes. He has been a visiting professor at Stanford University, Brown University, the University of Pretoria (South Africa), American University in Cairo, Central European University, and the Getulio Vargas Foundation (Brazil). He is a board member of WITNESS, the Business and Human Rights Resource Center, *OpenGlobalRights* and the

Business & Human Rights Journal. He has been an adjunct judge of the Constitutional Court of Colombia, and writes a weekly op-ed for *El Espectador*. He holds a PhD and an MS (sociology) from University of Wisconsin-Madison, an MA from NYU's Institute for Law and Society, an MA (Philosophy) from the National University of Colombia, and a JD from University of the Andes. His recent publications include *Radical Deprivation on Trial: The Impact of Judicial Activism on Socioeconomic Rights in the Global South* (CUP, coauthor), *Compliance with Socioeconomic Rights Judgments* (CUP, coed.), and "The Future of Human Rights: From Gatekeeping to Symbiosis" (*Sur* Journal).

John Gerard Ruggie is the Berthold Beitz Professor in Human Rights and International Affairs at Harvard's Kennedy School of Government and affiliated professor in international legal studies at Harvard Law School. He has received numerous awards for his scholarship, including a Guggenheim Fellowship, and is a Fellow of the American Academy of Arts & Sciences. From 1997–2001 he served in the UN Administration of Kofi Annan as assistant secretary-general for strategic planning. His responsibilities included overseeing the creation of the UN Global Compact and the Millennium Development Goals, as well as leading Annan's institutional reform efforts and liaising with the US government. From 2005–2011 he served as special representative of the secretary-general for business and human rights, in which capacity he produced the UN Guiding Principles on Business and Human Rights. His book reflecting on that experience, *Just Business: Multinational Corporations and Human Rights* (W.W. Norton), has been translated into Chinese, Japanese, Korean, Portuguese, and Spanish. A previous book, *Constructing the World Polity*, contributed to the establishment of the social constructivist approach to the study of international relations.

Claret Vargas is a researcher and director of internationalization at the Center for the Study of Law, Justice and Society (Dejusticia), an international global south NGO based in Colombia. Before joining Dejusticia she served as executive director at the Stanford Human Rights Center. Vargas's research focuses on the design of effective implementation mechanism in business and human rights and in the context of strategic litigation. Her advocacy work includes alien tort statue litigation, the inter-American system, and the intersection of corporate responsibility, environmental degradation and human rights. She is currently completing a textbook on the inter-American system, written jointly with Professor James Cavallaro and other inter-American system experts. She earned her BA in social studies, and MA and PhD in Latin American literature from Harvard University. She holds a JD from Harvard Law School. She clerked for the Honorable Mark L. Wolf, former Chief Judge of the United States District Court for the District of Massachusetts. She has also worked with the Centro de Estudios Legales y Sociales (CELS) in Argentina and was a legal fellow at the Center for Justice and Accountability (CJA).

Acknowledgments

This book is the result of several years of collective work, not only of the authors of the different chapters, but also of three institutions and groups of people that made possible the research and action project that led to this volume. The Center for Law, Justice and Society (Dejusticia), a human rights research and advocacy organization based in Bogota, Colombia, was the home base of the project and provided much of the intellectual and organizational impetus for the book. I am particularly grateful to Dejusticia members who have staffed our business and human rights area (Meghan Morris, Sean Luna, Claret Vargas, and Tatiana Andia) for their superb research assistance and key contribution to establishing Dejusticia's voice in the global discussion on business and human rights. The Watson Institute for International and Public Affairs at Brown University was the ideal partner institution in the project. As part of the South-North Dialogue Series co-sponsored by Brown and Dejusticia, Peter Evans and I organized the workshop where the draft versions of the book's chapters were presented and discussed. With his unparalleled mix of altruism, intellectual acuity, and enthusiasm, Peter has been a source of unconditional encouragement and support over the years, and participated in every aspect of the conception and execution of the workshop. At Brown, the generous support of Rick Locke (then director of the Watson Institute) and Patrick Heller also proved essential to the success of the workshop. The Ford Foundation generously sponsored Dejusticia's international program, of which this book is a result. At Ford, Martín Abregú and Louis Bickford have been thought partners through the years and provided essential encouragement to new research and advocacy on business and human rights and other emerging fields.

During the production of the manuscript, Sean Luna and Celeste Kauffman provided outstanding editorial support. At Cambridge University Press, the advice and support of John Berger, two anonymous reviewers, and Malcolm Langford as co-editor of the Globalization and Human Rights Series encouraged me to improve, expand, and update the original manuscript.

To all of them, my deepest thanks and appreciation.

César Rodríguez-Garavito

Introduction: A Dialogue Across Divides in the Business and Human Rights Field

César Rodríguez-Garavito

As business and human rights (BHR) has evolved into a global field of research and practice over the last two decades, it has tended to operate at two clearly recognizable levels. On the one hand, a wealth of international regulatory initiatives – from UN norms and guiding principles to industry-specific codes of conduct to regional standards – has produced a veritable global "regime complex,"[1] in which highly diverse regulations and institutions coexist without a coordinating node or an overarching set of principles. The regime complex includes a wide range of regulations and institutions, from the hard law global and regional organizations have adopted (such as the UN, the EU, and the WTO) to soft law initiatives groups of states (such as the OECD's guidelines on conflict minerals and human rights) and private bodies (such as the codes of conduct adopted by individual corporations or transnational business associations) have undertaken.

What they have in common is their location in the field. Whether "soft law" or "hard law," such top-down, norm-making, and norm-implementation processes have remained largely confined to traditional centers of power, from Geneva (as in the case of the UN standards), to Washington (as in the case of industry codes such as the Fair Labor Association), to Paris (as in the case of the OECD Guidelines for Multinational Enterprises). Mirroring its object of study, international law and global governance scholarship on BHR has focused on theoretical and legal arguments in defense of different global regulatory approaches.[2]

On the other hand, myriad communities along with local and national organizations around the world engage in campaigns, litigation, negotiations, and information politics aimed at preventing and redressing corporate violations of human rights. Whether efforts to regulate pharmaceutical companies' patent rights so as

---

[1] Robert Keohane and David Victor, "The Regime Complex for Climate Change," *Perspectives on Politics* 9 (1) (2011).

[2] For useful examples of this approach, see Jena Martin and Karen Bravo (eds.), *The Business and Human Rights Landscape: Moving Forward, Looking Back* (Cambridge: Cambridge University Press, 2016); Surya Deva and David Bilchitz (eds.), *Human Rights Obligations of Business Beyond the Corporate Responsibility to Respect?* (Cambridge: Cambridge University Press, 2013).

to make essential medicines accessible, peoples' tribunals aimed at protecting indigenous peoples' lands in the face of extractive economies' expansion into their territories, or new waves of transnational antisweatshop campaigning, such bottom-up corporate accountability strategies rarely draw on the global standards that dominate the attention of global governance analysts and practitioners. Rather than legal analysis, empirical sociolegal research tends to dominate the scholarly literature on these bottom-up initiatives.[3]

The contrast between these two locations in the BHR field is clear to those who circulate between them, including several contributors to this volume.[4] It has certainly been patent in my experience as a scholar-practitioner. The dominant debates at the UN level – such as those on the implementation of the UN Guiding Principles on Business and Human Rights (GPs) and the future of the ongoing discussion within the intergovernmental working group tasked by the UN Council with developing a treaty on BHR – do feel oftentimes a world away from litigation, campaigning or fieldwork on human rights violations stemming from corporate practices in indigenous territories in Colombia, Central American sweatshops, Indian tea plantations, or policy debates regarding intellectual property rights and access to medicines in the Americas.[5]

Against this background, the idea behind this collective volume is threefold. First, participants and topics were chosen so as to foster dialogue, reflection, and circulation between the aforementioned two levels, in order to contribute to increasing the collective capacity of the BHR field to regulate, prevent, and effectively remedy human rights abuses related to corporate activity. Thus, contributors include scholars, practitioners, and scholar-practitioners who explicitly engaged with each other both in their chapters and the workshop that led to this volume. Second, given the intense (and sometimes acerbic) debates between different approaches within the field, the workshop and the book brought together analysts and practitioners espousing diverging views with regard to both theoretical issues – such as the conceptual underpinnings of the UN Guiding Principles and of proposals for a binding treaty – and practical trade-offs – such as which next international regulatory steps would be most effective for protecting human rights, as well as viable in light of current and

[3] See, for instance, Boaventura de Sousa Santos and César Rodríguez-Garavito, *Law and Globalization from Below: Towards a Cosmopolitan Legality* (Cambridge: Cambridge University Press, 2005).
[4] See, for instance, Jochnik (Chapter 7), Kweitel (Chapter 10), and Mehra (Chapter 8).
[5] César Rodríguez-Garavito, "Ethnicity.gov: Global Governance, Indigenous Peoples and the Right to Prior Consultation in Social Minefields," *Indiana Journal of Global Legal Studies* (Winter, 2011); César Rodríguez-Garavito, "Global Governance and Labor Rights: Codes of Conduct and Anti-Sweatshop Struggles in Global Apparel Factories in Mexico and Guatemala," *Politics & Society* 33 (2005); César Rodríguez-Garavito, "Empowered Participatory Jurisprudence: Experimentation, Deliberation and Norms in Socioeconomic Rights Adjudication," in Katharine Young (ed.), *The Future of Economic and Social Rights* (Cambridge: Cambridge University Press, 2017); Rochelle Dreyfuss and César Rodríguez-Garavito (eds.), *Balancing Wealth and Health: Global Administrative Law and the Battle over Intellectual Property and Access to Medicines in Latin America* (Oxford: Oxford University Press, 2014).

foreseeable future geopolitical circumstances. As readers will note, contributors accepted this challenge by engaging each other – sometimes wholeheartedly agreeing, sometimes sharply disagreeing – and making an explicit effort to explain what they see as the right conceptual frames and regulatory strategies. Third, in order to counter the dominance of Global North voices in the scholarly debate on BHR, the discussion and the book include authors from or with a long experience of working in the Global South.

Given the wide diversity of regulations and institutions in the BHR field, this dialogue was possible only by narrowing down the focus of discussion. Interestingly for the theory and practice of human rights and global governance, BHR has been the subject of one of the most explicit efforts to restructure a regime complex in order to provide it with a focal point and "orchestration" mechanisms. As he explains in Chapter 2, John Ruggie led the development of the UN GPs with these purposes in mind. The GPs were explicitly inspired in models of polycentric and experimental global governance. The UN Human Rights Council endorsed them in 2011 at the end of Ruggie's mandate as the UN Secretary-General's Special Representative on Business and Human Rights (SRSG), and have since been gradually adopted by public and private regulatory institutions; from the OECD, to national governments and business associations.

In his final report to the Human Rights Council, the SRSG noted that the GPs were not intended to be the final word on the regulation of business, but rather "the end of the beginning: by establishing a common global platform for action, on which cumulative progress can be built, step-by-step, without foreclosing any other promising longer-term developments." Keeping this in mind, I argue in Chapter 1 that scholars and practitioners should evaluate the conceptual and empirical achievements and limitations of the GPs not only in terms of their static dimension (such as the content of the standards they include), but also in terms of their dynamic dimension (such as their capacity to push the development of new norms and practices that might go beyond the initial content of the GPs and improve corporate compliance with human rights).

This book is a collective effort by BHR scholars and practitioners from different parts of the world to take stock of the static and dynamic dimensions of the GPs and the broader theoretical, legal, and policy debates and initiatives they have sparked. To that end, the book combines conceptual analysis and empirical work. From a conceptual standpoint, it brings to the surface the theoretical underpinnings of the heated debate around the GPs and other approaches to BHR. From an empirical standpoint, several contributions to the book examine whether, in practice, the GPs' orchestration mechanisms and regulatory incentives are taking the practice of BHR beyond the "end of the beginning," that is, whether there is early evidence of rule convergence and dissemination of better state and corporate practices with regard to human rights. Given that, by design, the GP framework is polycentric, contributors examine its implementation through multiple channels, from the practices of individual businesses or sector-based business associations to the Working Group on the Issue of Human Rights and Transnational Corporations and Other Business Enterprises, the official channel established by the UN for the specific purpose of disseminating and implementing the GPs.

THE STRUCTURE AND CONTENTS OF THE BOOK

This volume is the result of an organized collective effort, guided by a common set of questions. It stemmed from a conference coconvened by the Center for Law, Justice, and Society (Dejusticia, Colombia) and Brown University's Watson Institute for International Studies in March 2014. At the conference, held at Brown University, contributors presented the first drafts of their chapters, and engaged in a two-day discussion of their texts and broader debates on BHR. They subsequently revised the original papers in light of the workshop's discussions.

To strengthen the coherence of the volume and the focus of the discussion, the book's editor authored a chapter that served as the background paper of the workshop and the volume (Chapter 1). Contributors engage to different extents, from different angles, and with very diverse levels of agreement or disagreement with the background chapter and with each other.

The book has two organizing themes. Part One discusses the intersection between global governance and BHR. Chapters in this section explore the conceptual and legal underpinnings of global governance and human rights approaches to BHR, with an emphasis on the GPs, but also including the current efforts at the UN level to develop a binding treaty on the matter. Part Two provides more empirical and grounded accounts of how these different governance arrangements work in practice, again with an emphasis on the GPs: how their stakeholders can be spurred into action, which institutions can serve as orchestrators, and what sorts of initiatives can ensure transnational norm-uptaking and compliance.

Rodríguez-Garavito's Chapter 1 opens the first part of the book. He takes as his point of departure the analytical distinction between integrated and polycentric approaches to regulation, as developed by global governance theorists over the last two decades. While endorsing the GP's polycentric, experimentalist approach, he criticizes the weakness of civil society participation in the GP's design, as well as in its implementation by the WG. He proposes institutional mechanisms embodying an "empowered participatory" approach to the work of the WG, as well as a range of alternatives regarding the content and scope of the emerging binding treaty at the UN level that, while building on the GPs and being politically feasible, would go beyond and improve upon the GPs' normative content and actual impact on the ground.

In Chapter 2, John Ruggie's revisits the GPs and the logic behind them, with particular attention to the work of aligning distinct governance systems that influence corporate conduct, and providing the basis upon which these systems can play a mutually reinforcing role and compensate for each other's weaknesses. He collects and explains the significance of some of the most salient examples of the GPs being taken up at all levels, showing, by example, how implementation through distributed networks has begun to bear tangible fruit. He then turns to two concerns regarding the GPs that must be addressed in order to push forward implementation: civil society participation, and the push for international legalization of the business and human rights agenda. He addresses the treaty process and the obstacles it faces, and makes the case for principled pragmatism and redoubling efforts to implement the GPs regardless of the outcome of the treaty process in the long term.

Surya Deva (Chapter 3) questions the line of division between the dynamic and static dimensions of the background chapter and argues that the static dimension frames (and potentially limits) the reach of the dynamic dimension of the GPs. It also suggests that an "either or" view of the treaty and the GPs is not characteristic of keen observers of the BHR arena, who favor both sets of tools. The chapter analyzes what ought to be the role of international law in addressing governance gaps and considers the friction between core corporate principles and fundamental requirements for the protection of human rights, arguing that companies should have the duty to respect, protect and fulfill human rights. Deva's chapter argues for a move away from overly state-centric answers and which will be undermined by states' failures to enforce human rights norms. He closes by proposing the adoption of a Declaration on the Human Rights Obligations of Business that would provide normative basis for why companies have such rights obligations and clarify their extent and implementation mechanism.

In Chapter 4, Tara Melish argues for a reframing of the GPs debate, moving away from ordering competing visions along an experimentalist versus command-and-control spectrum and toward a discussion of competing theories of how social change or system transformation can best be achieved. Melish argues that, from a human rights viewpoint, approaches underlying initiatives such as the GPs reveal a top-down structure in decision-making, and argues that they contemplate no power shift. She views efforts toward the adoption of a treaty as calls to remedy these weaknesses and to reinforce global expressive commitments to human rights in the context of corporate activities. Melish proposes the inclusion of a fourth "participate" pillar into the GPs, as well as a simultaneous push for a treaty in the model of the UN Convention on the Rights of Persons with Disabilities, for this treaty is flexible, but has expressive commitments, embeds participants' rights, and specifies states' obligations.

From a viewpoint that stands in contrast with those of Deva and Melish, Larry Catá Backer (Chapter 5) argues that a call for a binding treaty must be resisted; instead, the polycentric character of the BHR field must be reinforced and deepened. In order for polycentric governance to work, he argues, there is a need for a central orchestration mechanism that interprets transnational normative governance instruments, including the GPs, and further argues that representative civil society organizations must have the ability to bring cases and advocate before such an interpretive body. Backer justifies his proposal historically first, outlining the evolution of a trend toward building integrated metagovernance orders (the GPs being a prime example of such an order) and the trend toward the abstraction of the individual, the rise of mass movements, and the rise of civil society as the figure that protects individual dignity. The chapter points to recent lost opportunities by the WG to take on the role of a quasi-judicial body empowered to interpret the GPs and proposes a path to move in that direction.

In the closing chapter of Part One, Claret Vargas inquires into the central concerns that animate civil society and communities' support for a binding treaty on BHR and considers whether and how binding human rights treaties have been found to address similar concerns in other contexts. She examines the work that a treaty can do to reduce the implementation gap, as compared to a nonbinding instrument, and identifies factors that tend to improve the implementation of human rights treaties. Vargas considers whether those factors exist or can be activated in the GPs implementation processes and concludes that it may be less helpful to think of these agreements as part of a binary of hard and soft law instruments. Instead, she argues that it is more helpful to view these two types of instruments as located in a continuum of agreements, with those with the most access to tools that facilitate implementation on one end, and those with the least at the other end. She presents some case studies and makes recommendations for more effective implementation of BHR norms, whether in the treaty context or in the GPs implementation context.

Switching to a focus on BHR practice, in Chapter 7, Chris Jochnik focuses on the issue of shifting power and uses a specific measuring stick for progress: does it affect the day-to-day circumstances and capacities of people on the ground? The chapter distinguishes two sectors and approaches within the BHR field: Human Rights (top-down, engaging the global human rights architecture) and human rights (bottom-up, seeking to empower local stakeholders and movements). While acknowledging that this framework simplifies several issues, Jochnick uses it to illustrate the reasons for the pushback and disappointment in all top-down regulatory processes on the part of civil society organizations and communities and to look at the tensions through the lens of power. While questioning the capacity of the GPs to address power differentials, this chapter places similar doubt on the capacity of a treaty, ensconced in the UN system as it is, to address issues of power any more effectively. Jochnick concludes by exploring the spaces where progress can be made, including grassroots mobilization, empowering advocates, and strengthening institutional support for corporate accountability at the national level.

In Chapter 8, Amol Mehra recognizes the layered complexity and diversity of business enterprises, and argues that advocates must be creative and systematic: creative in developing models that push businesses to respect human rights, and systematic in the use of the full panoply of avenues and tools that are currently available to advocates. He highlights tools and levers beyond sanctioning harmful behavior. Mehra begins by emphasizing the nature of the GPs as a floor upon which stakeholders must build up and proposes to look beyond the WG to address implementation gaps. He highlights the wide range of international, regional, and national standards that can be used to embed respect for human rights in the practices of businesses. He also argues for developing preventative measures along-side remedial measures, and for a better understanding of the particular challenges of litigating against corporations in specific contexts. Mehra's chapter concludes by arguing for an "always in all ways" approach to implementing human rights norms in the business context.

In Chapter 9, Louis Bickford's considers how the field of BHR will move to its next level of impact. Drawing on social movement literature, the chapter argues that international norms and standards that undergird the field of business and human rights, including the GPs, have generated a coherent set of "external symbols" that can serve human rights advocates in the work of developing a global frame. Indeed, while advocates have already begun using the external symbols to demand better accountability of corporate actors, Bickford argues that a wider swath of civil society organizations – from NGOs to universities – can contribute to legitimize and give heft to the standards that the GPs capture and contribute to the work of framing. The chapter then presents two additional angles to engage the GPs and their implementation: political opportunity structures, as well as organized action and how NGOs can help build frame resonance globally and in specific societies.

In Chapter 10, Juana Kweitel considers the avenues currently available to advocate for a more effective regulatory environment on business and human rights. Kweitel reviews the treaty proposal, and, in particular, the participation of organizations and "nontraditional players" in processes in Geneva for the first time and provides an assessment of both the potential and risks that the process carries. The chapter offers a similarly exacting analysis of the GPs and the performance of the WG in its early work, and turns to outline the ways in which human rights organizations should re-engage in monitoring the WG, and underscores five priorities for CSOs' work in business and human rights: documenting violations, campaigning, litigation, new tools for GP enforcement at the national level, and new coalitions.

Bonita Meyersfeld opens Chapter 11 with an analysis of structural flaws in the architecture of the GPs. It compares the ideal implementation of the GPs with the realities on the ground, for example, the vulnerabilities of states with high levels of poverty and incentives to lower regulatory protections in order to attract investment. Meyersfeld also examines the design flaws in the construction of the GPs, and the multiple forms of exclusion during consultations, brought on by practical reasons, but resulting in the lack of consultation of people living in poverty. She argues that, in order to address structural flaws, the players must be disaggregated and the diagnosis of the harms to be addressed must be more accurate. Symptoms of the harm, such as the Bhopal gas leak case in India, are more visible, but the harm, as Meyersfield argues, is one of economic hegemony where poverty is not viewed as a human rights violation. The chapter then proposes two specific approaches to address the BHR problem successfully: regional alliances and a reassessment of the value of human labor.

The book closes with a concluding, prospective commentary by César Rodríguez-Garavito about BHR as a field of research and practice. From an external point of view, that of observers interested in a sociological understanding of a field, he begins by characterizing BHR in terms of the conceptual, normative, and strategic positions that are at play in it. He conceives BHR as an emerging field whose analytical and practical boundaries are still being actively contested, with different actors offering contrasting frames to understand and influence regulatory frameworks such as GPs and a potential binding treaty. Rodríguez-Garavito further argues that BHR can be viewed as an illustration of broader discussions about transformation of human rights at large. He closes by proposing an ecosystemic conception of BHR, one that embraces the rich diversity of strategies and frames within the field, and that strives to create synergies among them and with other social justice fields concerned with corporate accountability.

PART I

Global Governance meets Business and Human Rights

Conceptual Debates and Regulatory Alternatives

1

Business and Human Rights: Beyond the End of the Beginning

César Rodríguez-Garavito[*]

One of the main challenges for human rights and governance today is the regulation of business in the global economy. The challenge is to close the gap between transnational economic processes, on the one hand, and the regulation of state and corporate duties and responsibilities, on the other, in order to protect, respect, and fulfill human rights in the context of corporate activity and ensure accountability for violations.

The UN Guiding Principles on Business and Human Rights (GPs) were developed in order to help close this regulatory gap. The Human Rights Council adopted the GPs in 2011, at the end of John Ruggie's mandate as the UN Secretary-General's Special Representative on Business and Human Rights (SRSG). In his final report to the Human Rights Council, the SRSG noted that the GPs were not intended to be the final word on the regulation of business, but rather "the end of the beginning: by establishing a common global platform for action, on which cumulative progress can be built, step-by-step, without foreclosing any other promising longer-term developments."[1]

Keeping this in mind, the achievements and limitations of the GPs should be evaluated both conceptually and empirically not only in terms of their *static dimension* (such as the content of the foundational and operative standards they include), but also in terms of their *dynamic dimension* (such as their capacity to push the development of new norms and practices that go beyond the initial content of the GPs and improve companies' compliance with human rights standards). Since the adoption of the GPs and the establishment of the Working Group (WG) charged with implementing them, the debate in academic, advocacy, and policy circles has focused on the static dimension of the GPs. For example, the growing academic literature on the issue consists in large part of analyses of the language, conceptual foundations, and scope of the GPs as adopted by the UN, along with historical

---

[*] I gratefully acknowledge Meghan Morris for her crucial support and contribution to the project that led to this chapter. I also thank Sean Luna, Tatiana Andia, and Claret Vargas for outstanding research support.
[1] Par 13. A/HRC/17/31

accounts of the SRSG mandate.[2] There is a similar emphasis in advocacy circles, which can be noted in controversies that unfolded during the SRSG mandate and have since reemerged (for example, around the desirability of a binding treaty regarding corporate human rights obligations) and that continue to inform the critical stances toward the GPs of a significant number of human rights NGOs.

Although these retrospective debates have scholarly and practical importance, in this chapter, I focus on the dynamic dimension of the GPs. My emphasis here is on what has unfolded after the adoption of the GPs, as well as on what should unfold in the future, in order to enable the business and human rights field as a whole to effectively contribute to the protection of rights-holders on the ground.[3]

From this prospective point of view, and using the notion that the GPs are only the "end of the beginning" as an entry point, I analyze their potential to generate "cumulative progress," examining the steps that have been taken and that would need to be taken in order to make their promise to advance "step-by-step" a reality. I also discuss whether, in practice, they have opened or closed spaces for "other promising longer-term developments" in the business and human rights (BHR) field.

In assessing the GPs, I view them as one component of a global "regime complex"[4] that regulates corporations' duties and responsibilities with regard to human rights. As I argue in the concluding chapter of this volume, the human rights field in general, and the BHR in particular, have become considerably more plural, as new actors, strategies, and types of regulations proliferate in a more multipolar and interconnected world.[5] Thus, I propose to view the BHR field as an ecosystem where different actors, regulatory models, and political strategies coexist, rather than as a vertically integrated, law-centered global system.[6] Although I focus on the GPs, my analysis of their potential and limitations is made against the background of that ecosystem, in which the GPs coexist with other soft-law and hard-law standards and are mobilized, appropriated, and contested by a wide array of actors, from states and corporations to grassroots communities, NGOs, and transnational advocacy networks.

---

[2]   See, among many others, the contributions in Radu Mares (ed.), *Business and Human Rights at a Crossroads: The Legacy of John Ruggie* (Leiden: Martinus Nijhoff, 2011); Surya Deva and David Bilchitz (eds.), *Human Rights Obligations of Business Beyond the Corporate Responsibility to Respect?* (Cambridge: Cambridge University Press, 2013).

[3]   While the retrospective trend I describe has not ended, recent scholarship has seen a growing body of work that engage with the dynamic aspects of the GPs. See, for example, Jena Martin and Karen E. Bravo (eds.), *The Business and Human Rights Landscape* (Cambridge: Cambridge University Press, 2015); Damiano de Felice, "Business and Human Rights Indicators to Measure the Corporate Responsibility to Respect: Challenges and Opportunities," *Human Rights Quarterly* 37, no. 2 (2015), 511–555.

[4]   Robert Keohane and David Victor, "The Regime Complex for Climate Change," *Perspectives on Politics* 9 (1) (2011).

[5]   See also César Rodríguez-Garavito, "The Future of Human Rights: From Gatekeeping to Symbiosis," *SUR International Journal of Human Rights* 20 (2015).

[6]   Ibid.

This chapter combines conceptual analysis and empirical work. From a conceptual standpoint, I posit that the intense debates around the GPs are representative of a broader, ongoing discussion in academic, policy, and advocacy circles between different approaches to global governance and human rights. As de Búrca, Keohane, and Sabel have argued, similar debates pervade other regulatory fields such as climate change and labor rights.[7] On the one hand, proponents of what these authors call "integrated and comprehensive regimes" tend to favor "the idea of negotiating a comprehensive, universal and legally binding treaty that prescribes, in a top-down fashion, generally applicable policies."[8] On the other hand, proponents of "experimentalist governance" tend to favor a polycentric approach, oftentimes taking as a starting point voluntary standards enforced through pressure by states, private actors, and civil society.

The BHR field exhibits a particularly spirited and explicit form of this debate, as contributions to this volume evince. Although many participants in the debate favor a hybrid approach that takes elements from both the integrated and the experimentalist views, there are discernible differences in their conceptual and practical emphases. As we will see, while some anchor their proposals in one version or another of binding comprehensive regulations, others explicitly favor a more gradual and experimentalist model.

The GPs can be inscribed in the experimentalist camp, as the former SRGS states in this chapter. My conceptual argument focuses, therefore, on whether the GPs possess the institutional mechanisms which, according to the global experimentalist paradigm, are necessary to generate cumulative progress.

Given the discussion about and different usages of experimentalist governance in this literature (including this volume), two conceptual clarifications are in order. First, the debate between integrated and polycentric approaches long preceded the GPs. Indeed, a vast body of literature has developed over the last two decades that theorizes and empirically studies the contrast between these approaches, and makes a case for an experimentalist governance paradigm under a variety of labels, among them "democratic experimentalism,"[9] "post-regulatory law,"[10] "responsive

7 Grainne de Búrca, Robert Keohane, and Charles Sabel, "New Modes of Pluralist Governance," *NYU Journal of International Law & Policy* 45 (2013).
8 Robert Falkner, Hannes Stephan, and John Vogler, "International Climate Policy After Copenhagen: Towards a 'Building Blocks' Approach," *Global Policy* 3 (2010), 252.
9 Michael Dorf and Charles Sabel, "A Constitution of Democratic Experimentalism," *Columbia Law Review* 98 no. 2 (1998), 267–473; Charles Sabel, "Learning by Monitoring: The Institutions of Economic Development," in Neil Smelser and Richard Swedberg (eds.), *The Handbook of Economic Sociology* (Princeton: Princeton University Press, 1994), 137–165; Charles Sabel, "Bootstrapping Reform: Rebuilding Firms, the Welfare State, and Unions," *Politics & Society* 23 no. 1 (1995), 5–48.
10 Gunther Teubner, "After Legal Instrumentalism? Strategic Models of Post-Regulatory Law," in G. Teubner (ed.), *Dilemmas of Law in the Welfare State* (Berlin: De Gruyter, 1986), 299–326.

regulation,"[11] "collaborative governance,"[12] "reflexive law,"[13] "new governance"[14] or simply "governance."[15] Contrary to what some critics in scholarly circles have suggested, neither the SRGS nor the GP process generated this conceptual debate and framing. Rather, they inherited it.

It is also important to bear in mind that the discussion between integrationist vs. experimentalist approaches cannot be simplistically reduced to one between preferences for mandatory vs. experimental standards, respectively. The "softness" or "hardness" of international regulations is only one factor in the debate. Equally important are variables such as the centralized or polycentric nature of the implementation process of such regulations, the importance of rules aimed at diminishing power asymmetries among actors in the BHR regulatory field, and the relevance of principled as opposed to pragmatic considerations for or against a given regulatory approach, among others. Given the specific purposes of this chapter, I do not attempt to offer a more complex typology, but rather leave that effort for the final chapter of this book. Here I take as my point of departure the abovementioned, well-established typology and characterize it in terms of integrationist vs. experimentalist approaches to BHR. Fully mindful that most approaches fall somewhere between these two ideal types (in the Weberian sense of this term), I aim to shed new light on the BHR by connecting it to the preceding, broader discussion in the global governance literature.

From an empirical standpoint, I examine if, in practice, the GP's experimentalist mechanisms have worked during the process of implementation of the GPs, and if this process appears to be aimed at cumulative progress. Given that, by design, the GP framework is polycentric, it is implemented through multiple entities, from national state institutions to intergovernmental organizations to individual businesses and sector-based business associations. In terms of experimentalist governance theory, these and other entities play an "orchestration" role by enforcing existing standards and creating new ones, engaging the social actors involved in

[11] Ian Ayres and John Braithwaite, *Responsive Regulation: Transcending the Deregulation Debate* (New York: Oxford University Press, 1992).
[12] Jody Freeman, "Collaborative Governance in the Administrative State," *UCLA Law Review* 45, no. 1 (1997): 1–98.
[13] Gunther Teubner, "Substantive and Reflexive Elements in Modern Law," *Law and Society Review* 17 no. 2 (1983), 239–285; Ralf Rogowski and Ton Wilthagen (eds.), *Reflexive Labour Law: Studies in Industrial Relations and Employment Regulation* (Boston: Kluwer, 1994).
[14] Orly Lobel, "New Governance as Regulatory Governance," in David Levi-Four (ed.), *The Oxford Handbook of Governance* (Oxford: Oxford University Press, 2012).
[15] Bob Jessop, "The Rise of Governance and the Risk of Failure: The Case of Economic Development," *International Social Science Journal* 155 (1998), 29–45; Michael Mac Neil, Neil Sargent, and Peter Swan (eds.), *Law, Regulation, and Governance* (Don Mills, Ontario: Oxford University Press, 2002); Joseph Nye and John Donahue (eds.), *Governance in a Globalizing World* (Washington, D.C.: Brookings Institution, 2000);

the field of business and human rights, promoting collaboration and discussions among them, and disseminating standards and practices.[16]

In light of the multiplicity and diversity of orchestrators, empirical studies need to focus on one or a limited set of them in order to remain manageable. In this chapter, I focus on the WG, the entity established by the UN for the specific purpose of promoting the dissemination and implementation of the GPs.[17] Although other nodes of orchestration and implementation are equally relevant – for instance, national contact points implementing the OECD's Guidelines, regional courts incorporating the GPs into their jurisprudence, or national human rights institutions entrusted with the task of coordinating BHR policies by virtue of national action plans currently being developed by numerous countries to domesticate the GPs – I cannot pursue a detailed analysis of them in this chapter.[18]

My empirical evidence is based on a combination of systematic analysis of the documents produced by the WG over the course of its mandate with participant observation and interviews in the four forums organized by the WG in Geneva between 2012 and 2015. With the goal of counterbalancing the emphasis of Global North voices in the literature,[19] I also use data from interviews and participant observation in international events on the issue held in the Global South over this period: the 2013 WG's Regional Forum on Business and Human Rights for Latin America held in Medellín, Colombia; the Alternative Forum organized by civil society organizations in Medellín parallel to the WG Regional Forum; and the annual versions of the Peoples' Forum on Human Rights and Business held in Bangkok (2013), Bogotá (2014), and Nairobi (2015) with NGOs and victims' organizations that address corporate violations of human rights in order to discuss specific cases, strategies, and civil society proposals for advancing corporate accountability.

This chapter is divided in four sections, each one of which details one of the arguments I present. In the First Section, I discuss the history of the GPs and the WG. In this discussion, I argue that the GPs have made tangible progress in creating

[16]   Kenneth Abbott and Duncan Snidal, "Taking Responsive Regulation Transnational: Strategies for International Organizations," *Regulation and Governance* 7 (2013).

[17]   By concentrating on the WG, I do not mean to argue that it is the sole or even the main orchestration mechanism of the GPs. A thorough prospective assessment of the GPs would need to encompass other equally important implementation mechanisms that are discussed in other contributions to this volume, from national actions plans to regional standards like those of the OECD to sector-specific, multistakeholder arrangements. Although I allude to these and other mechanisms below, offering a systematic assessment of their operation is beyond the scope of this chapter and the empirical study that underlies it. For a discussion of the WG as one among several orchestrating mechanisms, see Ruggie, Chapter 2, in this volume. For an analysis of some of those mechanisms, see Mehra, Chapter 8.

[18]   For a discussion of national action plans, see Mehra, Chapter 8 in this volume. For civil-society-led initiatives drawing on the GPs, see Jochnik, Bickford, and Kweitel (Chapters 7, 9, and 10).

[19]   A telling illustration is that over 90 percent of works compiled in the Oxford Bibliography on business and human rights were produced by scholars based in the Global North. See Michael Santoro and Florian Wettstein, *Business and Human Rights Bibliography* (Oxford: Oxford University Press, 2013). I am grateful to Juana Kweitel for bringing this to my attention.

an authoritative focal point for an issue that is highly controversial and divisive. These achievements are due to their steady dissemination in diverse spaces, from national plans of action developed by states to OECD principles and corporate codes of conduct, as well as national and regional court rulings. That said, due to a narrow interpretation of its mandate and a focus on the dissemination of the GPs, the WG has not done enough to advance the normative agenda and the effective implementation of the GPs such that there are increased protections for victims of corporate abuse. In this sense, they have remained at the "end of the beginning," without substantial attempts to go beyond it.

In the second section, I detail the reasons for these limitations. Through contrasting my analysis of WG events and reports with the promises of experimentalist governance, I find that the limitations emerge from two sources, one of which was embedded in the GPs, and the other of which emerged from work that remains to be done in terms of their implementation. First, neither the GPs nor the WG have explicitly and systematically incorporated an essential element of experimentalist governance: the empowered participation of civil society. Second, there is confusion and ongoing debate regarding who counts as "civil society" for the purpose of participation in the implementation of the GPs.

In the Third Section, I address another side of the debate, focusing on those who, from an integrationist approach, tend to dismiss the GPs and propose a binding treaty as the main mechanism to advance the protection of human rights in the context of business activities. Although it has the advantage of putting upward pressure on global regulation of companies and keeping the normative status of human rights on the agenda, I argue that, from a dynamic and prospective point of view, this position has its own limitations. A dominant focus on an international treaty leaves to the side the possibilities to effectively protect rights that might emerge from other forms of regulatory pressure, including the GPs, as well as the fact that these might complement binding domestic and international rules. In addition, with regard to the possibility of broad participation of civil society, this focus on a treaty can privilege the voices of specialized organizations with significant experience in this type of negotiation, to the detriment of grassroots organizations located far from the spaces where this kind of instrument is discussed. Finally, although this position is solidly based on legal considerations, it often pays insufficient attention to political viability and actual impact.

In the Fourth Section, I outline some conceptual and practical alternatives that, in my view, could combine the strengths and help to correct the limitations of the integrationist and experimentalist positions, offering intermediate paths toward the protection of human rights in the global economy. With respect to the GPs and the WG, I propose compliance mechanisms and the broadening of the WG agenda, as well as participatory implementation of the GPs. With respect to the question of a binding treaty, I propose a combination of participatory implementation of the GPs with a push toward a treaty that builds on and offsets some of the limitations of the GPs, while remaining sensitive to considerations of political feasibility, opportunity costs, and actual impact on the ground.

IMPLEMENTING THE GUIDING PRINCIPLES

The Origins of the Guiding Principles and the Working Group

The WG's mandate and orientation are in part a product of institutional history. Specifically, the history of the UN's engagement with the issue of business and human rights, and debates regarding the nature of that engagement, laid the groundwork upon which the mandate of the WG was crafted, as well as the way in which the WG has interpreted that mandate.

UN involvement in the question of the relationship between private enterprise and human rights began in the 1970s, with the establishment of the UN Commission on Transnational Corporations and the UN Centre for Transnational Corporations (UNCTC). In response to public frustration with the inadequacy of a purely state-centric approach to accountability, these bodies were charged with researching the impacts of transnational business activity, strengthening the ability of host countries to negotiate terms with these enterprises, and developing draft normative frameworks for transnational business activities. The work of the Commission eventually led to a draft Code of Conduct on Transnational Corporations, which was debated in a series of special sessions between 1983 and 1990. Due to significant opposition to the Code, particularly by host states of transnational corporations based in the North, it was finally abandoned in 1994, and the UNCTC was dismantled.[20]

Under the leadership of Kofi Annan, the UN embarked on a new effort to address the corporate sector, leading to the eventual development of the UN Global Compact in 2000. The Global Compact established ten nonbinding principles to guide businesses in the development of socially and environmentally sustainable practices. Many human rights advocates opposed the voluntary nature of the Global Compact, arguing that binding regulation was necessary to stem harmful corporate activity. Some of these advocates formed a now-defunct coalition called Alliance for a Corporate-Free UN, opposing the environmental and social records of the businesses with which the UN had formed relationships through the Global Compact. The Global Compact, however, was relatively well received by the business community, and a significant number of companies joined the voluntary initiative.[21]

In light of the critiques of voluntary initiatives in dealing with corporate accountability for human rights violations, the UN Sub-Commission on the Promotion and

[20]   Scott Jerbi, "Business and Human Rights at the UN: What Might Happen Next?" *Human Rights Quarterly* 31 (2009).

[21]   The UN Global Compact website states that since its launch in 2000, it has grown to over 12,000 participants, including 9,000 businesses. See https://www.unglobalcompact.org/what-is-gc/partici pants (accessed 5 March 2017).

Protection of Human Rights began in the early 2000s to develop a set of Norms on the Responsibilities of Transnational Corporations and Other Business Enterprises with Regard to Human Rights (UN Draft Norms).[22] As the product of an expert group, the UN Draft Norms did not have a directly binding effect, but they represented the first UN attempt to identify human rights legal standards that would apply to corporations. The Norms became a lightning rod for debate, with human rights advocates and some academics strongly supporting the attempt to establish corporate human rights obligations,[23] and businesses and other scholars rejecting it for a variety of reasons, including the shift of responsibility from states to the private sector.[24] Eventually, the UN Draft Norms were scuttled through a UN Commission on Human Rights resolution that refused to grant the norms legal status and mandated that the Sub-Commission abstain from performing monitoring functions with respect to the Norms.

In light of the failure of the Norms, the UN Economic and Social Council requested that the Office of the High Commissioner for Human Rights compile and assess existing human rights standards related to business activity. In its resulting report, the Office of the High Commissioner noted increased interest in discussing such standards; on the heels of this report, the Commission on Human Rights requested that the Secretary-General appoint a special representative on the subject. In 2005, Kofi Annan appointed John G. Ruggie – who had formerly worked for Annan as chief adviser for strategic planning, and had been involved in the development of the Global Compact – as Special Representative on Business and Human Rights (SRSG).

The initial mandate of the SRSG was relatively limited in scope, and focused largely on the identification and clarification of standards of corporate accountability with respect to human rights and the identification of state and corporate best practices. Unlike other UN special procedures, the SRSG's mandate did not include country visits or the examination of specific situations of human rights issues related to business. That said, the SRSG's approach to the mandate in certain senses broadened it; he culminated his first three-year mandate with the development of the Protect, Respect, and Remedy Framework (PRR), which clarified the state duty to protect against human rights abuses, corporate responsibility to respect human rights, and victims' need for greater access to judicial and nonjudicial remedy.

---

[22] Larry Catá Backer, "Multinational Corporations, Transnational Law: The United Nations' Norms on the Responsibilities of Transnational Corporations as a Harbinger of Corporate Social Responsibility in International Law," *Columbia Human Rights Review* 37 (2005).

[23] ESCR-Net, UN Human Rights Norms for Business: Briefing Kit (New York: ESCR-Net, 2005); David Weissbrodt and Muria Kruger, "Norms on the Responsibilities of Transnational Corporations and Other Business Enterprises with Regard to Human Rights," *American Journal of International Law* 97 (2003).

[24] See the Interim Report of the Special Representative of the Secretary-General on the Issue of Human Rights and Transnational Corporations and Other Business Enterprises. E/CN.4/2006/97.

The SRSG developed the Framework in part through consultations with governments, businesses, and civil society groups over the course of his mandate.

The mandate was then extended for another three years, and expanded with the idea that the SRSG would "operationalize" the PRR Framework through concrete guidelines for both states and businesses. The SRSG used the extension of his mandate to develop what are now known as the UN Guiding Principles on Business and Human Rights, a set of nonbinding standards based on the PRR Framework that the UN Human Rights Council adopted in 2011. While civil society had partially welcomed the PRR Framework, as it dealt directly with some of the issues human rights advocates had previously highlighted, the GPs became the subject of significant debate. The GPs were endorsed and supported by the OECD, the European Commission, and numerous corporations. However, human rights advocates, some still frustrated by the failure of the Draft Norms, were disappointed that there had not been more significant movement toward binding standards for corporations,[25] and many rejected the GPs entirely. In addition, there was broad critique from human rights organizations that the GPs actually represented a step backward in the protection of human rights, as they did not incorporate long-standing international human rights protections relevant to corporate activity. There were also recurrent complaints that the SRSG had not taken into sufficient account the views of civil society on these matters.[26]

Despite these criticisms, the GPs were unanimously endorsed by the UN Human Rights Council and became the centerpiece of efforts related to human rights and business at the UN. And the Working Group on Business and Human Rights was established by the UN Human Rights Council to guide their implementation.

The Work of the Working Group

The WG is a five-member expert group, made up of representatives from each region. It was initially given a three-year mandate, focused on the dissemination and implementation of the GPs, the promotion of best practices and capacity-building regarding business and human rights, the initiation of country visits, and the development of recommendations regarding access to effective remedy for people whose human rights are affected by business activity.[27]

---

[25]   FIDH et al. 2011 "Joint Civil Society Statement on the Draft Guiding Principles on Business and Human Rights" (3 March 2011); Connie de la Vega, et al., "Holding Businesses Accountable for Human Rights Violations: Recent Developments and Next Steps," *International Policy Analysis* (2011). See the analysis of this issue in David Bilchitz and Surya Deva, "The Human Rights Obligations of Business: A Critical Framework for the Future," in *Human Rights Obligations of Business Beyond the Corporate Responsibility to Respect?* (eds.), Surya Deva and David Bilchitz (Cambridge: Cambridge University Press, 2013)

[26]   See, for instance, Human Rights Watch "U.N. Human Rights Council: Weak Stance on Business Standards" (16 June 2011).

[27]   See A/HRC/17/L.17/Rev.1 (2011) for the full text of the mandate.

In general, the first years of the WG have been characterized by a relatively narrow interpretation of its mandate. Despite the fact that the WG is considered to be a "special procedure" of the Human Rights Council, and the relative openness of its mandate, it has largely focused on the dissemination and implementation of the GPs. This has been a point of critique of the WG by civil society groups, which have argued that it has placed insufficient emphasis on engaging individuals and groups affected by business activities. Also, these groups argue that it has been slow to take on the question of effective remedy – arguably the element of its mandate that is most directly connected to affected groups and their needs.

The substance of the beginning of the WG mandate – and how its members have carried it out – is reflected in part through the WG's ongoing reports to the UN Human Rights Council and the General Assembly. Its first report to the Human Rights Council had a clear focus on strategy, an approach that was also present in its first report to the General Assembly. This latter report presented the WG's plans to support business efforts to conduct human rights due diligence, as well as its intention to support the development of national action plans around human rights and business. There were not, however, clear plans outlined to deal with issues such as regulation and effective remedy.

An additional issue that emerged in the WG reports was the extent to which it was unlikely to consider individual cases of human rights violations in the context of business activity. In its first report, the WG stated that it "was not in a position to investigate individual cases of human rights violations."[28] Although the WG subsequently backtracked on this statement, agreeing to meet with affected individuals and groups on country visits and receiving individual submissions, it has not approached a position such as that taken by other special procedures that consider individual cases. The procedures by which the submissions it receives are considered have not been made clear, which has also emerged as a point of concern for human rights NGOs.

The WG's first thematic report was on the issue of indigenous peoples.[29] The report assessed the question of indigenous peoples, business, and human rights, following an analysis of the three pillars of the GPs (state duty to protect, corporate responsibility to respect, and effective remedy). This report includes the most detailed discussion of effective remedy of any of the WG reports that preceded it, particularly regarding the state duty to adopt measures that remove obstacles to access to judicial remedies for indigenous peoples. However, the report's approach to the topic of free, prior, and informed consultation represents in certain areas a step backward in the protection of this right, failing to mention the cases in which international law requires that consent be obtained. The report also fails to distinguish between the notions of "consent" and "consultation," leaving to one side the

---

[28] See A/HRC/WG/12/3/1. See also the letter from Conectas and Amnesty International to the WG on this question (sent 13 July 2012).
[29] See A/68/279.

significant domestic and regional jurisprudence on this point and disregarding the binding nature of these rights.[30]

The WG's most recent thematic report focuses on metrics. The report highlights the dearth of data to measure and understand the "nature, scale or extent" of the human rights impacts by business activities on a global level, and by country. Similarly, it highlights the lack of data to measure the efforts of states to "prevent and remedy" business-related harm.[31] With the benefit of four years of implementation efforts, it offers a look at the lag in implementation, research, and collection of information regarding Pillar 3: remedy, confirming, implicitly, the fears of civil society, and grassroots organizations that access to justice would remain as elusive as they were under previous voluntary regimes.

Nonetheless, the report does open up possible spaces for stronger advocacy as it calls for more serious collection of data, and a focused attention on metrics that actually matter: the impacts on affected communities: "Research in the field of business and human rights lacks comprehensive data on the number and nature of complaints against companies for their adverse impacts and the effectiveness of the bodies tasked with investigating and remediating those impacts."[32] Importantly, the WG notes that such metrics, while difficult to obtain, would be "what is meaningful to know" and must include "taking into account assessments by affected individuals and communities themselves."[33]

The report also highlights the lack of attention by states and companies on actual impacts (as opposed to reporting on enacting a policy) and on the effects on indigenous, minority, and other vulnerable communities, as well as on human rights defenders.[34] The inclusion of affected communities' perspectives in the implementation of the GPs, as in the panels and debates sponsored by the WGs, has been a point of strong contention for affected communities. The WG's 2015 report shows an emergent acknowledgment of the importance of these communities' participation in the process, but still is a significant distance from incorporating them as active stakeholders with an influential voice in the shape that implementation policies – from states and within companies – should take. On the other hand, this report is a step forward in shifting the conversation from expressions of "commitment" to human rights to the measurement of actual impacts on prevention or redress.[35] It could provide a useful tool for civil society to hold states accountable for

---

[30] Dejusticia, Conectas, and Justiça Global, "Commentary on the UN Working Group on Human Rights and Transnational Corporations and Other Business Enterprises' first report to the United Nations General Assembly (A/67/285)" (August 2013), accessed 15 January 2014, www.businesshumanrights.org/Links/Repository/1024544

[31] United Nations, General Assembly *Report of The Working Group on the Issue of Human Rights and Transnational Corporations and Other Business Enterprises*, A/70/216 (30 July 2015) *available from* UNdocs.org/A/70/216

[32] *Report of the* WG, A/70/216 (30 July, 2015), at ¶ 88.   [33] Ibid., ¶ 89.   [34] Ibid., ¶ 51–52.

[35] Ibid. ¶ 52.

the disjuncture between professed commitments and results felt by affected communities.

As noted, the arc of the international debate described above regarding business and human rights has long been marked by a divide between integrationist and experimentalist approaches. While this debate has indeed been central, one can also view the history of the UN developments on this issue as a debate over who can and should have a voice at the UN policy making table. The following sections will discuss how these two aspects of the debate have taken shape over the course of the WG mandate. I begin by analyzing the issue of participation in the implementation of the GPs and then move to examining new proposals for a binding treaty. I keep my prospective vision and analytical focus on the dynamic aspect the GPs by honing in on the potential and limitations of the implementation of the GPs by the WG, on the one hand, and civil society proposals for a binding treaty, on the other, for taking norms and practices on business and human rights beyond the "end of the beginning."

THE DYNAMIC LOGIC OF THE GUIDING PRINCIPLES: THEORY AND PRACTICE

Experimentalist Governance and the Guiding Principles

The question of who participates in the GP framework, and how they participate, is not simply empirical, but rather sits at the heart of the theory of governance that inspired the GPs. As opposed to the classical integrationist, state-centered mode in international law, experimentalist governance scholars propose a gradual and poly-centric approach.[36] Given the legal and political fragmentation of contemporary globalization, they propose governance arrangements that align the multiple reg-ulatory systems that make up global "regime complexes," in fields ranging from climate change to intellectual property.[37] Importantly, the dynamic logic of this model follows a building blocks approach, based on regulatory standards and institutional mechanisms that strengthen and orchestrate different governance systems.

The BHR field is a clear example of the global legal pluralism that experimentalist governance identifies. National and international, hard-law and soft-law, public and private regulations have developed without a coordinated node or overarching framework. Compounding the breadth and diversity of this regulatory field is the fact that it encompasses widely different industries (from agriculture and apparel

---

[36] Grainne de Búrca, Robert Keohane and Charles Sabel, "New Modes of Pluralist Governance," p. 739.

[37] K. Raustiala and David Victor, "The Regime Complex for Plant Genetic Resources," *International Organization* 58 (2004); Robert Keohane and David Victor, "The Regime Complex for Climate Change," *Perspectives on Politics* 9 (2011).

production to financial services and information technology) and human rights (from the right to life to labor rights to indigenous rights to environmental rights).

The SRSG's strategy in developing the GPs to serve as an authoritative focal point for this regime complex was admittedly akin to such a building blocks approach.[38] The building blocks are three governance systems: (1) state law (domestic and international), (2) corporate governance, and (3) a "civil governance system involving stakeholders affected by business enterprises and employing various social compliance mechanisms such as advocacy campaigns and other sources of pressure."[39] Continuing with the architectural metaphor, the idea behind the GPs is that each building block is placed in such a way that it compensates for the weaknesses of the others and exercises pressure for upward movement, or continual improvement in the protection of human rights affected by business activities.[40]

Writing from a "new governance" perspective, Melish and Meidinger note that the structure of the GPs is solidly based in the first two columns (public and corporate), but the third column is weak (civil society). The "protect" and "respect" pillars of the framework pertain to states and corporations, respectively, and the absence of civil society pressure is not compensated by the "remedy" pillar. Given that the purpose of the remedy principles is to offer ways for civil society actors to seek redress for specific violations of human rights, the dominant role they envisage for such actors is as potential grievance holders, rather than subjects empowered to actively participate in the processes of norm creation, revision, monitoring, and enforcement. As theorized by experimental governance proponents, civil society participation in these processes is an essential source of pressure for compliance with existing standards and cumulative regulatory progress.[41] Although the GPs do move in that direction – for instance, by stating that corporations should "consult" with potentially affected communities in assessing human rights "risks"[42] – they do not incorporate civil society participation as a systematic institutional feature.

In line with my focus on the dynamic aspects of the GPs, I am mainly concerned with how public, corporate, and civil society pressure for compliance has been brought to bear on the implementation of the GPs. As noted, in polycentric governance arrangements, this entails several entities playing "orchestration" roles. Cumulative regulatory progress hinges on orchestration, which is supposed to "ratchet up" internalization of and compliance with human rights standards.[43]

The WG is one of the orchestration mechanisms of the GPs, the one explicitly created for this purpose within the UN system. Since the beginning of its mandate in

[38] Ruggie, "Global Governance."   [39] Ibid., p. 9.
[40] John Ruggie, *Just Business: Multinational Corporations and Human Rights* (New York: Norton, 2013).
[41] Tara Melish and Errol Meidinger, "Protect, Respect, Remedy and Participate: 'New Governance' for the Ruggie Framework," R. Mares (ed.), *Business and Human Rights at a Crossroads: The Legacy of John Ruggie* (Leiden: Martinus Nijhoff, 2011).
[42] A/HRC/17/31, Principle 18.
[43] Archon Fung, Dara O'Rourke, and Charles Sabel, *Can We Put an End to Sweatshops?* (Boston: Beacon Press, 2001).

2011, the WG has adopted what it has called a "multistakeholder, consultative, and inclusive approach" to this task.[44] This strategy has had substantial success with bringing states and business to the table through consultations, workshops on best practices, and forums. It has met with less success in engaging active participation of civil society organizations and affected groups.

Before examining the WG's record on this regard, it is important to remark on the significance of this asymmetry for the governance model that the GPs embody. For this model may neglect power inequalities among actors in regulatory frameworks, and view the global public sphere as a depoliticized arena of engagement among generic "stakeholders." The stark inequalities marking the local and international contexts that pose the most difficult governance challenges (e.g., those between transnational corporations, on the one hand, and workers and affected communities, on the other) translate into deep asymmetries among participants in multistakeholder arrangements and venues, from local consultations to global conferences.[45]

A promising complementary approach is Fung and Wright's "empowered participatory governance," as one of its central concerns is to theorize and empirically study the role of countervailing power in governance systems.[46] This approach acknowledges that some experimentalist governance frameworks "are often inattentive to problems of powerlessness and domination, thus seeming to suggest that if only the institutional designs can be constructed just right, then gross imbalances of power in the context of these institutions will be neutralized."[47] Therefore, institutional arrangements and advocacy strategies are needed that facilitate the deployment of countervailing power, a concept "that describes how powerful actors with privileged access to decision-making venues may be challenged and even defeated from time to time by the weak and less organized.[48] Without countervailing power mechanisms, multistakeholder arrangements are likely to frustrate the goals of experimentalist governance: "writ large, the shift from top-down adversarial governance to collaborative governance, when there is no countervailing power or capacity, can amount in practice to a state-shrinking, deregulatory maneuver in which oppositional forces are co-opted and neutralized and the collaborative participation becomes mere window dressing."[49]

Given the power asymmetries among states, corporations, and rights-holders, durable improvements in the protection of human rights with regard to business activities hinge on the development of institutional mechanisms that bolster the

---

[44] See A/HRC/WG/12/3/1.
[45] This critique of experimentalist governance theory is drawn from César Rodríguez-Garavito, "Global Governance and Labor Rights: Codes of Conduct and Anti-Sweatshop Struggles in Global Apparel Factories in Mexico and Guatemala," *Politics & Society* 33 (2005).
[46] Archon Fung and Erik Olin Wright, "Countervailing Power in Empowered Participatory Governance," in *Deepening Democracy: Institutional Innovations in Empowered Participatory Governance* (eds.), Archon Fung and Erik Olin Wright (London: Verso, 2003).
[47] Ibid., p. 259   [48] Ibid., p. 260   [49] Ibid., p. 265

countervailing power of rights-holders, affected communities and civil society organizations, such that they can play the role envisaged in the "building blocks" approach. In playing such a role, civil society organizations do not follow a single path. Depending on their methods of work, constituencies, and type of expertise, some choose to engage with the WG, others to confront it, and yet others to do both.[50] As Elliot and Freeman have shown with regard to global labor standards,[51] from the point of view of the effective protection of human rights, the coexistence of "confronters" and "engagers" is an asset rather than a liability in global governance fields. For the optimal strategy for advancing the twin goals of compliance and dissemination is some form or adversarialism (to put continuous pressure on states and corporations to comply with the GPs and international law at large) and collaboration (to promote the diffusion of higher human rights standards within states and corporations).

From the viewpoint of the WG, this entails opening up avenues for participation not only for engagers (i.e., civil society organizations that aid in the dissemination of the GPs), but also for confronters (i.e., victims' and advocacy organizations capable of bringing specific cases and complaints to its attention, and to continually pressure for the ratcheting up of the content of and compliance with human rights obligations). As Keck and Sikkink have shown, by exercising "accountability politics,"[52] confronters are key sources of countervailing power – for instance, by holding states and corporations to the GPs and other obligations under hard-law and soft-law, national and international standards, and by putting pressure on them to adopt more effective norms and practices.

As I have shown in a study of international labor standards, institutional arrangements embodying this type of empowered participatory governance have a better prospect of contributing to sustainable improvements in human rights practices on the ground.[53] Contrary to Ruggie's conclusion, in Chapter 2, of this volume, such arrangements can be and have been established not only at the local or national level, but also at the global scale. Relevant recent precedents can be found in the climate change regime that emerged from the 2016 Paris Conference of the Parties, the UN Convention on the Rights of People with Disabilities, the Montreal Protocol on Substances that Deplete the Ozone Layer and the Worker Rights Consortium's

---

[50]   On this point, see Kweitel, Chapter 10 in this volume.
[51]   Kimberly Elliot and Richard Freeman, *Can Labor Standards Improve Under Globalization?* (Washington, D.C.: Institute for International Economics, 2003), 50, 64.
[52]   Margaret Keck and Kathryn Sikkink, *Activists Beyond Borders* (Ithaca: Cornell University Press, 1998).
[53]   Rodríguez-Garavito, César "Global Governance and Labor Rights," op. cit. For a related argument with regard to the global regulation of intellectual property as it impinges upon access to medicines, see Rochelle Dreyfuss and César Rodríguez-Garavito, "The Battle Over Intellectual Property Law and Access to Medicines: Global Administrative Law, Contestation and Innovation in Latin America," in *Balancing Wealth and Health: Global Administrative Law and the Battle over Intellectual Property and Access to Medicines in Latin America* (eds.), Rochelle Dreyfuss and César Rodríguez-Garavito (Oxford: Oxford University Press, 2014).

code of conduct and monitoring system for labor rights in the global apparel industry.[54]

In sum, the dynamics of the GPs is founded upon the overlap and complementarity among public, corporate, and civil society forms of governance. To that end, the WG, as one of its orchestration mechanisms, needs to both disseminate and encourage the uptake of the GPs among states and corporations, and to create channels for collaboration with and the exercise of accountability politics by civil society. Whereas dissemination taps into ideational incentives for compliance, accountability politics unleashes material incentives for compliance. However, for accountability politics to work, the WG's institutional arrangements and practices need to facilitate the exercise of countervailing power, lest power differentials vis-à-vis states and corporations render civil society pressure moot.[55]

How does the empirical record of the implementation of the GPs measure up against the promises of the new governance model? How has the WG engaged with multiple stakeholders? How has it dealt with power differentials among them? I now turn to these questions.

The Asymmetrical Implementation of the GPs

Since the beginning of its mandate, the WG's efforts focused on the dissemination of the GPs, as outlined in its initial reports. In its first report to the General Assembly, the WG notes that a pillar of its dissemination strategy has been to work with key "multipliers," which it identifies as regional institutions, business associations, development agencies, corporate social responsibility, and sustainability platforms. It notes its efforts at dissemination among industry, and prioritizes the business sector for further dissemination. The WG also remarks that it will "support Governments, business associations and other collectives in the elaboration and implementation of plans of action designed to disseminate and implement the GPs."[56] Similarly, this report outlines implementation efforts by states and businesses, highlighting two projects that the WG would take on to support such efforts: the elaboration of national action plans, and "peer discussion and learning among States and business enterprises" regarding implementation.[57]

The WG's emphasis on dissemination, alongside previous efforts by the SRSG to this effect, has made tangible and rapid progress toward normative convergence around the GPs among governments and business, thus getting off to a promising

---

[54]   Ibid. See also de Búrca, Keohane and Sabel, "New Modes of Pluralist Global Governance," pp. 744–773.
[55]   The WG is only one of many leverage points to which countervailing power can be applied. For a discussion of a broader array of institutional and political opportunities for bottom-up pressure for corporate accountability, see Backer, Bickford, Jochnick, and Vargas (Chapters 5, 9, 7, and 6) respectively, in this volume.
[56]   See A/67/285, para. 35.   [57]   See A/67/285, para. 39.

start in fulfilling one of the central tasks of orchestration mechanisms within regime complexes. For instance, the new human rights chapter of the OECD's Guidelines for Multinational Enterprises all but replicates the GPs. The International Financial Corporation Sustainability Principles and Performance Standards, which set conditions on the loans it extends to the private sector, recently incorporated human rights clauses drawn from GP concepts. And a new social responsibility standard, ISO26000, has been developed that includes a human rights chapter modelled after the GPs.[58]

Similarly, national action plans (NAPs) for the implementation of the GPs are being discussed in several countries. European countries have been leading the charge: The European Commission had announced its intention to develop an action plan at the EU scale,[59] and, at the time of this writing, nine out of the ten nations that had produced a NAP were EU countries. Colombia produced the tenth NAP. In its December, 2015 report, the WG noted with concern the lack of National Baseline Assessments in the development of NAPs and praised Chile, South Africa, Zambia, Germany, and Scotland, among others, for putting an emphasis on baseline assessments to inform the development of their respective NAPs. Currently, nineteen more states have committed to developing a NAP and are in the process of producing one, while eight more states have national human rights institutions or civil society organizations that have taken steps toward producing a NAP.[60] However, as the WG's own 2015 report notes, there is little information on the actual impacts that state actions that broadcast a public commitment to human rights principles have on affected communities. This includes NAPs.[61]

The counterpoint to the WG's initial emphasis on dissemination and collaboration with state, corporate, and civil society "multipliers" has been its relative inattention to the participation of affected communities and civil society organizations focusing on accountability politics, let alone power differentials between these types of stakeholders and those deemed capable of playing a multiplier role. Despite the most recent increased attention to affected communities, it remains important to look back at the WG's mode of interaction with affected communities and its insufficient attention to them, by comparison to other stakeholders. This imbalance

---

[58] Ruggie, "Global Governance," p. 11.

[59] International Corporate Accountability Roundtable and the Danish Institute for Human Rights, "Interim Report: National Action Plans on Business and Human Rights" (Washington, DC: ICAR, 2013).

[60] For the most updated information on NAPs, see www.ohchr.org/EN/Issues/Business/Pages/NationalActionPlans.aspx (accessed March 5, 2017).

[61] "[N]ational action plans are a means, not an end. [...] For national action plans processes to be effective, they must be regularly reviewed and updated, with inbuilt monitoring mechanisms. In addition, the process by which they are carried out, that is one that includes comprehensive mapping of State duties and extensive stakeholder consultation, is just as important as the final product. The Working Group encourages States to view national action plans as a tool for continuous improvement and to carry them out with inclusion and comprehensiveness in mind." *Report of the WG*, A/70/216 (30 July 2015), at ¶ 73.

is particularly striking in light of two facts. First, the WG mandate requires it to "develop a regular dialogue and discuss possible areas of cooperation with Governments and all relevant actors, including relevant United Nations bodies, specialized agencies, funds, and programmes [. . .], as well as transnational corporations and other business enterprises, national human rights institutions, representatives of indigenous peoples, civil society organizations, and other regional and subregional international organizations."[62] Second, the WG's status within the UN system is that of a "special procedure" of the Human Rights Council, which mandate holders have traditionally interpreted as privileging engagement with victims of human rights violations.

Given the breadth and complexity of the global regulatory regime it contributes to orchestrating, the WG had no choice but to make strategic decisions about priorities, for it would have been unfeasible to attempt to undertake all of its tasks with regard to all stakeholders at once. In light of the above discussion, in making those decisions, a key criterion should be the need to ensure "participation of relevant entities ('stakeholders') in a nonhierarchical process of decision-making."[63] This would entail adopting working methods and institutional mechanisms aimed to explicitly bring in affected individuals and communities, as well as civil society organizations working with them. Drawing on the tradition of special procedures of the UN Human Rights Council, such mechanisms could include receiving and responding to individual submissions and complaints, prioritizing topics that are likely to address the concerns and elicit the participation of such communities and organizations (e.g., access to remedy for victims), and fostering forms of engagement with stakeholders that help counter power differentials among them (e.g., meetings with victims of human rights violations and assistance for the latter to meaningfully participate in regional and global consultations).

The WG's initial strategic decisions did not move in this direction and embodied a narrow interpretation of its mandate. In terms of the tension between principles and pragmatic considerations encapsulated by the "principled pragmatist"[64] approach that the former SRSG took in developing the GPs, the WG has erred on the side of pragmatic considerations rather than on the side of the principle of creating further space for the effective enforcement of human rights. For instance, as noted, the WG initially asserted that it "was not in a position to investigate individual

---

62 U.N. General Assembly, Human Rights Council, 17th Session, "Promotion and Protection of All Human Rights, Civil, Political, Economic, Social and Cultural Rights, Including the Right to Development." ((A/HRC/17/L.17/Rev.1), 15 June 2011), p. 3.

63 de Búrca, Keohane, and Sabel, "New Modes of Pluralist Global Governance," p. 739.

64 According to the former SRSG, principled pragmatism entails "an unflinching commitment to the principle of strengthening the promotion and protection of human rights as it relates to business, coupled with a pragmatic attachment to what works best in creating change where it matters most in the daily lives of people." See Interim Report of the Special Representative of the Secretary General on the Issue of Human Rights and Transnational Corporations and Other Business Enterprises, E/CN.4/2006/97, 2006, para. 81.

cases of human rights violations." At the prompting of some NGOs, it later revised its view and stated that it would meet with victims during country visits.[65]

This trajectory – initial inattention to empowered civil society participation, followed by a gradual opening to it in response to criticism – has marked the first few years of the operation of the WG. This is evident, for instance, in the evolution of the regional and global forums it convenes, which vividly illustrate two challenges of civil society participation in multistakeholder arrangements: who gets to participate and who gets to counts as civil society in such dialogues.

With regard to *who gets to participate*, the format of the first global and regional forums limited the extent to which all stakeholders were able to contribute to the discussion. The WG made efforts to place representatives of each stakeholder group on panels. However, given the weak participation in the forums as a whole by affected groups and civil society – due to their own disengagement, to their possible lack of trust in the process, and to the limited possibility of attending given the cost and logistics – the panels at the first global forum in 2012 often featured the same civil society members repeatedly, and included only one panel with the participation of affected individuals.

Although the WG in its first report of April 2012 recognized the challenges faced by vulnerable communities to participate,[66] it did not implement measures to address the imbalances early enough, opening the door for civil society organizations to begin to call for more opportunities for participation. For example, in a statement issued right before the launching of the first UN regional forum on business and human rights in Medellín, Colombia, in August 2013, a group of NGOs demanded that the WG "generate real and effective mechanisms for participation in order to ensure that the representatives of the affected communities from various sectors and social movements have the ability to express their views and present their cases in the United Nations Framework."[67] Similar concerns were expressed in a civil society declaration issued after the event, and have been discussed in several civil society coordination meetings.[68]

---

[65] See joint letter from Conectas and Amnesty International to the WG (13 July 2012), accessed 23 April 2014, www.businesshumanrights.org/media/documents/un-working-group/conectas-and-amnesty-intl-ltr-to-un-working-group-13-jul-2012.pdf. The response of the WG (30 July 2013) is available at: www.business humanrights.org/media/documents/un-working-group/un-working-group-on-business-human-rights-response-toamnesty-conectas-jul-2012.pdf.

[66] In particular, the report highlights the need for the WG to pay more attention to affected people and the obstacles they face in access to justice. U.N. Working Group, "Report of the Working Group on the Issue of Human Rights and Transnational Corporations and Other Business Enterprises."

[67] See the "NGO declaration re forthcoming UN Regional Forum on Business and Human Rights for Latin America & Caribbean," accessed 5 March 2017, https://business-humanrights.org/en/ngo-declaration-re-forthcoming-un-regional-forum-on-business-and-human-rights-for-latin-america-caribbean-others-invited-to-sign-on#c75407

[68] See the "Declaration of civil society organizations that participated in the First Regional Forum on Business and Human Rights in Latin America and the Caribbean," accessed 27 January 2014, www .business-humanrights.org/Links/Repository/1022144; see also the "Joint letter on suggestions for the

In response to the concerns expressed by civil society groups, the WG gradually began to change some of its procedures to broaden participation. It secured limited funds to support travel of selected participants from under-represented regions and countries at the annual forum in Geneva, and introduced other methods of engagement, such as smaller side events, issue-focused expert workshops, and preforum stakeholder meetings.[69] Additionally, after suggestions made by civil society organizations and other stakeholders, the WG modified the format of the plenary sessions at the 2013 UN global forum so as to include more community and civil society participants on panels and to clearly differentiate questions coming from business, states, and civil society when opening the floor, guaranteeing that each of these groups had an equal opportunity to participate.

As noted, a second issue of contention is *who gets to count as part of civil society* for the purposes of these forums and other engagements with the WG. Differences over the boundaries of civil society arose at the consultations and forums convened by the WG. Human rights advocacy organizations with the longest engagement on this issue – some dating to UN efforts prior to the Draft Norms – have critiqued the inclusion in the "civil society" category of new consulting firms and think tanks advising corporations and states on the issue of business and human rights.

With the adoption of the GPs and other multistakeholder governance systems, a number of entities of this type have been established, with some operating as consultants for businesses working with the latter to ensure compliance with the GPs and other international regulatory standards.[70] This hybrid role has sparked debate over the boundaries of the category of civil society, with more established human rights advocacy organizations questioning the extent to which engagement and participation by these newer groups in the process has a secondary consequence of edging more long-standing (and more critical) groups out of the picture. Some groups have also questioned the extent to which the work of these new entities dilutes rather than strengthens the positive effects of the GPs.

Initially, the WG was impervious to this criticism and tended to conflate all nonstate, noncorporate entities under the category of civil society. This was evident in the discrepancies between the WG's headcount of civil society participants at the first UN regional forum and the one provided by human rights NGOs. While the latter did not count as civil society participants those firms and organizations that worked as consultants for business and states, the former did include them.

2013 UN Forum on Business and Human Rights" www.business-humanrights.org/Links/Repository/1019929; similar concerns were expressed in the People's Forum held in Bangkok-Thailand in November 2013, and the civil society coordination meetings held in Geneva in 2012 and 2013 and in Medellín.

69   See the "Response to the civil society organizations who have sent submissions in relation to the 2013 Regional Forum on Business and Human Rights for Latin America and the Caribbean," accessed 27 January 2014, www.business-humanrights.org/UNWorkingGroupPortal/Events/RegionalForums.

70   Examples of such organizations are Business for Social Responsibility, the Global Business Initiative and Rights Advice.

The result of these contrasting calculations makes evident the dispute over boundaries and its consequences for empowered participatory governance. In the calculation by human rights NGOs, only 10 percent of the panelists came from communities affected by business activities or NGOs that work with such communities, while 43 percent represented companies or human rights consulting firms. The WG's reply provided a different assessment, stating that 32 percent of the speakers belonged to business organizations and 23 percent to civil society.[71] Although some of the discrepancies are due to the fact that civil society groups took into account only the main panel sessions (forty-seven speakers) and the WG took into account also expert workshops and side sessions (seventy-three speakers), the bulk of the difference is explained by contrasting conceptions of the boundaries between business and civil society.[72] While human rights NGOs counted some organizations that offer consultancy services to corporations as being part of the business sector, the WG counted them as civil society participants.

Boundaries are always contested (especially in such a historically and conceptually charged category as "civil society") and hybrid entities of all types cannot be easily classified. Yet boundary debates can have tangible consequences in practice. For instance, the discussion about numbers had the positive result of generating more transparent information about registered participants and speakers at the 2013 UN forum in Geneva. In contrast to what had happened in the 2012 global forum and the 2013 regional forum, the WG disclosed a full list of registered participants, classifying them under such labels such as "Consultant," "Civil Society Organization," and "Other."[73]

In sum, multistakeholder initiatives such as the one centered around the WG tend to both encourage the engagement and limit the participation of relevant actors. As the trajectory of the WG suggests, engagers and multipliers tend to be have a predominant role over confronters. This predominance is compounded when the two types of actors and strategies are lumped together under the category of civil society. This, in turn, may widen power disparities among stakeholders, as the voice of more powerful actors (e.g., corporations and states) gets further amplified by civil society actors working for them (e.g., consulting firms).

---

[71] See the "Declaration of civil society organizations that participated in the First Regional Forum on Business and Human Rights in Latin America and the Caribbean" www.business-humanrights.org /Links/Repository/1022144; and the "Response to the civil society organizations who have sent submissions in relation to the 2013 Regional Forum on Business and Human Rights for Latin America and the Caribbean" www.business-humanrights.org/UNWorkingGroupPortal/Events/RegionalForums.

[72] There are far smaller discrepancies when it comes to government and UN participants. According to the NGO count, 26 percent of the speakers represented regional governments, and 21 percent came from various United Nations agencies. According to the WG count, 23 percent belonged to governments and national human rights institutions and 22 percent to UN agencies.

[73] See the list of participants at www.ohchr.org/Documents/Issues/Business/ForumSession2/ ListOfParticipants.pdf.

As a result, such institutional arrangements may fail to incorporate the voice of and empower less powerful stakeholders, such as affected individuals and communities.[74] And the chances for accountability politics to serve as a source of upward pressure in new governance regimes may be consequently reduced.

In order to avoid these risks of governance failure, such regimes need to incorporate institutional mechanisms aimed to bolster countervailing power. In the final section of the chapter I propose specific ways in which the WG could move in this direction.

A COMPLEMENTARY ROUTE: A BINDING TREATY

As noted in the introduction, in addition to whether it exerts upward pressure, the dynamic aspect of the GPs should be assessed in terms of whether they effectively open spaces for "other promising, longer-term developments." Taking into account the history of UN engagement with the issue of business and human rights, as well as ongoing debates regarding the need for binding norms related to the obligations of business, it is clear that a central long-term development in this area will be the adoption of a binding international treaty. Such a treaty, in addition to the dissemination and empowered civil society participation in the implementation of the GPs discussed in the previous section, would be a fundamental step beyond the "end of the beginning" in law and governance regimes related to business and human rights.

In this section, I examine this complementary route and the debate surrounding it. Although some proponents of a binding treaty do not oppose the GPs, others have criticized the GPs and the governance model they represent as insufficiently effective in protecting the rights of people and groups negatively affected by business activities.[75] Likewise, some defenders of the GPs tend to discount the political viability and legal desirability of this type of binding norm, as well as the doctrinal and "legalist" model of governance, which, in their view, undergird proposals for a treaty.[76]

My argument is located between the two sides of this debate. On the one hand, I suggest that an effort to adopt a binding treaty – if equally mindful of normative and pragmatic considerations, written at an adequate level of generality, and aimed at the right target – could result in a fundamental step forward toward the protection of human rights in the context of business activities, and could serve to add specificity to the GPs' content on key points, as well as strengthen their implementation and enforcement. On the other hand, I argue that the dominant focus on a binding treaty

---

[74] For a related discussion of power imbalances in the GPs and international law at large, see Meyersfeld, Chapter 11 in this volume.

[75] See, for example, Alianza Social Continental et al. "Statement to the Delegations on the Human Rights Council, "Final Report of the SRSG on the issue of human rights and transnational corporations and other business enterprises" (2011).

[76] See Ruggie, Chapter 2 in this volume.

that some scholars and advocacy organizations have adopted in their proposals fails to take advantage of concrete progress that could result from the effective, expansive, and empowered implementation of the GPs.

My arguments regarding the implementation of the GPs and a binding treaty have similar conceptual roots. As global governance theorists have argued, it is possible to combine polycentric and centralized or voluntary and mandatory mechanisms in the same regulatory regime.[77] If adequately orchestrated, these distinct approaches can be complementary.

There are multiple reasons to believe that such complementarity exists with respect to the implementation and expansion of the GP regulatory framework. First, in terms of the tripartite (public, corporate, and civil society) governance scheme undergirding the GPs, a binding treaty would specify obligations and reinforce compliance mechanisms with respect to the first, while opening remedy and participation mechanisms that currently exist in international human rights law for civil society. Second, the adoption of a treaty would improve the GPs' alignment with international human rights norms and institutions. Since the GPs specify exclusively "responsibilities" (and not duties) of companies with respect to human rights, companies might use the GPs to deny their obligations under international law (such as, for example, Shell argued with respect to *jus cogens* in the *Kiobel* v. *Royal Dutch Shell* case before the U.S. Supreme Court).[78] Also, as Deva argues in this volume, the GPs are under-inclusive in terms of the range of sources of international human rights obligations they acknowledge, as they refer only to those "expressed in the International Bill of Human Rights and the principles concerning fundamental rights set out in the International Labour Organization's Declaration on Fundamental Principles and Rights at Work,"[79] thus leaving out core human rights treaties on the rights of women, victims of racial discrimination, children, and people with disabilities. Thus, a binding treaty would bring BHR obligations in line with international law. Third, a viable and targeted treaty, in addition to having a greater chance of approval at the UN, would establish a regulatory floor that would recognize and take advantage of the normative power of human rights standards, which could unleash the type of polycentric and experimental regulation embedded in the GPs and favored by experimentalist governance scholars. Finally, if such a treaty clarified extraterritorial obligations for states and companies with respect to such human rights violations, it would help to close a structural regulatory gap – the territoriality of state jurisdiction – that is unlikely to be overcome through decentralized and gradual mechanisms such as the GPs.

---

[77] de Búrca, Keohane, and Sabel, "New Modes of Pluralist Global Governance," p. 727.

[78] *Kiobel v. Royal Dutch Petroleum*, 133 S.Ct. 1659 (2013). The former SRSG intervened with a brief in this case to clarify that the GPs should not be interpreted in this fashion.

[79] GPs, Principle 12.

Background: the GPs and the Idea of a Binding Treaty

The proponents of regulation in the form of a binding treaty are, in large part, civil society groups and academics that have long been engaged in efforts to further the regulation of corporations at the domestic and international level. The case for a treaty comes from a long history of efforts to hold corporations accountable for the negative impacts of their operations. These efforts, particularly by civil society and affected groups, have consistently been hindered by the lack of binding rules applicable to corporate entities, as well as complications arising from the lack of extraterritorial application of domestic rules that do exist. The notion of an international binding instrument thus has long held broad appeal within civil society groups.

Many of these groups narrate the history of their approach to the matter in the SRSG mandate and the WG mandate as one grounded partially in the failed Draft Norms in the mid-2000s. The Draft Norms were and are interpreted by these groups to have at least reasonably effectively incorporated existing international human rights obligations relevant to business activity, unlike the GPs, which they perceive as regressive to the extent that they do not fully incorporate existing binding obligations.[80]

Groups who had dedicated significant energy to the development and promotion of the Draft Norms were also dissatisfied with the extent to which the Norms themselves were discounted in the process of developing the GPs. From the beginning of the SRSG's mandate, civil society insisted on the centrality of the Draft Norms, specifically arguing that voluntary initiatives should not be "seen as a substitute for the reaffirmation of the obligations imposed to all under the international law of human rights."[81]

The former SRGS identified a "deeply divisive debate between human rights advocacy organizations and the business community"[82] regarding the possibility of binding obligations on companies as one triggered by the Norms, and one that his mandate would need to overcome in order to be successful. The SRSG coupled his reading of the political context of the Norms with a legal interpretation that further justified his distance from them (which he calls his commission of "Normicide"),[83] arguing that corporations' duties under the Norms were insufficiently determinate, and that there was not a clear distinction in the Norms between state and corporate duties.[84]

---

[80] See, for example, FIDH et al. "Joint Civil Society Statement on the Draft Guiding Principles on Business and Human Rights" (3 March 2011); Oxfam, "Oxfam International's Perspective on the Draft Guiding Principles for the Implementation of the United Nations 'Protect, Respect, and Remedy' Framework" (2011); European Center for Constitutional and Human Rights, "SRSG John Ruggie's Draft Guiding Principles for the implementation of the United Nations 'Protect, Respect, and Remedy Framework'" (2011).

[81] FIDH, "Contribution of the FIDH to the discussion with the UN Special Representative on human rights and transnational corporations" (2005).

[82] Ruggie, *Just Business*, xviii.   [83] Ibid., p. 54   [84] Ibid., pp. 49–51.

This distancing of the mandate from the Draft Norms, and what this meant both in terms of the form of the GPs (voluntary rather than binding) and their content (new principles rather than a restatement of established norms), was a central point of civil society critique of the SRGS mandate. As the mandate continued and it became clear that the Norms would not figure in the frameworks emerging from it, some groups remained engaged in the process, providing feedback on the evolving GPs in an attempt to influence their content. This feedback was consistently focused, among other issues, on recommending that the draft GPs incorporate existing human rights standards, as groups argued that the draft principles took "a more regressive approach toward the human rights obligations of States and the responsibilities of nonstate actors than authoritative interpretations of international human rights law and current practices."[85] The final content of the GPs, however, was unsatisfactory to the majority of human rights advocacy groups on these points, and some called for their wholesale rejection as a result.[86]

The Working Group and the Persistent Relevance of a Treaty

Despite the distance the SRGS took from the Draft Norms in his mandate and the nonbinding nature of the GPs, in his Recommendations on Follow-Up to the Mandate (2011), he outlined what he saw as a way forward with respect to the advancement of human rights and business through international legal mechanisms. In this document, he outlined two main recommendations: first, the embedding of the GPs at different levels, and second, the clarification of international legal standards related to business and human rights. He identified one possibility in this regard as "an intergovernmental process of drafting a new international legal instrument."[87]

Civil society groups dissatisfied with the voluntary nature of the GPs pushed politically on this point, referencing the SRSG's statement, but the WG did not take up this request in the first years of its mandate. As the WG focused these first years on the dissemination and implementation of the GPs, rather than the next steps toward developing binding mechanisms, these groups became increasingly frustrated with the WG, with some distancing themselves entirely from the Working Group and its efforts. For the first several years of the WG mandate, this distancing characterized civil society engagement with the WG and the GPs, and the question of a binding treaty remained on the back burner.

The issue, however, did not disappear from the civil society agenda, and emerged once again in force at the WG Regional Forum on Business and Human Rights in

---

[85] FIDH et al. 2011 "Joint Civil Society Statement on the Draft Guiding Principles on Business and Human Rights" (3 March 2011).

[86] See, for example, Alianza Social Continental et al., "Statement to the Delegations on the Human Rights Council 2011."

[87] Ruggie, "Recommendations on Follow-Up to the Mandate" (2011:5).

Medellín, Colombia, in August 2013. At this forum, participants expressed a revived push for a treaty on several fronts. First, the government of Ecuador manifested its intention to pursue renewed efforts toward an international treaty on the subject, bringing more than twenty other states together to push for a binding international treaty regarding the human rights obligations of businesses. Second, the WG itself raised the possibility of beginning conversations regarding a treaty process for grave human rights abuses related to business activity. And third, civil society organizations engaged in internal conversations regarding the possibility of renewing their own efforts toward a treaty process.[88]

The Forum was also an interesting example of the range of support that the possibility of a binding international treaty has among civil society organizations. The list of signatories of the civil society declaration that emerged included Geneva-based international human rights organizations as well as national-level and more grassroots civil society groups. This range is indicative of a diversity of motivations for supporting such an initiative. For civil society groups working on specific cases and doing grassroots organizing, there is significant distrust of corporations and a desire to end the impunity they are seen to enjoy; this impunity is understood to be fostered by voluntary initiatives and reduced by binding rules. For more international NGOs, an additional driving force is their comparative advantage in doing the political work necessary to push for a binding instrument. In particular, groups based in Geneva are structured around UN work, and have been some of the longest and most persistent participants in efforts toward an international binding instrument.

This mix is evident also in the more recent civil society Treaty Alliance, which gained momentum after the idea of a binding treaty revived at the Human Rights Council. In June 2014, the Council approved a resolution Ecuador had proposed the previous year to create an intergovernmental working group to negotiate a binding instrument on BHR. Since then, the Treaty Alliance has served as a platform for civil society organizations to coordinate efforts, engage with the intergovernmental working group, and submit inputs for the latter's meetings in July 2015 and October 2016.

The Drawbacks of a Dominant Focus on a Treaty

Despite its ability to bring together diverse actors within civil society, as well as its importance for effectively regulating corporate activity, the proposal for a binding

---

[88] Many civil society groups supported the Ecuador-led effort to push for an international treaty; see, for instance, FIAN International et al. "Statement to the Human Rights Council in support of the initiative of a group of States for a legally binding instrument on transnational corporations" (2013). However, some groups withdrew their support upon the summary closure of the offices of the Fundación Pachamama in December 2013, citing the hypocrisy of Ecuador's efforts to further international regulation of businesses for human rights abuses while shutting down a civil society organization promoting the protection of human rights in extractive industry.

treaty, when taken as the dominant or even exclusive focus of advocacy and norm making, has limitations of its own. As demonstrated through the lengthy process of developing the Draft Norms, pushing for a binding international treaty related to business and human rights is costly in terms of politics, resources, and time. Civil society meetings frequently include references to such a treaty process as a twenty-year effort, which requires substantial political maneuvering, knowledge, and resources. It also requires significant state support, which can emerge through leadership efforts such as Ecuador's, but also must be broad-based in order to be successful.

It is also often difficult for smaller organizations without large operating budgets or significant political connections to do the political heavy lifting in Geneva that such a treaty process requires, leaving Geneva-based organizations at the helm of such efforts. On the one hand, this takes advantage of their comparative strengths, long history of work on the issue, and resulting accumulated knowledge regarding such processes, as well as their strategic location. In many ways, these organizations serve a crucial and unique purpose. At the same time, organizations without a base in Geneva can easily become alienated from the political work involved in pushing for a treaty. If efforts toward a binding instrument become an exclusive or primary focus of civil society strategy around the issue of business and human rights, these dynamics risk pushing to the margins the priorities, perspectives, and political strategies of smaller or more regional or local organizations (such as local organizing, work on specific cases, or local and national legislative campaigns) from the center of civil society efforts to address human rights violations by business. When taken as the sole or dominant focus as opposed to a key component of a broader range of policy and advocacy alternatives, this emphasis can thus reproduce the power asymmetries – within civil society, as well as between civil society, on the one hand, and states and corporations, on the other – that hinder progress in experimentalist governance arrangements.[89]

A final potential limitation of an international instrument that might involve binding human rights obligations for corporations is the extent to which establishing additional state-like duties for corporations (a goal of a number of participants in the Treaty Alliance) might in turn lead to their eventual accumulation or assertion of additional state-like powers (such as, for example, the authorized use of force). This concern is infrequently discussed in civil society circles, in part because to a large extent corporations are already perceived to de facto possess such powers to a certain degree, and thus should be regulated accordingly (i.e., with power comes responsibility). However, such a concern about the slippery slope and consequences that may emerge from shifting or sharing duties between states and nonstate entities is not unwarranted. Indeed, the increased and unprecedented role that business has

---

[89] See Bickford and Vargas (Chapters 9 and 6 respectively) for a complementary strategic assessment of the focus on a binding treaty.

taken at the UN as a result of the GP process, as discussed in the previous section, is an initial indication of the types of power shifts that are possible as even merely voluntary responsibilities are imputed to corporations.

While incurring some of these costs may well be worth it, particularly if efforts toward a binding international instrument prove successful, it is important to recognize the simultaneous relevance of efforts other than a binding instrument. For this reason, in line with my conceptual and empirical argument, I propose to see a binding treaty as one tool in a broader toolkit, or a medium-term strategy that is best combined with other short-term strategies that are likely to improve effective protection of human rights vis-à-vis corporate activities. Among such strategies are local political organizing and litigation around particular business and human rights cases and disputes, sector-specific multistakeholder initiatives, systematization, and further elaboration of UN treaty bodies' recommendations on states' extraterritorial obligations, and efforts toward effective domestic regulation of business activity. The fact that the political viability of a binding international treaty is also perennially in question renders it even more important to diversify approaches and strategies, even while supporting efforts toward an eventual binding international instrument.

For these reasons, in closing the chapter in the following section, I make the case for a gradual, multipronged approach to a binding treaty, which entails simultaneously advancing the aforementioned empowered, expansive implementation of the GPs, on the one hand, and the adoption of a UN-sponsored binding instrument that expands and complements the foundation laid by the GPs, on the other.

Parameters and Alternatives for Positive-Sum Efforts Around a Treaty and the GPs

An ecosystemic view such as the one proposed in this and the concluding chapters – which seeks to foster symbiotic relationships between the GPs, a potential new treaty and other norms and leverage points in the BHR field, – takes as a starting point conceptual and practical parameters that narrow down the range of alternatives currently under discussion in the intergovernmental working group on a BHR treaty.

First, this view acknowledges the fact of the fragmentation of global governance regimes, and the likelihood that this trend will continue to mark international regulatory fields, including BHR. In the face of increasing multipolarity, not only emerging regimes such as BHR or climate change, but also more established ones like international labor rights will probably be constituted by a plural array of institutions and norms, without a single institution or instrument having an uncontested coordination or orchestration role. Contrary to the former SRGS's view, the GPs will not become "the" focal point in the field, but one among several normative focal points. Contrary to the premises embraced by numerous proponents of a comprehensive binding treaty, the evidence suggests that rationalizing the field from the top down through an instrument with superior, overarching normative status, will be as unlikely as in other regulatory fields – if not more, given the thematic breadth, the diversity of legal subjects, and the blurring lines of geopolitical interest between countries in the Global North and emerging powers in the Global South. Therefore, from this perspective, the short-term task for BHR scholars and practitioners is more akin to a carpenter's, who carefully adjusts loose pieces so as to improve their fit and mutual support, as opposed to an architect concerned with constructing a perfect roof (be it the GPs, a treaty or something else). For those of us who spend part of our time in academia and part in practice, everyday work certainly looks and feels more like a carpenter's shop (see, for instance, Jochnik's and Mehra's Chapters 7 and 8 in this volume).

Second, this view plays down the difference between "soft" and "hard" law. In practice, the distance is much less clear than the analytical distinction would suggest, as courts, governments, rights-holders, corporations and civil society organizations invoke soft and hard regulations oftentimes interchangeably. As Shelton has noted, "nonbinding norms have a complex and potentially large impact on the development of international law."[90] To cite just one recent illustration within the BHR field, in November 2015, the Inter-American Court of Human Rights drew on the GPs in the *Kaliña and Lokono Peoples v. Suriname* judgment.[91] In analyzing Suriname's duties with regard to the regulation of corporate activity in its territory, specifically, the actions of two mining companies that had caused environmental damage and infringed upon indigenous peoples' rights, the Court relied on the commentary to Principle 18, which ultimately supported the Court's ruling against Suriname.

What does this mean for the debate on a treaty and the work of the intergovernmental working group currently discussing it? It means that proposals on the content, scope, and implementation mechanisms of the new binding instrument should be evaluated in light of their potential to build upon, expand, and reinforce existing regulations in the field, including the whole range of human rights treaties and soft-law instruments such as the GPs. This view runs counter the framing of the problem proposed by the former UN Rapporteur on the Right to Food, Oliver de Schutter, in his statement on the Ecuadorian proposal for a binding treaty. While convincingly positing that "the negotiation of such an instrument is one among many alternative ways through which the fight against impunity for human rights violations could be further strengthened," he argued that "the need for a new international instrument should be assessed [...] not in comparison to what was achieved by the Guiding Principles, which in any case did not have the intention of moving international law forward by imposing new obligations on States or on

---

[90]   Dinah Shelton, "Normative Hierarchy in International Law," *American Journal of International Law*, 100 (2006), 292–293.

[91]   *Case of the Kaliña and Lokono Peoples v. Suriname*. Judgment, Merits, Reparations and Costs. Inter-Am. C.H.R. Ser. C No. 309 (25 November 2015), ¶¶ 223–226.

private actors, but in comparison to the existing tools already provided by international human rights law."[92] Given that the contours of international human rights
law are contested (de Schutter includes, for instance, soft-law recommendations by
UN treaty bodies), and that difference in "bindingness" between soft-law and hard-
law standards is more tenuous in practice than in the books, I posit that any new
international law instrument should indeed be concerned with its fit with other such
instruments, but also with its capacity to build upon and go beyond other types of
regulations in the field, including the GPs. As we will see, de Schutter himself has
made insightful proposals to this effect.

Third, ongoing efforts to negotiate a binding treaty should incorporate the aforementioned legal and empirical lessons from the debate around the GPs. They
should be nonregressive vis-à-vis existing international human rights norms (which
include not only the ones recognized by the GPs, but all the core human rights
conventions), be wary of directly imposing international duties on corporations, aim
to incorporate institutional mechanisms to facilitate empowered participation by
affected individuals and civil society at large, and be realistic about prospects for
state endorsement at the UN level.

The last consideration – political feasibility in light of facts and empirical trends –
deserves additional comment, as scholars with a normative bent often pay insufficient attention to it. As shown by the fact that the work of the intergovernmental
working group has divided UN Council members, and that the Ecuadorian proposal
wrongly excluded national corporations as objects of regulation, there are no clear
signs of an emerging consensus around a treaty. In these circumstances, BHR
advocates and scholars would do well to heed Alston's warning:

> The history of state engagement with human rights regimes is one of determined
> incrementalism, not one of dramatic leaps forward. In the past, the factors that have
> facilitated significant new initiatives include conviction that a proposal is largely
> toothless (in the sense that it will not soon return to bite the governments that voted
> for it), a coherent geo-political or ideological bloc that comes together to provide
> strong support for it, or a sense of overwhelming public concern or unrest over the
> failure of governments or the international community to act in a given situation.
> Otherwise organic evolution has been the hallmark of change.[93]

Although egregious corporate abuses should certainly warrant overwhelming public
concern and decisive state action, including regulation at the international level,
none of Alston's conditions empirically hold at this moment. Thus, incrementalism

---

[92] Olivier de Schutter, "Contribution of the Special Rapporteur on the Right to Food, Mr. Olivier De
    Schutter, to the Workshop 'Human Rights and Transnational Corporations: Paving the Way for
    a Legally Binding Instrument' Convened by Ecuador, 11–12 March 2014, During the 25th Session of
    the Human Rights Council. Available at www.srfood.org/images/stories/pdf/otherdocuments/
    20140311_Ecuador.pdf.
[93] Philip Alston, "Against a World Court for Human Rights," *NYU Public Law and Legal Theory
    Research Paper Series* 13 (2013), 20.

and organic evolution would probably be the approach to a BHR treaty that would have the greatest chance of advancing human rights protection in the global economy.

CONCLUSION: SOME POTENTIAL WAYS FORWARD

In this chapter, I have argued that the GPs framework cogently identifies an endemic feature of contemporary globalization: the fragmentation of governance evident in the coexistence of multiple formal and informal regulations within regime complexes. In line with experimentalist governance theory, it proposes a polycentric approach to this challenge, in which public, corporate, and civil society governance complement each other through an authoritative focal point (the GPs) and various orchestrating mechanisms (the WG, international public and private standard-setting bodies, national governments, industry-specific multistakeholder governance systems, etc.).

I have focused on the dynamic aspect of the GPs by assessing the potential and limitations of such a polycentric approach, as implemented by the WG, to (1) create pressures for continues improvement in the protection of human rights on the ground, and (2) open spaces for longer-term regulatory developments. In examining pressures for continuous improvement, I delved into the governance mechanism of the GPs framework that, in my view, has been least developed: empowered participation of affected communities and individuals, as well as civil society organizations exercising accountability politics. In inquiring into longer-term developments, I concentrated on the possibilities for a binding treaty as a complementary route to the expanded, participatory implementation of the GPs.

In line with the theoretical, legal, and policy arguments I have offered, I close by sketching some specific institutional steps that can be pursued, among others, in order to take the GPs framework beyond its starting point and strengthen the broader system of international human rights and governance regarding business activities.

With respect to empowered participation by civil society, I propose three mechanisms.[94] In line with the empirical focus of the chapter, I focus on the WG, although principles and institutional arrangements of empowered participation could, and should, be incorporated into other orchestrating mechanisms of the BHR, from OECD national contact offices to domestic human rights institutions responsible for the implementation of national action plans.

---

[94] See also Dejusticia, Conectas, and Justiça Global, "Working Group on the Issue of Human Rights and Transnational Corporations and Other Business Enterprises: A Review of the First Two-and-a-Half Years of Work" (2013), accessed 20 January 2014, www.business-humanrights.org/Links/Repository/1024544.

First, following the tradition of UN special procedures, the WG should craft and publicize a substantive agenda that explicitly prioritizes areas and topics for short-term progress. As noted, the WG has successfully elaborated a procedural agenda that privileges dissemination and multistakeholder consultations. This agenda should be complemented with one that undertakes the task of detailing substantive standards and effective practices with regard to specific GPs and other international standards. Although failing to incorporate the highest standards of existing international law, the WG report on indigenous peoples moves in this direction. Additional steps in this direction have been visible in the increasing strength with which the WG has called for a consideration of actual impacts on affected communities, first tepidly in its 2014 report focused on NAPs, which called for baseline assessments that went beyond "identifying existing policy, laws and regulations" and also assess "the effectiveness of a policy and the practicalities of enforcement within the legal, regulatory, and adjudicative frameworks."[95] The report also took up an issue that remains largely unaddressed in the process of GP implementation and dissemination: baseline studies "should cover all three pillars of the Guiding Principles."[96] In its 2015 report, the WG took up the issue with somewhat greater force, detailing the types of metrics and other variables that matter most when measuring business impacts on human rights, as well as the effectiveness of policies meant to implement the GPs.[97] While this sets an interesting new tone, it remains unclear if the call for better metrics will be part of a longer-term strategy to provide more specific guidance on the implementation of the GPs, so that there are tangible positive effects on affected communities.

A welcome and natural next step to these three thematic reports would be for the WG to take up the issue of access to remedy as the focus of a participatory process and produce a substantive report. This focus would not only comply with the WG mandate, which provides the WG with the authority to elaborate on the remedy pillar, but would also be particularly conducive for the type of empowered civil society engagement I have outlined. Victims and civil society organizations are particularly well positioned to contribute the necessary information, demands, and proposals to advance on this front.

Second, the WG should continue to strengthen its institutional mechanisms for interacting with and effectively incorporating the demands of victims of human rights violations into its work. In addition to specific meetings and consultations in the context of country visits and international forums, a particularly important step would be to disseminate widely that the WG now has a process for considering individual submissions.[98] Indeed, that the WG is now open to receiving individual

---

[95] United Nations, General Assembly, *Report of the Working Group on the Issue of Human Rights and Transnational Corporations and Other Business Enterprises*, A/69/263 (5 August 2014), available at UNdocs.org/A/69/263, ¶ 20.

[96] Ibid.   [97]   See *Report of the WG*, A/70/216 (30 July 2015).

[98] See Backer, Chapter 5, in this volume for a related argument in favor of processing individual submissions. See also the guidelines for individual submissions alleging violations of human rights

submissions speaks to the productive debate that the implementation process has created, and the growing awareness of the WG about the dangers and obstacles affected communities and individuals face. If the WG is to systematically incorporate local knowledge and incentives for compliance with the GPs that can only come from affected persons in new governance systems, the WG must follow the lead of other UN special procedures in creating a transparent, explicit system for processing individual submissions.[99] By early 2013, the WG had done just that: it began to accept individual communications, publicized its procedures regarding such communications, and to report on communications three times a year, similar to the methodology of other UN special procedures.[100] The information available in these reports includes the names of the corporations and states in question, the actions taken by the WG, and the rate of response on the part of the WG. More information is needed to understand the degree to which these individual complaints have provided information to the WG that is relevant to its overall mandate, and has informed the thematic choices of its post-2013 reports.

Third, the WG should create specific institutional mechanisms to bring the voices of victims and civil society organizations into its consultations and outputs. To this end, it could follow the lead of both mandatory and voluntary governance systems. A particularly relevant example of these mechanisms is the regime of the UN Convention on the Rights of Persons with Disabilities, whose main innovations are institutional mechanisms for empowered participation of civil society actors.[101] Similarly, lessons from corporate codes of conduct for labor in the apparel sector can be useful, as two decades of experimentation have allowed scholars and practitioners to single out institutional mechanisms – such as the combination of public and private regulation, independent monitoring, transparency of information, and civil society participation – that lead to enhanced protection of human rights.[102]

With regard to longer-term developments, specifically the ongoing intergovernmental work toward a binding treaty, several alternatives have been formulated that would fall within the legal and political parameters I outlined the previous section. In other words, the ecosystemic view of BHR would be compatible with several proposals regarding the content and scope of a possible binding instrument.

to the Working Group, available at www.ohchr.org/EN/Issues/Business/Pages/Submittingcomplaints.aspx.

[99] In 2012, the WG reported that it had received forty communications regarding disputes around corporate activities that impinge upon human rights. See para. 13, A/HRC/23/32. However, it is unclear how it received and processed them; for instance, whether it requested information from states or companies.

[100] These communications reports are available at www.ohchr.org/EN/HRBodies/SP/Pages/CommunicationsreportsSP.aspx (last visited on 8 June 2016).

[101] Grainne de Búrca, "The European Union in the Negotiation of the UN Disability Convention," *European Law Review* 2 (2010).

[102] See Richard Locke, *The Promise and Limits of Private Power: Promoting Labor Standards in a Global Economy* (Cambridge: Cambridge University Press, 2013); Rodríguez-Garavito, "Global Governance and Labor Rights."

One alternative that many have defended, myself included, is a limited binding treaty addressing (1) corporate involvement in the most serious human rights abuses and (2) extraterritorial application of domestic regulation in this field, which could be a concrete step forward in the short term that would be able to garner political support. In line with the proposals a number of human rights NGOs have advanced, the former SRSG has supported both elements of this alternative, suggesting that a top priority for the WG should be proposing that governments craft an instrument addressing when "international law prohibitions of the worst human rights abuses are violated by legal persons."[103] In his Opening Address at the first United Nations Forum on Business and Human Rights in Geneva, he also highlighted the importance of addressing extraterritorial obligations.

This proposal has been criticized on conceptual and empirical grounds.[104] Rather than defending this particular option, my interest lies in finding a broader array of options that would be at least as politically realistic, represent clear normative progress, and, most importantly, offer concrete and effective tools for preventing and redressing corporate human rights violations.

De Schutter has insightfully laid out two alternative courses of action along these lines.[105] First, a binding treaty could be adopted that clarified *states'* duties to protect, respect, and fulfill human rights with respect to corporate activity. Importantly, this treaty would make explicit states' extraterritorial duty to protect, by imposing on the parent corporation based in a given state's territory obligations to control its subsidiaries oversees. Second, the same treaty could specify states' duties to provide one another with legal assistance and to cooperate with each other in order to guarantee that victims have access to effective remedies. Such cooperation and assistance would revolve around the issue areas that currently frustrate transnational corporate accountability: collection of evidence and the seizure of assets and execution of rulings against corporate violators of human rights.

These three alternatives (and others that fall within the parameters proposed above) would also have at least some state support, as demonstrated by those that joined Ecuador's recent initiative, and would also garner support from civil society.[106] Although a number of corporations and states will likely mount opposition to any effort that includes binding rules, it is more difficult to mount such

---

[103] Ruggie, *Just Business*, p. 200. See also Ruggie, Chapter 2 in this volume.
[104] James Stewart, "A New Instrument on "Gross" Violations? Enthusiasm and Apprehension," 2 February 2015. Available at http://jamesgstewart.com/a-new-instrument-on-corporate-responsibility-for-gross-human-rights-violations-enthusiasm-and-apprehension/
[105] Oliver de Schutter, "Towards a New Treaty on Business and Human Rights," *Business and Human Rights Journal* 1 (2016).
[106] See Daniel Augenstein and David Kinley, "When Human Rights 'Responsibilities' Become 'Duties': The Extra-Territorial Obligations of States that Bind Corporations," in Surya Deva and David Bilchitz (eds.), *Human Rights Obligations of Business Beyond the Corporate Responsibility to Respect?* (Cambridge: Cambridge University Press, 2013). Civil society groups and academics, among others, have undertaken significant work specifically on the issue of extraterritoriality; the Maastricht Principles on Extraterritorial Obligations of States in the area of Economic, Social and

opposition effectively in the realm of gross human rights abuses or with regard to states' duties or efforts to mutually assist each other. It is these pragmatic considerations, rather than any conceptual or moral prioritization of a subset of rights or duties, that underlie my view in this regard.

Such proposals also take seriously the notion of a step-by-step approach toward building international law, with the idea that the GPs should be a step toward furthering standards, and that limited instruments can and should, be a step on the way toward future additional instruments with a broader scope that include other, equally important rights, from socioeconomic to environmental rights, which corporate activities can seriously and negatively affect.[107] Again, I emphasize that work toward a treaty of any scope should not be an exclusive strategy, and should be combined with other, diverse types of work on the issue of business and human rights. In this way, the GPs mark the end of the beginning of one form of engagement among many, allowing for a truly polycentric, and hopefully, in the aggregate, successful, set of efforts to advance human rights in the context of business activity.

Cultural Rights are a particularly comprehensive statement of extraterritorial state obligations in the realm of ESC rights.

[107] For arguments in favor of including these rights on par with gross human rights violations in an international regulatory instrument, see Deva's, Kweitel's, and Melish (Chapters 3, 10, and 4) respectively, in this volume. For an opposing view, see Backer, Chapter 5.

2

Hierarchy or Ecosystem? Regulating Human Rights Risks of Multinational Enterprises

John Gerard Ruggie

Calls to regulate multinational enterprises through a single overarching international treaty instrument go back to the 1970s. Over time, pressure for such a treaty has come most persistently from activists, and more intermittently from developing countries.[1] A recent civil society assessment sums up the record to date: "All these efforts met with vigorous opposition from TNCs and their business associations, and they ultimately failed."[2] This includes a 2003 initiative known as the Norms on the Responsibilities of Transnational Corporations and Other Business Enterprises with Regard to Human Rights, developed by an expert subsidiary body of the then UN Commission on Human Rights (now the Human Rights Council), but dismissed by its intergovernmental parent body, the Commission.[3]

In contrast, in June 2011 the Human Rights Council unanimously endorsed the Guiding Principles on Business and Human Rights (UNGPs), which I developed over the course of a six-year mandate as Special Representative of the UN Secretary-General for Business and Human Rights. It involved nearly fifty international consultations in all regions of the world, extensive research, as well as site visits to business operations and affected communities.[4] The UNGPs are the first authoritative guidance that the Council and its predecessor body, the Commission on Human Rights, have issued for states and business enterprises on their respective obligations in relation to business and human rights; and it marked the first time

---

[1] See Tagi Sagafi-nejad, *The UN and Transnational Corporations: From Code of Conduct to Global Compact* (Bloomington: Indiana University Press, 2008).

[2] "Corporate Influence on the Business and Human Rights Agenda of the United Nations," Working paper issued by Misereor, Global Policy Forum, and "Brot für die Welt," June 2014, p. 5, www .globalpolicy.org/home/221-transnational-corporations/52638-new-working-paper-corporate-influence-on-the-business-and-human-rights-agenda-of-the-un.html.

[3] The Commission stated that it had not requested the text and that it had no legal standing. It also instructed that no monitoring by UN human rights bodies take place (UN Document E/CN.4/DEC/ 2004/116, 20 April 2004).

[4] For the full text of the GPs, see UN document A/HRC/17/31 (21 March 2011). I elaborate on the thinking and activities that produced the UNGPs in my book, *Just Business: Multinational Corporations and Human Rights* (New York: W.W. Norton, 2013).

that either body "endorsed" a normative text on *any* subject that governments did not negotiate themselves.

In comparison with normative and policy developments in other complex and difficult domains, such as climate change, the uptake of the UNGPs has been relatively swift and widespread: by other international standard-setting bodies, governments, businesses, civil society and workers' associations, law societies, institutional investors, and most recently by FIFA (International Federation of Association Football), the governing body of the world's most popular sport.

Some observers attribute the success of the UNGPs to the fact that they were not legally binding. Undoubtedly this made Council endorsement easier. But it does little to explain subsequent developments. More to the point, the UNGPs were not conceived as a static document, to be adopted by governments, which then would be expected to impose them on businesses. Instead, they were designed to generate a new and different regulatory dynamic, one in which public and private governance systems – corporate as well as civil – each come to add distinct value, compensate for one another's weaknesses, and play mutually reinforcing roles – out of which a more comprehensive and effective global regime might evolve, including specific legal measures. The spatial imagery embedded in the UNGPs is a regulatory ecosystem, not hierarchy.

The chapter by Rodríguez-Garavito in this volume addresses several key issues concerning how to build on the foundations established by the UNGPs to keep advancing the business and human rights agenda. I appreciate his understanding the UNGPs as a dynamic process, rather than assessing them purely as a static document. I also find myself in agreement with much of his argument regarding the desirability of continuing to pursue the "polycentric approach" embodied in the UNGPs; identifying ways of dealing with the attendant "orchestration" problems; the challenge of institutionalizing what he calls "accountability politics" in order to "ratchet up" the internalization and compliance by business with human rights standards; and his conclusion that any move toward further international legalization in this space is no substitute for continuing to address ongoing needs in the here and now, and that it should focus as a matter of priority on gross human rights abuses.

In what follows, I begin with a reprise of the UNGPs and the logic behind them. Then I elaborate on two important issues raised elsewhere in the book. The first is the criticism by Rodríguez-Garavito as well as others that the UNGPs don't do enough to ensure what they call "the empowered participation of civil society." The second is the role and forms of international law that would reinforce and build on the UNGPs rather than positioning the two in opposition and thereby threatening to repeat past failures yet again. I begin with a reprise of the UNGPs and the logic behind them.

THE UNGPS

Human rights discourse is infused with the assumption of a rights-based hierarchy – the idea that human rights trump not only in a moral sense but that they also do, or at least should, in terms of the law. Yet in an influential report to the UN General Assembly, the authoritative International Law Commission concluded that "no homogenous hierarchical metasystem is realistically available" within the international legal order to resolve the problem of incompatible provisions among different bodies of law, including when different tribunals that have overlapping jurisdictions address exactly the same set of facts and yet reach different conclusions.[5] Thus, the UNGPs took a different tack.

Polycentric Governance

The UNGPs are based on the observation that corporate conduct at the global level is shaped by three distinct governance systems. The first is the system of public law and governance, domestic and international. The second is a civil governance system involving stakeholders affected by business enterprises and employing various social compliance mechanisms such as advocacy campaigns and other forms of pressure, but also collaborating with them. The third is corporate governance, which internalizes elements of the other two (unevenly, to be sure) as constraints and opportunities. Lacking was an authoritative basis whereby these governance systems become better aligned in relation to business and human rights, compensate for one another's weaknesses, and play mutually reinforcing roles – out of which cumulative change can evolve over time.

To foster that alignment, the UNGPs draw on the different discourses and rationales that reflect the different social roles these governance systems play in regulating corporate conduct.[6] Thus, for states the emphasis is on the legal obligations they have under the international human rights regime to protect against human rights abuses by third parties, including business, as well as policy rationales that are consistent with, and supportive of, meeting those obligations. For businesses, beyond compliance with legal obligations, the UNGPs focus on the need to manage the risk of involvement in human rights abuses, which requires that companies act with due diligence to avoid infringing on the rights of others and address harm where it does occur. For affected individuals and communities, the UNGPs stipulate ways for their further empowerment to realize a right to remedy.

Drawing these foundational elements together, the UNGPs rest on three pillars:

1. The state duty to protect against human rights abuses by third parties, including business, through appropriate policies, regulation, and adjudication;

---

[5]   International Law Commission, "Fragmentation of International Law: Difficulties Arising from the Diversification and Expansion of International Law," UN Doc. A/CN.4/L.682 (13 April 2006).

[6]   For an interesting discourse analysis of the development of the GPs, see Karin Buhman, "Navigating from 'train wreck' to being 'welcomed': negotiation strategies and argumentative patterns in the development of the UN Framework," in Surya Deva and David Bilchitz (eds.), *Human Rights Obligations of Business* (Cambridge: Cambridge University Press, 2013).

2. An independent corporate responsibility to respect human rights, which means that business enterprises should act with due diligence to avoid infringing on the rights of others and to address adverse impacts with which they are involved;
3. Greater access by victims to effective remedy, judicial and nonjudicial.

The UNGPs are comprised of thirty-one principles, each with commentary elaborating its meaning and implications for law, policy, and practice. They encompass all internationally recognized rights, and apply to all states and all business enterprises. They do not, by themselves, create new legally binding obligations for business but derive their normative force through the recognition of social expectations by states and other key actors, including business itself. Yet elements of them have already been incorporated into binding regulations and national laws.

Implementation through Distributed Networks

I was succeeded in my UN mandate by a five-person expert group, one from each of the geographic regions recognized within the UN, whose job it was to promote the UNGPs and facilitate their implementation. Rodríguez-Garavito discusses the Working Group in his Chapter. Here, I want to stress that the model of implementation I envisaged from the start involved a variety of other actors. Of course, this included individual governments and businesses. Some thirty states either have issued or are in the process of developing National Action Plans for the implementation of the UNGPs. Leading companies have aligned their policies and practices with them.[7] Beyond them, I worked closely with the Organization for Economic Cooperation and Development, to ensure that its Guidelines for Multinational Enterprises were made consistent with the UNGPs. The Guidelines are important because each of the forty-two adhering governments are required to establish a complaints mechanism, known as National Contact Points (NCPs). The previous Guidelines iterations lacked a human rights chapter; the 2011 has such a chapter, drawn directly from the UNGPs. Early evidence suggests that human rights complaints fare better in the NCP process than on other types of complaints.[8]

Similarly, I worked with the International Finance Corporation to include appropriate human rights criteria in their sustainability framework and performance standards to which clients are required to adhere. In turn, these are tracked by the so-called Equator banks, private financial institutions that account for three-fourths of global project lending – thus affecting the cost of capital. The European Union has

---

[7] The Business and Human Rights Resource Centre tries to keep track of undertakings by companies and governments. See http://business-humanrights.org/.

[8] John Gerard Ruggie and Tamaryn Nelson, "Human Rights and the OECD Guidelines for Multinational Enterprises: Normative Innovations and Implementation Challenges," *The Brown Journal of World Affairs* 22 (Fall/Winter 2015).

adopted a new mandatory nonfinancial reporting requirement for companies above a certain size, referencing the UNGPs.

Likewise, I sought to ensure that the human rights provisions of ISO26000, a new social responsibility guidance issued the International Organization of Standardization, was fully compatible with the UNGPs. Its importance lies in the heavy uptake it enjoys in Asia. The ASEAN Intergovernmental Commission on Human Rights is drawing on the UNGPs in its own work; so is the African Union, in relation to the Africa Mining Vision. The General Assembly of the Organization of American States has formally endorsed the UNGPs. The China Chamber of Commerce of Metals, Mineral and Chemicals Importers and Exporters, affiliated with the Ministry of Commerce, has issued Guidelines for Social Responsibility in Outbound Mining Investments, which instruct Chinese companies operating over-seas to "observe the UN Guiding Principles on Business and Human Rights during the entire life-cycle of the mining project."[9]

Ever-increasing numbers of companies report that they are bringing internal management and oversight systems into greater alignment with the UNGPs. Workers organizations and a number of global NGOs are using the UNGPs as legal and policy advocacy tools. The International Bar Association, UK Law Society, and the American Bar Association are promoting the UNGPs' incorporation into the legal profession, including through law firms' client advisory work.[10]

Perhaps the least expected convert to the UNGPs has been embattled FIFA. FIFA's decision to review the adequacy of its World Cup bidding requirements in relation to human rights goes back to 2011, not long after the selection of Russia and Qatar to host the 2018 and 2022 tournaments respectively. Amid other sources of external pressure, in June 2014 Mary Robinson, former President of Ireland and former United Nations High Commissioner for Human Rights, and I sent an open letter to then FIFA President Sepp Blatter. We recommended that FIFA incorporate the UNGPs into its policies, practices and relationships.[11] In early 2015, FIFA staff sought technical support from the UN Office of the High Commissioner for Human Rights on the UNGPs in relation to bidding documents for the 2026 Men's World Cup. In July 2015, FIFA issued a press release stating that its Executive Committee had decided that "future bids [for the Men's World Cup] will have to meet a number of important additional criteria. In particular, FIFA will recognize the provisions of

---

[9]   See https://business-humanrights.org/en/guidelines-for-social-responsibility-in-outbound-mining-investments.

[10] For the official IBA guidance, see www.ibanet.org/LPRU/Business-and-Human-Rights-for-the-Legal-Profession.aspx.

[11] Mary Robinson and I sent the letter on behalf of the Institute for Human Rights and Business, of which she is the Patron and I chair the International Advisory Board. The letter is available at www.ihrb.org/pdf/2014-06-11-Open-Letter-FIFA.pdf. We attached a recent Institute report, "Striving for Excellence: Mega-Sporting Events and Human Rights," available at www.ihrb.org/pdf/2013-10-21_IHRB_Mega-Sporting-Events-Paper_Web.pdf.

the UN Guiding Principles on Business and Human Rights and will make it compulsory for both contractual partners and those within the supply chain to comply with these provisions."[12] FIFA subsequently asked me, as the author of the UNGPs to provide recommendations for "further embedding" them "into FIFA's policies and practices."[13] In February 2016, the FIFA Congress adopted a new provision in the FIFA Statutes that states, "FIFA is committed to respecting all internationally recognised human rights and shall strive to promote the protection of these rights."[14] And the bidding requirements for the 2026 Men's World Cup are expected to include human rights criteria for the first time, broadly in line with the UNGPs.

My task was two fold. First, I was asked to provide advice on, among other things, human rights language planned for inclusion in the FIFA Statutes and the 2026 Men's World Cup bidding requirements, as well as identifying key gaps in current FIFA's policies and practices. Second, we agreed that I would publish a comprehensive and independent public report on what it means for FIFA to embed respect for human rights across the full range of its activities and relationships, using the UNGPs as the template. The report was published in April 2016.[15]

Candidate countries would not be peremptorily excluded from hosting a World Cup. The way future bidding requirements are expected to work in relation to human rights is for FIFA to conduct human rights diligence of all bidders. If serious risks are identified, FIFA would then ask the bidder(s) to develop effective mitigation strategies for the purposes of the Cup. If these are judged adequate, the bid would be considered along with others; if they were not adequate, FIFA would move on the next bidder. For tournaments that have already been awarded, FIFA is expected to use its leverage to reduce existing human rights harm – which FIFA has begun to address in Russia and Qatar.[16] Nothing like this has ever happened in the history of international sports.

---

[12] See www.fifa.com/about-fifa/news/y=2015/m=7/news=fifa-executive-committee-sets-presidential-election-for-26-february-20–2666448.html/.

[13] See www.fifa.com/governance/news/y=2015/m=12/news=fifa-to-further-develop-its-human-rights-approach-with-international-e-2744747.html.

[14] See http://resources.fifa.com/mm/document/affederation/bodies/02/74/76/37/draftfifastatutesextraordinarycongress2016en_neutral.pdf, Article 3.

[15] See John Gerard Ruggie, "'For the Game. For the World.' FIFA and Human Rights," available at www.hks.harvard.edu/content/download/79736/1789834/version/1/file/Ruggie_humanrightsFIFA_reportApril2016.pdf.

[16] On a visit to Moscow, FIFA President Gianni Infantino was asked about Russia's "gay propaganda" law. He said FIFA is not the world's welfare agency but "we need to be responsible about these things, we have to be responsible about the position we take about human rights." A few days later in Qatar, when asked about the migrant workers' situation in that country, he announced a FIFA led oversight committee that was to include civil society members. See, respectively, "FIFA's Infantino Wants Video Assistance at 2018 World Cup," *New York Times*, 19 April 2016, and Owen Gibson, "FIFA Promises Panel to Ensure Decent Working Conditions for 2022 World Cup Workers," *The Guardian*, 22 April 2016.

The two component elements of the UNGPs that have enjoyed the most rapid uptake are human rights due diligence requirements for companies, and expanding the role of nonjudicial grievance mechanisms, including at the operational or site level established by or otherwise involving companies. The reason is simple. At least in principle, each of the three main stakeholder groups has an interest in making these work, even though their rationales for doing so may differ. For states, promoting or requiring human rights due diligence and grievance mechanisms serves the duty to protect; for businesses, they are a means to manage stakeholder-related risk; and for affected individuals and communities, they offer the promise of reducing the overall incidence of corporate-related harm while also serving as one possible source of remedy where harm occurs. I expect this kind of dynamic interaction to continue to drive change. Changes in judicial remedy are moving much more slowly.

I now turn to two key challenges raised by other contributors to this volume.

CIVIL SOCIETY IN THE UNGPS

The UNGPs were developed through a "polycentric" process, involving representatives of states, business, and civil society.[17] With regard to civil society specifically, I held numerous bilateral meetings with NGOs as well as with individuals and communities adversely affected by business operations. Civil society groups typically accounted for the largest single number of participants in the multistakeholder consultations I convened, many of which were held in the Global South. But still the question is sometimes asked: where is civil society in the UNGPs? Rodríguez-Garavito argues that the future success of the UNGPs depends in no small measure on the "empowered participation of civil society," and he finds that the UNGPs fall short in this respect. Tara Melish and Errol Meidinger have suggested that the UNGPs should have had a fourth pillar, officially recognizing civil society's critical role.[18] Melish, in Chapter 4 in this volume, repeats that proposal and argues that there are insufficient "expressive commitments" to civil society participation in the UNGPs, as a result of which NGOs are unable to use of the UNGPs sufficiently to press for changes in state and corporate conduct.

I certainly agree with the proposition that civil society participation is critical, and from the start conceptualized and articulated the UNGPs with that in mind: hence their very foundation in the idea of polycentric governance. Moreover, neither

[17] I elaborate on the analytics framing the GPs process in my article "Global Governance and 'New Governance Theory': Lessons from Business and Human Rights," *Global Governance*, 20 (Jan.–Mar. 2014).
[18] Tara J. Melish and Errol Meidinger, "Protect, Respect, Remedy and Participate: 'New Governance' Lessons for the Ruggie Framework," in Radu Mares (ed.), *The UN Guiding Principles on Business and Human Rights* (Leiden: Martinus Nijhoff, 2012). Curiously, the authors claim that even the third pillar was a victory "hard-fought by the human rights community" (p. 314). The claim is incorrect. The "Protect, Respect, and Remedy" framework was developed and presented as one piece from the outset.

NGOs nor workers organizations have had the slightest difficulty in using the UNGPs as a tool to press for changes. But there are also several logical, practical, and empirical issues in play here that require clarification.

For starters, Rodríguez-Garavito takes his concept of "empowered participation" from an important study by Archon Fung and Erik Olin Wright on institutional innovations in democratic countries that are intended to achieve more direct citizen involvement in devising and implementing public policies affecting their daily lives.[19] There is much to be learned from the cases on which that study's conclusions and generalizations are based. But let us also recall the cases themselves and their settings: neighborhood councils in Chicago, addressing issues related to policing and public schools; habitat conservation planning under the U.S. Endangered Species Act; participatory budgeting in Porto Alegre, Brazil; and certain steps toward administrative and fiscal devolution from the states of West Bengal and Kerala, India, to villages. Fung and Wright believe these innovations to be transferable and scalable in some contexts. Indeed, the UNGPs provisions for nonjudicial grievance mechanisms involving companies and affected individuals and communities embody some of Fung and Wright's insights.[20] But there are strict limits to the applicability of the institutional innovations they identify to the level of the global polity itself, including (or perhaps above all) to the state-based United Nations system.

What about a "Participate" pillar, as recommended by Melish and Meidinger? There are two problems with that idea in this context. First, it might have made sense if the UNGPs were a discrete multistakeholder membership initiative like the Kimberley Process to stem the trade in conflict diamonds or the Forest Stewardship Council. But they are not. They are a soft-law instrument that prescribes minimum standards of conduct for all states and all businesses in relation to all human rights. There is no central governing institution as such. Moreover, Rodríguez-Garavito suggests that introducing such a fourth pillar into the UNGPs might have required including standards for civil society actors as well – which would have delighted some states and many businesses, but I suspect would have been resisted by civil society.

Second, and in a more practical vein, I seriously doubt that a "Participate" pillar would have survived the UN political process of getting the UNGPs approved. More and more countries are limiting the degrees of freedom of human rights

---

[19] Archon Fung and Erik Olin Wright (eds.), *Deepening Democracy: Institutional Innovations and Empowered Participatory Governance* (London: Verso, 2003).

[20] One of the most successful such efforts with which I am familiar is the creation of eight Regional Development Councils under a Global Memorandum of Understanding established between Chevron Nigeria Limited and communities in Delta, Rivers, Bayelsa, Ondo, and Imo States, Nigeria. My UN mandate produced a short and award-winning documentary on this initiative, which is available at http://shiftproject.org/video/only-government-we-see-building-company-community-dialogue-nigeria. The documentary was funded by a grant from the government of Norway.

organizations, especially those with international ties, and are requiring the latter to register with and be monitored by the authorities. This is happening in China, India, Russia, several Middle Eastern countries and even Ecuador, which for a time had become a hero to NGOs when it proposed an international business and human rights treaty. It strains credulity to believe that in this environment governments would agree to establish NGOs on equal footing with them in a "Participate" pillar to govern the business sector.

But if not a pillar, what about more extensive "expressive commitments" in the UNGPs text in support of civil society participation? Melish references the Convention on the Rights of Persons with Disabilities as a precedent, contending that the UNGPs are weaker in this regard and don't give civil society enough hooks.[21] Indeed, Article 4.3 of that Convention provides that "States Parties shall closely consult with and actively involve persons with disabilities, including children with disabilities, through their representative organizations."[22] Here I would make two points:

First, I did in fact embed affected individuals and communities, together with civil society actors that may represent them, within the three pillars. There are specific references to the need to engage with, consult, and report to affected persons and communities as part of the UNGPs human rights due diligence requirements. Moreover, detailed legitimacy and effectiveness criteria are laid out for nonjudicial grievance mechanisms, state-based and private, on the premise that "a grievance mechanism can only serve its purpose if the people it is intended to serve know about it, trust it and are able to use it" (Commentary to GP 31). Finally, the UNGPs as a whole do provide (and are being used as) a public and judicial advocacy tool, an authoritative basis for making demands on states and businesses. This includes leading global human rights and workers organizations, as well as legal advocacy groups.[23] None of this may be enough, as Melish and Meidinger and to a lesser extent Rodríguez-Garavito contend. But it reached the limits of my imagination of what was achievable – not as a theoretical exercise, but in actual practice – regarding civil society empowerment within the UNGPs' provisions.

---

[21]   See Melish and Meidinger, *supra* note 18, and Melish in this volume.

[22]   www.un.org/disabilities/convention/conventionfull.html.

[23]   The International Corporate Accountability Roundtable (ICAR) has done impressive work using the GPs as a platform to further advance corporate accountability, including through national regulation. ICAR is a coalition of leading global human rights organizations; its Steering Committee includes EarthRights International, Human Rights Watch, Human Rights First, Global Witness, and Amnesty International. Also see International Trade Union Confederation, "The United Nations 'Protect, Respect, Remedy' Framework and the United Nations Guiding Principles for Business and Human Rights: A Guide for Trade Unionists," available at www.ituc-csi.org/IMG/pdf/ 12-04-23_ruggie_background_fd.pdf; and Advocates for International Development, "The UN Guiding Principles on Business and Human Rights: A Guide for the Legal Profession," www .europarl.europa.eu/meetdocs/2014_2019/documents/droi/dv/411-un_projectrespectremedy_/411-un _projectrespectremedy_en.pdf .

My second point again concerns inappropriate (and therefore misleading) analogizing from one setting to another. There are substantial differences in scope, scale and political dynamics between the disabilities convention and attempts to regulate multinational corporations. The former addresses one group of persons and enumerates the rights relevant to their being able to lead lives of dignity. As is true of other economic, social and cultural rights treaties, states' undertakings are subject to "progressive realization," linked to state capacity. Moreover, broad consensus exists on the underlying aims. In contrast, business and human rights deals with all rights of all people, with all states, and with all businesses. It is characterized by extensive problem diversity, significant institutional variations, and conflicting interests across and within states. Not least are the interests and influence of multinationals themselves. Consequently, straight analogizing from the disabilities convention to business and human rights is questionable on both substantive and methodological grounds.

Ultimately, my main concern with the line of criticism contending that the UNGPs do not provide enough hooks for civil society is its potential risk of creating a self-fulfilling prophecy. Rodríguez-Garavito notes that many human rights organizations in developing countries lack the capacity to fully track and engage in global governance processes, such as the evolving UNGPs. Therefore, they look for cues to opinion leaders whose views and preferences broadly reflect their own. It would be far more helpful, not only to the UNGPs but more importantly to those suffering corporate-related human right harm, if those opinion leaders provided further guidance on how such organizations can use and build on the UNGPs, instead of relitigating the question about whether the UNGPs text adopted in 2011 says enough regarding the role of civil society.

INTERNATIONAL LEGALIZATION

As the business and human rights agenda continues to evolve, further legalization is an inevitable and necessary component of future developments. But, in light of the failure of past treaty efforts in this domain, we need to ask ourselves what form legalization should take at the international level. What approach does experience tell us would yield the most benefit for affected individuals and communities? This is no mere academic question. In September 2013, Ecuador proposed that the UN Human Rights Council establish an intergovernmental working group to negotiate just such a treaty instrument, and some 600 NGOs formed a "treaty alliance" to support it.[24] In a sharply divided vote, the Council adopted the proposal on June 26, 2014.

Will this latest attempt to impose binding international law obligations on transnational corporations turn out to be another instance of the classic dysfunction

---

[24] www.treatymovement.com. It is noteworthy that the major global human rights organizations, such as Amnesty and Human Rights Watch, did not join the alliance, reflecting doubts about the timing and efficacy of the Ecuador proposal.

of doing the same thing over and over again and expecting a different result? Or might the negotiations come to reflect more deeply on the reasons for this prior record and move in a productive direction? In the heat of the moment, treaty advocates and opponents seem to be on a collision course. Going forward, the answer hinges on whether the initiative's supporters are more interested in making a difference than in making a point, and whether its opponents can accept that some form of further international legalization in business and human rights is both necessary and desirable. I elaborate on these scenarios below.

Let's begin with the Ecuador resolution and the vote on it. The resolution calls for the establishment of an open-ended intergovernmental working group within the Human Rights Council, "the mandate of which shall be to elaborate an international legally binding instrument to regulate, in international human rights law, the activities of transnational corporations and other business enterprises."[25] Thus, the resolution is not addressed to any specific human rights abuses. Rather, it seeks to establish an overarching international legal framework – a global constitution of sorts – governing business conduct in relation to human rights. It then goes on to define "other business enterprises" in a way that is intended to exclude national companies, so that the new legal framework would apply only to transnational corporations.[26] Thus, to illustrate, the language of the proposed treaty would have covered international brands buying readymade garments from the factories housed in the collapsed Rana Plaza building, but not the owners of the local factories in which they are produced.

In addition to Ecuador, the resolution was cosponsored by Bolivia, Cuba, South Africa, and Venezuela. The vote in the Council was twenty in favor, fourteen against, with thirteen abstentions. A majority of African members voted for it, as did China, India, and Russia. Apart than the sponsors, all other Latin American countries, notably Brazil, abstained. The European Union and the United States voted against the resolution, which they thought counter-productive and polarizing; both stated that they would not participate in the treaty negotiating process.[27] Japan and South Korea also voted no. Representatives of the civil society coalition were euphoric, though several NGOs criticized the exclusion of national companies.[28]

---

[25] UN Document A/HRC/26/L.22/Rev. 1 (24 June 2014).

[26] A footnote in the resolution states the following: "'Other business enterprises' denotes all business enterprises that have a transnational character in their operational activities, and does not apply to local businesses registered in terms of relevant domestic law." The resolution is silent on the subject of joint ventures with domestic partners, including state-owned enterprises, and on other forms of host state involvement with transnational corporations.

[27] The U.S. statement is posted at https://geneva.usmission.gov/2014/06/26/proposed-working-group-would-undermine-efforts-to-implement-guiding-principles-on-business-and-human-rights/.

[28] See Arvind Ganesan of Human Rights Watch: "Dispatches: A Treaty to End Corporate Abuses," available at www.hrw.org/news/2014/07/01/dispatches-treaty-end-corporate-abuses: "A fundamental flaw lies in Ecuador's insistence that the treaty focus on multinational companies, even though any company can cause problems and most standards, including the UN [guiding] principles, don't draw this artificial distinction."

China's explanation of its vote was no rousing endorsement. China's delegate stated that the vote was based on the following "understanding": that the issue of a business and human rights treaty is complex; that differences exist among countries in terms of their economic, judicial, and enterprise systems, as well as their historical and cultural backgrounds; and that it will be necessary, therefore, to carry out "detailed and in-depth" studies, and for the treaty process itself to be "gradual, inclusive, and open."[29] China, of course, is no more likely than the United States to impose human rights standards on its multinationals that it has not accepted for itself as a state.[30]

In short, a sizeable majority of Council members did not vote in favor of the Ecuador resolution. The home countries of the vast majority of the world's transnational corporations opposed and are boycotting the proposed treaty negotiations, abstained, or in China's case signaled significant conditionality. Thus, as of now this latest treaty effort looks very much like a case of dysfunction redux. But is there nothing to be learned from forty years of history – indeed, from international lawmaking generally – that could ensure additional remedy to victims of corporate-related human rights harm? I believe there is, but it would require key doctrinal preferences to yield to practical reality. I briefly flag three.

The first is for treaty supporters, states and NGOs, to recognize that no treaty of any kind will emerge in the near future. Ecuador itself, in informal consultations leading up to the vote, estimated that it could take a decade or more. Indeed, if the current impasse is not bridged we may well witness a replay of the 1970s TNCs Code of Conduct negotiations, which drifted on for years until they were finally abandoned in 1992. Recall that even the nonbinding Declaration on the Rights of Indigenous Peoples took twenty-six years from conception to adoption. That's not a reason to delay. But it does raise an obvious question for treaty supporters: what do they propose to do between now and then – whenever the then may be? The obvious answer should be to implement and build on the UN Guiding Principles on Business and Human Rights. But this poses a dilemma for many treaty proponents. Let me explain.

Virtually every country that spoke during the Council debate stressed the importance of implementing the UNGPs. Indeed, the day after the deeply divided vote on the Ecuador proposal the Council adopted a second resolution, introduced by

---

[29] See http://webtv.un.org/search/ahrc26l.22rev.1-vote-item3-37th-meeting-26th-regular-session-human-rights-council/3643474571001?term=humanrightscouncil&sort=date.

[30] This raises a fundamental point that civil society treaty advocates and their academic supporters have ignored when criticizing what they consider to be the "weakness" of Pillar 2. All Council members in 2011 were able to endorse the corporate responsibility to respect *all* human rights because within the UNGPs' framework that responsibility is based in a global social norm, not a legal obligation. In contrast, if the corporate responsibility to respect human rights were turned into an international treaty obligation, its applicability and the range of human rights to which it would apply would be determined by individual instances of state treaty ratification – not only involving the proposed new treaty, but also the variable human rights standards that individual states currently recognize as international legal obligations.

Argentina, Ghana, Norway, and Russia along with forty additional cosponsors from all regions of the world. It extends the mandate of the expert working group the Council established in 2011 to promote and build on the UNGPs, and requests the High Commissioner for Human Rights to facilitate a consultative process with states, experts, and other stakeholders exploring "the full range of legal options and practical measures to improve access to remedy for victims of business-related human rights abuses."[31] It also asks the expert working group to report on UNGPs implementation – lack of awareness of what is actually happening being a main reason for the belief by many that not much is. This resolution was adopted by consensus, requiring no vote.

But here is the problem: many of the countries supporting the treaty process have done little if anything to act on the UNGPs. Similarly, many of the NGOs in the treaty alliance have done little to promote them – some even campaigned against their endorsement by the Human Rights Council in 2011. Both groups all along have simply held to the doctrinal position that only international legal measures can produce significant change, and since the UNGPs do not by themselves create new international law obligations, a treaty is necessary. But given Ecuador's own conjecture that a business and human rights treaty may be a decade or more away, will treaty proponents now take implementing the UNGPs more seriously – as an interim measure, if nothing else? If not, what will they say to victims, in whose name these battles are waged?

A second doctrinal position stands in the way of progress: the very scale of the proposed treaty. The idea of establishing an overarching international legal framework through a single treaty instrument governing all aspects of transnational corporations in relation to human rights may seem like a reasonable aspiration and simple task. But neither the international political or legal order is capable of achieving it in practice. The crux of the challenge is that business and human rights is not so discrete an issue-area as to lend itself to a single set of detailed treaty obligations. Politically, the problem diversity, institutional variation, and conflicting interests across states only increase as the number of TNC home countries grows (note, for instance, China's remarks previously). Legally, the category of business and human rights simply encompasses too many complex areas of national and international law for a single treaty instrument to resolve across the full range of human rights.[32] Any attempt to do so would have to be pitched at such a high level of abstraction that it would be devoid of substance, of little practical use to real people in real places, and with high potential for generating serious backlash against any form of further international legalization in this domain – as we already began to witness in the recent Council debate.

---

[31]   UN Document A/HRC/26/L.1, Rev.1.
[32]   For starters, I count human rights law, labor law, antidiscrimination law, health and safety law, privacy law, consumer protection law, environmental law, anticorruption law, humanitarian law, criminal law, investment law, trade law, tax law, property law and, not least, corporate and securities law.

This brings me to a third doctrinal impediment. Treaty opponents need to face up to the reality that international law in this domain cannot and will not remain frozen in place forever. If some of the arguments by Ecuador and the treaty alliance sounded like a blast from the past, so too did some rejoinders from the other side. For example, the delegate of the United Kingdom stated that "this issue is one of the rule of law, the national rule of law in individual states."[33] Similarly, the International Chamber of Commerce stated in a press release that "no initiative or standard with regard to business and human rights can replace the primary role of the state and national laws in this area."[34] Both statements are absolutely correct as far as they go. But if national law and domestic courts sufficed, then why do TNCs not rely on them to resolve investment disputes with states? Why is binding international arbitration necessary, enabled by 3,000 bilateral investment treaties and investment chapters in free trade agreements? The justification for this has always been that national laws and domestic courts are not adequate and need to be supplemented by international instruments.

In their response to Ecuador's resolution, the United Kingdom and ICC both expressed strong support for the Guiding Principles. Indeed, both have actively promoted and contributed to their implementation – the United Kingdom being the first country to adopt a National Action Plan. But we must remain clear about what the UNGPs are and do. The UNGPs established an evidence- and consensus-based foundation. They have generated new national and international policy requirements as well as some new legal requirements. Where they are being acted upon and developed further, they help reduce the overall incidence of corporate-related human rights harm and also provide for sources of nonjudicial remedy that did not exist before. But they were never intended to foreclose other necessary or desirable future paths.

Early on in my mandate I identified an approach to international legalization in business and human rights consistent with the principled pragmatism that brought us the Guiding Principles.[35] Principled pragmatism views international law as a tool for collective problem solving, not an end in itself. It recognizes that the development of any international legal instrument requires a certain degree of consensus among states. And it holds that before launching a treaty process its aims should be clear, there ought to be reasonable expectations that it can and will be enforced by the relevant parties, and that it will turn out to be effective in addressing the particular problem(s) at hand. This suggests narrowly crafted international legal

---

[33] The statement may be viewed at http://webtv.un.org/search/ahrc26l.22rev.1-vote-item3-37th-meeting -26th-regular-session-human-rights-council/3643474571001?term=human rights council&sort=date.

[34] "ICC disappointed by Ecuador Initiative adoption," available at: www.iccwbo.org/News/Articles/ 2014/ICC-disappointed-by-Ecuador-Initiative-adoption/.

[35] John Gerard Ruggie, "Business and Human Rights: The Evolving International Agenda," *American Journal of International Law* 101 (October 2007).

instruments for business and human rights – "precision tools" I called them – focused on specific governance gaps that other means are not reaching.[36]

One obvious candidate would be the worst of the worst: business involvement in gross human rights abuses, including those that may rise to the level of international crimes, such as genocide, extrajudicial killings, and slavery as well as forced labor. I made a proposal to this effect in a note I sent to all UN member states in February 2011, conveying my recommendations for follow-up measures to my mandate.[37] In the case of natural persons, broad consensus exists on the underlying prohibitions, which generally enjoy greater extraterritorial application in practice than other human rights standards. But further specificity is required as to what steps states should take with regard to business enterprises – legal persons – and about the role that international cooperation could play in helping states to take those steps. A legal instrument with this focus would have the secondary effect of heightening state and corporate awareness of the need for businesses to more broadly avoid human rights harm, much as the Alien Tort Statute did before the U.S. Supreme Court restricted its extraterritorial applicability in the recent *Kiobel* case.[38]

In short, the issue for me has never been about international legalization as such; it is about carefully weighing what forms of international legalization are necessary, achievable, and capable of yielding practical results, all the while building on the UNGPs' foundation.

This discussion leads to several conclusions. First, if Ecuador and its supporters hold fast to the terms and intent of their resolution, there are only two possible outcomes. Either the negotiations drag on for a decade or more and follow the path of the 1970s Code of Conduct negotiations; or they manage to persuade enough developing countries to adopt such a treaty text, but which home countries of most TNCs do not ratify and by which they will not be bound. Whatever outcome prevails, it would represent another dead end, delivering nothing to individuals and communities adversely affected by corporate conduct.

Second, if treaty opponents hold fast to their position that national law and voluntary initiatives suffice, and that no further legalization of any kind is acceptable now or in the future, they will contribute to the resurgent polarization that we have witnessed over the past year, and in the process undermine the Guiding Principles – not because the UNGPs lack value, but because discounting or dismissing their value is politically expedient for treaty proponents.

---

[36] I am well aware of what some call the "expressive" function of law, in contrast to its regulative role. But the field of international human rights does not lack for expressive legal instruments; what is in short supply are actionable paths to cumulative change.

[37] www.ohchr.org/Documents/Issues/TransCorporations/HRC%202011_Remarks_Final_JR.pdf.

[38] In *Kiobel v. Royal Dutch Petroleum Company* the Supreme Court held that a presumption against extraterritoriality applies to the statute, and "even where the claims touch and concern the territory of the United States, they must do so with sufficient force to displace the presumption against extra-territorial application."

Third, the resolution introduced by Argentina, Ghana, Norway, and Russia – currently overshadowed by Ecuador's resolution – will play an important role going forward. In the short run, the consultations it calls for on "the full range of legal options and practical measures to improve access to remedy," led by the Office of the High Commissioner and involving all stakeholder groups, will contribute practical information, insights, and guidance as the treaty negotiations get under way. But if the treaty process ends up prizing doctrine over practical results, the consensus resolution might well generate a constructive parallel process in its own right.

However this plays out, governments, businesses, and NGOs need to redouble (or in many cases, begin) efforts to implement and further develop the Guiding Principles, including through National Action Plans that set out clear expectations for governments and all types of business enterprises.[39] No future treaty, real or imagined, can substitute for the need to achieve further progress in the here and now. Indeed, the more that is accomplished by building on this widely supported foundation, the less politicized and polarized the debate about international legalization will become. Principled pragmatism may yet continue to prevail.

Conclusion

The UN Guiding Principles on Business and Human Rights have succeeded in generating the beginnings of a new global regulatory dynamic in the area of business and human rights. Their success – modest except when compared to the alternatives – is due to the fact that the development of the UNGPs consciously reflected on and was informed by the reasons for past failures. It sought explicitly to devise a different approach, as described briefly earlier in this chapter. Thus, one of the great ironies for me from the very start of my UN mandate has been the desire by many human rights activists and some academic human rights lawyers to continually try to push the agenda back into the conventional mold. Why? Because that's simply how human rights has been done in the past and must be done in the future.[40] The chapter by Rodríguez-Garavito courageously recognizes not only the limits of the conventional posture, but also its potentially harmful consequences for impacted individuals and communities, particularly in the institutional contexts of the Global South.

---

[39] For excellent guidance, see International Corporate Accountability Roundtable, "National Action Plans on Business and Human Rights: A Toolkit for the Development, Implementation, and Review of State Commitments to Business and Human Rights Frameworks," available at http://accountabilityroundtable.org/wpcontent/uploads/2014/06/DIHR-ICAR-National-Action-Plans-NAPs-Report2.pdf.

[40] An academic exemplar is David Bilchitz, "A Chasm between 'Is' and 'Ought'? A Critique of the Normative Foundations of the SRSG's Framework and the Guiding Principles," in Deva and Bilchitz, *supra* note 6.

3

Business and Human Rights: Time to Move Beyond the "Present"?

Surya Deva

I INTRODUCTION

The endorsement of the Guiding Principles on Business and Human Rights (GPs) by the Human Rights Council in June 2011 is widely regarded an important step in ensuring that companies abide with their human rights responsibilities.[1] The GPs have definitely changed the lingua franca of the business and human rights (BHR) discourse. However, since the GPs are reflective of "the end of the beginning" in this area, they might not be able to do enough to change fundamentally corporate behavior. Nor might they be able to trigger sufficient changes – through national action plans (NAPs) or otherwise – in the present regulatory frameworks to offer victims of corporate human rights violations effective access to remedies. We would, therefore, need to look to beyond the GPs in the near future.

As part of this exploration of other regulatory initiatives which could fill in gaps left by the GPs, this chapter seeks to achieve two broad objectives. Firstly, it engages critically with the background Chapter to this volume written by César Rodríguez-Garavito (background Chapter).[2] Considering the space limit, I will confine myself to a few aspects of his Chapter which frame the BHR debate in ways that require some reflections. I also flag certain key issues – some of which were pushed under, what I will call, the "consensus carpet" – that must be addressed to ensure that companies comply with their human rights obligations.[3]

Secondly, by taking cue from the term "beyond" in the title of the background Chapter and the book,[4] this chapter explores what *ought* to be the role of

---

[1] Human Rights Council, "Guiding Principles on Business and Human Rights: Implementing the United Nations 'Protect, Respect and Remedy' Framework," A/HRC/17/31, March 21, 2011 (GPs).

[2] Chapter 1 in this volume: César Rodríguez-Garavito, "Business and Human Rights: Beyond the End of the Beginning."

[3] Some of these issues did not feature in the background Chapter as well, something which is understandable considering how much one could cover in a chapter of this much length.

[4] Coincidentally, the term "beyond" also features in the title of a recent book that I coedited: Surya Deva and David Bilchitz (eds.), *Human Rights Obligations of Business: Beyond the Corporate Responsibility to Respect?* (Cambridge: Cambridge University Press, 2013).

international law and civil society in dealing with the so-called governance gaps.[5] I propose that international law should move beyond the "state-centric" framework and that Civil Society Organizations (CSOs) should occupy a more central and institutionalized role in regulating the behavior of companies rather than operating from the periphery. As readers may notice, my plea to move beyond the "present" state of affairs in the area of BHR connects these objectives in several ways.

II FRAMING OF THE DEBATE: SOME CRITICAL REFLECTIONS

"Static" vs. "Dynamic" Dimensions

The background Chapter draws an important distinction between the "static" and "dynamic" dimensions of the GP. It focuses on the latter dimension, that is, on "what has unfolded after the adoption of the GPs, as well as on what should unfold in the future."[6] While such a focus seems sensible, we should not ignore the inter-relationship between the two dimensions, especially how the "static" dimension might influence the "dynamic" dimension. If we do not identify and adequately respond to the deficiencies of the GPs, such deficiencies are likely to impair the future progress in the form of evolution of other regulatory initiatives.

Let me offer a few examples to illustrate this point. The GPs are rooted in the belief that companies do not have legally binding human rights obligations under international law – rather they merely have a *"responsibility* to *respect"* human rights. Both aspects of this second pillar formulation are contestable: companies already do have certain legally binding human rights obligations and the nature of their obligations should not be limited to the "respect" category.[7] On the other hand, the GPs limit the obligations of states to the "protect" category,[8] implying thereby that their "respect" and "fulfill" kinds of obligations are not engaged in any significant way in the area of BHR. Furthermore, the GPs define "internationally recognized human rights" in a narrow manner so as to refer to the rights "expressed in the International Bill of Human Rights and the principles concerning fundamental rights set out in the International Labour Organization's Declaration on Fundamental Principles and Rights at Work."[9] Consequently, several other *core* international conventions – such as the Convention

---

[5] Although the "governance gaps" thesis is frequently used to denote challenges that we are experiencing today in the area of business and human rights, it seems to oversimplify the complexity of issues. Beyond a point, it is also not very illuminating because almost any past or current problem in the world could be explained with reference to governance gaps.

[6] Rodríguez-Garavito, Chapter 1 in this volume.

[7] See David Bilchitz, "A Chasm between 'Is' and 'Ought'? A Critique of the Normative Foundations of the SRSG's Framework and the Guiding Principles," in *Human Rights Obligations of Business* (eds.), Deva and Bilchitz, 107.

[8] The General Principles of the GPs though acknowledge that the GPs "are grounded in recognition of States' existing obligations to respect, protect and fulfil human rights".

[9] GPs, Principle 12.

on the Elimination of All Forms of Racial Discrimination (CERD), the Convention
on the Elimination of All Forms of Discrimination Against Women (CEDAW), the
Convention on the Rights of the Child (CRC), and the Convention of the Rights of
Persons with Disabilities (CRPD)[10] – do not form part of this "minimum" list. Rather
they may become relevant as "additional standards."[11]

Against this backdrop, any push for alignment solely with the GPs might inherit such
a narrow conception of obligations for both companies and states.[12] Although I have not
been an admirer of the UN Global Compact,[13] if the Compact Principles are today
aligned with the GPs, that would mean taking a regressive step, because the Compact
Principles in their current form encompass environmental responsibilities and are not
confined to the "respect" cage of responsibilities. Similarly, states which plan to
implement the GPs through NAPs might think that they do not need to look beyond
the three pillars of the GPs in discharging their human rights obligations – flowing from
both international law and constitutional law – in relation to the activities of business
actors. One can see evidence of this narrow focus, for example, in the 2013 version of the
NAP developed by the United Kingdom (UK):[14] while the Plan did contain some useful
steps,[15] it mirrored the three pillars and was silent as to the implications of the UK
government's obligations flowing from the CRC and CEDAW (including the Optional
Protocols related to these conventions) in relation to business. Moreover, the UK
government's 2013 NAP hardly said anything concrete to improve access to judicial
remedies in the UK,[16] though the 2016 update lists a few steps to promote access to
remedy.[17]

[10] It is pertinent to note that CERD (175), CEDAW (187) and CRC (193) have been ratified by more
states than the ICCPR (167) and the ICESCR (160).

[11] GPs, Commentary on Principle 12.

[12] The alignment may also bring positive results, e.g., the inclusion of a separate human rights chapter in
the OCED Guidelines of 2011.

[13] See Surya Deva, "Corporate Complicity in Internet Censorship in China: Who Cares for the Global
Compact or the Global Online Freedom Act?," *George Washington International Law Review* 39
(2007), 255.

[14] HM Government, "Good Business: Implementing the UN Guiding Principles on Business and
Human Rights", September 2013, accessed June 27, 2014, www.gov.uk/government/uploads/system/
uploads/attachment_data/file/236901/BHR_Action_Plan_-_final_online_version_1_.pdf.

[15] For example, extending the scope of directors' report under Section 172 of the Companies Act to
include human rights issues and taking into account the negative final National Contact Point
statements against a company when considering a project for export credit.

[16] See Richard Meeran, "Access to remedy: The United Kingdom Experience of MNC Tort Litigation
for Human Rights Violations," in *Human Rights Obligations of Business* (eds.), Deva and Bilchitz,
378. See also the recommendations made in this report to improve access to justice: Robert
McCorquodale, "Survey of the Provision in the United Kingdom of Access to Remedies for Victims
of Human Rights Harms Involving Business Enterprises" (17 July 2015), www.biicl.org/documents/
724_uk_access_to_remedies.pdf.

[17] HM Government, "Good Business: Implementing the UN Guiding Principles on Business and
Human Rights", May 2016, accessed February 20, 2017, https://www.gov.uk/government/uploads/
system/uploads/attachment_data/file/522805/Good_Business_Implementing_the_UN_Guiding_
Principles_on_Business_and_Human_Rights_updated_May_2016.pdf.

Remnants of the "Either/Or" Dichotomy

Another framing-related issue of the background Chapter that requires some clarification is the "either/or" formulation of two regulatory visions (which in the past used to be framed as "voluntary vs. obligatory" regulation): one wedded to the idea of a comprehensive, legally binding international treaty and the other under-pinned by diverse regulatory ideas such as polycentric governance, new govern-ance, reflexive regulation, and responsive regulation.[18] I think that keen observers of the BHR arena belong to a *third vision* rooted in the realization that we need both sets of regulatory tools, not either one of them.[19] Multinational corporations (MNCs) are difficult regulatory targets and we need a coherent combination of regulatory strategies to achieve an acceptable level of preventive and redressive efficacy.[20]

As reflective of the above juxtaposition (i.e., "those who dismiss the GPs and are proposing a binding treaty"),[21] the background Chapter examines whether an "exclusive focus" on an international treaty would be a viable alternative. Rodríguez-Garavito rightly rejects the idea of an exclusive or obsessive focus on putting in place a binding international treaty: the idea is as flawed as thinking that voluntary initiatives alone could tame the propensity of companies to ignore human rights norms. Rather, the author moots the idea of a binding international treaty as "one tool in a broader toolkit" to complement the GPs.[22]

Although I will revisit later the international treaty proposal, two observations can be made at this stage about the analysis of Rodríguez-Garavito and his proposal. Firstly, if certain CSOs do have an exclusive focus on a binding international treaty, this is mostly because of a "no choice" situation. As four decades of voluntary initiatives have not given much hope, CSOs have a legitimate skepticism about the efficacy of any *new avatars* of voluntary initiatives (including the GPs). Thus, proponents of voluntary initiatives – rather than CSOs – are largely responsible for this exclusive focus mind-set, if any.

Secondly, there can be at least two different senses in which a binding treaty can complement the GPs, but it is not entirely clear to me the sense espoused by the background Chapter. Ruggie has mooted one sense: that of putting in place an international treaty – as a "carefully constructed precision tool"– to deal with gross

[18] Rodríguez-Garavito, "Beyond the End of the Beginning," p. 3.
[19] See Surya Deva, "Connecting the Dots: How to Capitalize on the Current High Tide for a Business and Human Rights Treaty", in Surya Deva and David Bilchitz (eds.), *Building a Treaty on Business and Human Rights: Context and Contours* (Cambridge: Cambridge University Press, forthcoming in 2017).
[20] For these twin levels of efficacy as well as the idea of an "integrated theory" of regulation, see Surya Deva, *Regulating Corporate Human Rights Violations: Humanizing Business* (London: Routledge, 2012).
[21] Rodríguez-Garavito, "Beyond the End of the Beginning," p. 5.
[22] Rodríguez-Garavito, "Beyond the End of the Beginning," p. 35.

human rights abuses amounting to international crimes.[23] Taken in this sense, the treaty would try to cure the deficiency of Pillar 2, which (incorrectly) suggests that companies merely have a responsibility to respect human rights under international law. But a binding treaty could also complement the GPs in a much broader sense by going beyond their text, that is, by revisiting the nature and scope of corporate human rights obligations as well as the *modus operandi* of their enforcement. In this sense, the treaty would be conceived as a "logical extension" of the GPs, thus treating the GPs not as a sacrosanct document. It may be useful to clarify further the exact role and scope of an international treaty conceived by Rodríguez-Garavito, because while he embraces Ruggie's narrow treaty approach, at places a reference is made to the expansive or expanded implementation of the GPs – the latter seems to suggest that any future treaty might extend the contours of corporate responsibilities set by the GPs.

Guarding against the Business of Human Rights

My final reflections on the background Chapter are about a very important issue raised in it: "who gets to count as part of civil society." This issue relates to a wider problem, the emerging problem of *the business of human rights* in the area of BHR (or generally in the area of human rights).[24] Due to the perceived normative power enjoyed by human rights, almost everyone wishes to employ the currency of human rights to further personal goals, some of which might be even illegitimate or hidden. The emergence of consultancy firms of diverse kinds to guide companies to manage their human rights risks should be seen in this context.

A majority of companies (and their managers) lack the training and capacity to internalize human rights norms into their decision-making processes.[25] It is critical to build corporate capacity on this front. Nevertheless, we should also guard against consultancy firms that perform this task as a business activity but at the same time pretend to be neutral or independent experts committed to promoting the cause of human rights.[26] Making money and upholding human rights may go hand in hand on certain occasions, but not always.

---

[23] John Ruggie, "A UN Business and Human Rights Treaty? An Issue Brief," January 28, 2014, p. 5, accessed June 27, 2014, http://business-humanrights.org/media/documents/ruggie-on-un-business-human-rights-treaty-jan-2014.pdf. See also John Ruggie, "Recommendations on Follow-up to the Mandate" (11 February 2011), 4–5; and John Ruggie, *Just Business: Multinational Corporations and Human Rights* (New York: Norton & Company, 2013), 199–201.

[24] See Surya Deva, "Business and Human Rights, or the Business of Human Rights: Critical Reflections on Emerging Themes," in Bård A Andreassen and Vo Khanh Vinah (eds.), *Duties Across Borders: Advancing Human Rights in Transnational Business* (Intersentia, 2016), 21.

[25] The recent entry of CSR or business and human rights courses into the curriculum of both business schools and law schools may help in bridging this training deficit to some extent.

[26] Although it is not the focus of this chapter, even some CSOs and nonprofit organizations at times try to use human rights to pursue their nonhuman rights goals.

III ISSUES UNDER THE "CONSENSUS CARPET"

One of the most important contributions of the former Special Representative of the Secretary General on human rights and transnational corporations and other business enterprises (SRSG) was his ability to build some consensus in the area of BHR and secure a unanimous endorsement of the GPs by the Human Rights Council. However, this consensus was not without cost. Several complex key issues were sidestepped by the then SRSG: they were swept under the carpet to achieve consensus and unanimous acceptance of the GPs.[27] Considering the fact that there are already cracks in the consensus,[28] it is time to move beyond the glory of "unanimous endorsement" and confront issues which were either swept under the carpet for pragmatic reasons or were not considered. Moreover, unless policy makers confront these key inconvenient issues, we would only be performing cosmetic treatment of a deep-rooted problem. I briefly allude to some such issues here.

Reorienting the Corporation

Scholars have pointed out that corporate law has a critical role to play in promoting corporate compliance with human rights.[29] The former SRSG also realized this and integrated this aspect into his mandate as well as into the GPs.[30] This is a good start, but much more needs to be done to bring changes *from the inside* and in turn humanize business.[31] Let me mention two aspects which did not get enough attention in the GPs. Firstly, companies are not merely profit-maximizing machines which should respect human rights because of a "business case" for doing so: rather

---

[27] See David Bilchitz and Surya Deva, "The Human Rights Obligations of Business: A Critical Framework for the Future," in *Human Rights Obligations of Business* (eds.), Deva and Bilchitz, 1, 10–17; and Surya Deva, "Treating Human Rights Lightly: A Critique of the Consensus Rhetoric and the Language Employed by the Guiding Principles," in *Human Rights Obligations of Business* (eds.), Deva and Bilchitz, 78, 86–91.

[28] The initiative led by Ecuador, South Africa and other states from the Global South to negotiate a legally binding international treaty resulted in Human Rights Council adopting a resolution in June 2014. Out of the forty-seven members of the Council, twenty states supported the resolution, while fourteen voted against it and thirteen states abstained. See Business & Human Rights Resource Centre, "Binding Treaty: Pros and Cons," accessed July 22, 2014, http://business-humanrights.org/en/binding-treaty-pros-and-cons. These divisions have continued as most of the developed countries boycotted the first session of the open-ended intergovernmental working group held in July 2015.

[29] In an article published in 2004, I argued that the lack of human rights as part of corporate culture is one of the reasons why companies violated human rights and that this deficit was on account of non-sharing of landscape between corporate law and human rights law. Surya Deva, "Corporate Code of Conduct Bill 2000: Overcoming Hurdles in Enforcing Human Rights Obligations against Overseas Corporate Hands of Local Corporations," *Newcastle Law Review* 8 (2004), 87, 110–111. See also Andrew Keay, *The Enlightened Shareholder Value Principle and Corporate Governance* (London: Routledge, 2013).

[30] See SRSG, "Human Rights and Corporate Law: Trends and Observations from a Cross-national Study Conducted by the Special Representative", A/HRC/17/31/Add. 2, May 23, 2011; GPs, Principle 3 and the Commentary.

[31] Deva, *Humanizing Business*, 211–214.

society allows them to pursue diverse business activities subject to compliance with certain nonnegotiable rules such as human rights norms. These rules should be much more expansive than Milton Friedman's famous "rules of the game,"[32] Sternberg's twin principles of business ethics elaborated in *Just Business*,[33] and the expectations laid down in the GPs. Among others, Frank Bold's "The Purpose of the Corporation" project tries to grapple with this question.[34]

Secondly, the principles of limited corporate liability and separate personality— which were developed at a time when the concept of parent and subsidiary corporations was unknown and when corporations generally lacked the power to acquire and hold shares of other corporations[35] – should be refined, so that they are neither used by MNCs to outsource risks legally nor routinely employed by parent companies to delay or avoid their liability for human rights abuses. A number of alternatives are possible here. A direct duty of care, for example, may be imposed on parent companies in certain circumstances, thus bypassing the whole issue of piercing the corporate veil.[36] Alternatively, a parent company could be held accountable for human rights violations by its subsidiaries as a matter of principle, unless the parent company can show either that it did not know (or had no reason to know) about the human rights violations in question or that the violations took place despite the company having taken appropriate preventive and redressive due diligence steps.[37]

Nature and Extent of Corporate Obligations

Companies do (and should) have legally binding human rights obligations. It is problematic to conceive of municipal laws and international law as two watertight compartments and to claim that companies merely have social expectations – rather than binding obligations – under the latter.

Out of several potential reasons that could support the *obligation* thesis, one is that human rights are not uni-relational. All individuals have these inherent rights based on the idea of human dignity. For historic reasons, duties in relation to such rights

[32] Milton Friedman, *Capitalism and Freedom*, 40th anniversary edition (Chicago: University of Chicago Press, 2002), 133.

[33] Elaine Sternberg, *Just Business: Business Ethics in Action*, 2nd edition (Oxford: Oxford University Press, 2000).

[34] Environmental Law Service, "The Purpose of the Corporation," accessed June 27, 2014, http://en.eps .cz/our-work/campaign/purpose-corporation. See also University of Oslo, "Sustainable Companies Project," accessed 27 June, 2014, www.jus.uio.no/ifp/english/research/projects/sustainable-companies.

[35] Phillip Blumberg, *The Multinational Challenge to Corporation Law: The Search for a New Corporate Personality* (New York: Oxford University Press, 1993), 52.

[36] See, for example, *CSR v Wren* (1998) 44 NSWLR 463; *Chandler v Cape plc* [2012] EWCA (Civ) 525; *Choc v Hudbay Minerals Inc* 2013 ONSC 1414 (Ontario, 2014). See also Doug Cassel, "Outlining the Case for a Common Law Duty of Care of Business to Exercise Human Rights Due Diligence," *Business and Human Rights Journal* 1:2 (2016), 179.

[37] It is worth noting, incidentally, that the SRSG's due diligence is a more appropriate tool in relation to corporate obligations that fall into the "protect" category rather than the "respect" category.

developed mostly with reference to states. But it does not mean that other entities are free from such duties. In fact, every entity that could violate human rights ought to have corresponding obligations – the focus should be on the bearers of rights and not on violators. It matters little for victims whether states or other non-state actors infringed on their rights.

The Preamble of the Universal Declaration of Human Rights embodies this spirit (although yet to be developed and fulfilled), positing that "every individual and every organ of society [. . .] shall strive [. . .] to promote respect for these rights and freedoms," which are a "common standard of achievement for all people and all nations." Moreover, as Joseph Raz rightly points out, "there is no closed list of duties which correspond to the right [. . .] A *change of circumstances may lead to the creation of new duties based on the old right* [. . .] This dynamic aspect of rights, *their ability to create new duties*, is fundamental to any understanding of their nature and function in practical thought."[38] Raz's "change of circumstances" threshold could be easily satisfied now. The illustrative examples may include: (i) the outsourcing of essential public services by the state to private corporate actors and in turn create situations where profits considerations dictate the availability of, and access to, basic human needs;[39] (ii) the privatization of war and security allowing private military and security companies to violate human rights at will;[40] and the emergence of public-private partnerships for big infrastructure projects with direct impact on the human rights of people displaced by such projects.[41]

In terms of the extent of obligations, companies should have all three kinds of obligations to a varying degree: the duty to respect, protect, and fulfill human rights. While their obligations should not be identical to those that of states, the extent of such obligations should also not be so limited that individuals' human rights are not adequately realized in an era where companies perform pervasive functions, some of which used to belong to states. A precise demarcation of the extent of corporate obligations requires more work. But my preliminary thoughts are that companies should have state-like "respect" obligations, while their "protect" and "fulfill" types of obligations should be limited in comparison to states. For instance, a parent company should exercise the *protect* category of obligations to ensure that its

---

[38] Joseph Raz, *The Morality of Freedom* (Oxford: Clarendon Press, 1986), 171 (emphasis added).

[39] See Smita Narula, "The Right to Food: Holding Global Actors Accountable under International Law," *Columbia Journal of Transnational Law* 44 (2005), 691.

[40] See, for example, Human Rights Council, *Report of the Working Group on the Use of Mercenaries As a Means of Violating Human Rights and Impeding the Exercise of The Right of Peoples to Self-Determination*, A/HRC/15/25 (2 July 2010); F Francioni and N. Ronzitti (eds.), *War by Contract: Human Rights, Humanitarian Law and Private Contractors* (Oxford: Oxford University Press, 2011).

[41] See Surya Deva "Public-Private Partnerships: Keeping Human Rights on the Radar" in Pradeep Mehta (ed.), *Mainstreaming Public Private Partnership in India* (New Delhi: CUTS Institute for Regulation & Competition, 2012), 85.

subsidiaries or suppliers do not violate human rights violations.[42] Similarly, the *fulfill* type of obligations could be relevant in certain situations, e.g., a company operating a mine in a remote area where people lack access to basic needs.

Rights Beyond the International Bill of Rights and the ILO Declaration

Companies can (in)directly violate all human rights, as the former SRSG did point out.[43] Nevertheless, the rights that companies should respect – "at a minimum" – under the GPs are those enumerated in the International Bill of Human Rights and the ILO's Declaration on Fundamental Principles and Rights at Work. It is neither clear nor defensible why other core international conventions such as CERD, CEDAW, CRC, and CRPD or other instruments in the area of environmental rights and indigenous rights, were not included in the moral minimum. Despite being specifically requested by the Human Rights Council to "integrate a gender perspective throughout his work and to give special attention to persons belonging to vulnerable groups, in particular children," the GPs provides that companies *"may need to consider additional standards* ... where they may have adverse human rights impacts on them."[44]

The above unprincipled (or pragmatically principled) "pick and choose" approach adopted by the GPs to under-define "internationally recognized human rights" is highly problematic. Why should CEDAW and CRC, which are relevant to almost all corporate activities, be part of optional international human rights norms applicable to companies? Similarly, why should environmental rights be not the business of all business enterprises in all circumstances? Possible future regulatory international initiatives should remedy this defect of the GPs.

IV GOVERNANCE GAPS, INTERNATIONAL LAW, AND CIVIL SOCIETY

The former SRSG rightly identified "governance gaps" as a key problem created by MNCs' transnational and outsourcing-based operations.[45] He also noticed that most serious human rights violations were taking place in "weak governance zones" or "conflict zones."[46] Although the SRSG correctly diagnosed the illness plaguing the BHR area, the same cannot be said about the prescribed pill in the form of GPs.

[42] The approach adopted by the GPs – that each and every company has a responsibility to respect human rights – is desirable, but it is neither adequate nor does it take into account how companies in a group operate.
[43] In his 2008 Report, the SRSG observed: "there are few if any internationally recognized rights business cannot impact – or be perceived to impact – in some manner. Therefore, companies should consider all such rights." SRSG, "Protect, Respect and Remedy: A Framework for Business and Human Rights," Report of the Special Representative of the Secretary General on the Issue of Human Rights and Transnational Corporations and Other Business Enterprises, A/HRC/8/5, April 7, 2008, para 52. See also Ruggie, *Just Business*, pp. 95–96.
[44] GPs, Commentary on Principle 12 (emphasis added).   [45] SRSG, "2008 Report", paragraph 3.
[46] Ibid., paragraphs 47–49.

Like any regulatory initiative, the efficacy of the GPs is based on several assumptions such as the following: states will be both willing and capable to exercise their "protect" duty against all types of companies; companies will carry out their "responsibility to respect" diligently despite the absence of any legal bite flowing from the GPs or without CSOs having an institutionalized role as informal watchdogs;[47] non-judicial mechanisms can accomplish the effectiveness criteria stipulated in the GPs despite significant asymmetry between MNCs and the stakeholders affected by their activities.[48]

Against the backdrop of these assumptions, how realistic is it to expect those very states which are at the center of conflict or weak governance zones to exercise effectively their duty to protect people against violations perpetuated by companies? For instance, can we really rely on a state, whose agencies infringe human rights as a part of an institutionalized policy, to ensure that companies operating within or from its territory do not violate human rights? The sole or overreliance on government agencies as the custodian of human rights may be unrealistic even in democratic states with stable governance institutions.[49] Similarly, the "responsibility to respect" pillar will work only if a company is sincere about complying with its human rights responsibilities and there is a business case for doing so. If the business case for human rights was so straightforward and universal,[50] there would have been no need for the SRSG's mandate and even this book.

Therefore, I suggest that the GPs will fail to deliver where their help was/is needed the most, that is, in "hard cases." By borrowing Ronald Dworkin's term,[51] I use "hard cases" to refer to those instances where there is no clear business case for human rights and any action or omission on the part of states makes it more difficult for victims to hold companies accountable for violations of human rights. This difficulty – which can be framed in terms of obstacles to access to justice – would arise because not all companies are likely to walk the talk to respect human rights and some states will invariably be unable or unwilling to act robustly against such companies.

As I have argued elsewhere,[52] we need an international instrument to deal with corporate human rights violations for a number of reasons. But more critically, such

---

[47] Ruggie though thinks that there are "several bites." Ruggie, *Just Business*, pp. 101–102.

[48] The background Chapter also highlights this important point and stresses the need to empower CSOs to operate as a countervailing power. Rodríguez-Garavito, Chapter 1 in this volume.

[49] See Surya Deva, "Development, Sovereign Support to Finance and Human Rights: Lessons from India," in Juan Pablo Bohoslavsky and Jernej Letnar Černič (eds.), *Making Sovereign Financing and Human Rights Work* (Oxford: Hart Publishing, 2014), 289.

[50] For a critique of the business case, see Deva, *Humanizing Business*, 139–146.

[51] Ronald Dworkin, *Taking Rights Seriously* (Delhi: Universal Law Publishing Co. Pvt. Ltd., 1999), 81.

[52] Surya Deva, "The Human Rights Obligations of Business: Reimagining the Treaty Business," pp. 2–4, accessed July 22, 2014, http://business-humanrights.org/sites/default/files/media/documents/reimagi ne_int_law_for_bhr.pdf. See also David Bilchitz, "The Necessity for a Business and Human Rights Treaty," *Business and Human Rights Journal* 1:2 (2016), 203.

an instrument must neither be overly "state-centric" nor should it be confined to certain egregious human rights abuses.

We need to deviate from the current state-centric conception because states are not always consistent and reliable enforcers of human rights norms – this is one of the key reasons for the so-called governance gaps. If the international treaty gives states the exclusive charge of enforcing human rights norms against companies, it will do little to achieve the very goal for which the idea of a treaty is being mooted. In terms of norm creation at the international level, non-state actors have already started playing a crucial role. Regulatory schemes should harness the potential of non-state actors such as CSOs in enforcing international norms, especially in those cases where states falter to act against powerful companies.

Furthermore, we need an instrument with a wide scope that covers all human rights because the calls for negotiating a narrow treaty that deals with only egregious abuses reflects, among other factors, the Global North's prioritization of civil and political rights over social, economic, and cultural rights. For people living in the Global South – who suffer disproportionately due to corporate-related human rights abuses – the latter set of rights are as important as civil-political rights. Why should we take the displacement of indigenous people for mining, emission of (and/or exposure to) hazardous chemicals, compulsory pre-employment pregnancy test of women, and illegitimate land grab by companies less seriously than slavery or genocide? It seems that the background Chapter fails to capture this politics in international relations and governance.[53]

There are sound reasons why a majority of states should support the idea of negotiating a treaty to regulate human rights violative activities of companies.[54] The adoption of a resolution by the Human Rights Council in June 2014 to establish an open-ended intergovernmental working group (OEIGWG) to elaborate an international legally binding instrument opens the possibility of moving towards developing a treaty to redress the present situation of corporate impunity for human rights abuses.[55] It is difficult to predict at this stage whether this attempt, unlike previous such attempts, will result in adoption of an international instrument or not. Considering that most of the developed countries did not participate in the first two sessions of the OEIGWG and in wake of the continued opposition to the proposed treaty from business organizations, the initial signs are not very promising. It is also problematic that this Human Rights Council resolution seeks to limit – through a controversial footnote – the regulatory scope of an international legally binding

---

[53] To draw an analogy, it is suggested that the International Criminal Court (ICC) has mostly engaged with situations in Africa (i.e., the Global South) and ignored situations unfolding in, or involving, the Global North.

[54] Deva, "Reimagining the Treaty Business," pp. 4–6.

[55] Human Rights Council, "Elaboration of an international legally binding instrument on transnational corporations and other business enterprises with respect to human rights," A/HRC/26/L.22/Rev. 1 (26 June 2014).

instrument only to transnational corporations and other business enterprises with a transnational character. [56]

If the OEIGWG is unable to break the current deadlock, we should consider alternatives. One option may to develop international norms in this area the "bottom up."[57] For example, a diverse coalition of the *willing* stakeholders comprising states, scholars, practitioners, business representatives, CSOs, labor organizations, student unions, human rights defenders, and consumer/investor bodies could jointly draft an international instrument elaborating human rights obligations of business enterprises. Such an instrument, even though perhaps softer than the GPs, could be sounder normatively and closer to social expectations that people on the ground might have from business.

The other alternative option may to start with an overarching soft but more ambitious instrument.[58] In other words, instead of trying to negotiate a legally binding international instrument dealing only with selected gross human rights violations – akin to the Rome Statute – we should start with drafting a Declaration on the Human Rights Obligations of Business (Declaration) along the lines of the Universal Declaration of Human Rights.[59] This sequential order is crucial because a proposal to negotiate a narrow treaty not only puts the cart before the horse for pragmatic reasons, but it might also indicate that no binding treaty is perhaps required to deal with other human rights violations.

Such a Declaration should (i) provide a sound normative basis for why companies have human rights obligations, (ii) proclaim that human rights applicable to companies are not limited to only those mentioned in the International Bill of Rights but rather extend to those elaborated in all international instruments, (iii) outline the principles governing the extent of corporate obligations in relation to these rights, (iv) envisage a number of state-focal and non-state-centric mechanisms to implement and enforce human rights obligations against companies so as to provide victims with an effective access to a range of remedies, and (v) suggest ways to remove substantive, conceptual, procedural, and financial obstacles experienced by victims in holding companies accountable for human rights violations.

Once the Declaration is in place, simultaneous and/or sequential efforts should be made to concretize human rights obligations of companies in different areas.

[56] The footnote reads: "'Other business enterprises' denotes all business enterprises that have a transnational character in their operational activities, and does not apply to local businesses registered in terms of relevant domestic law." Ibid. For a detailed analysis, see Surya Deva, "Scope of the Proposed Business and Human Rights Treaty: Navigating through Normativity, Law and Politics", in Deva and Bilchitz (eds.), *Building a Treaty on Business and Human Rights*, forthcoming.

[57] See Surya Deva, "Multinationals, Human Rights and International Law: Time to Move beyond the 'State-Centric' Conception?" in *Human Rights and Business: Direct Corporate Accountability for Human Rights* (eds.), Jernej Letnar Černič and Tara Van Ho (The Hague: Wolf Legal Publishers, 2014), 27, 44–8.

[58] For further elaboration, see Deva, "Reimagining the Treaty Business."

[59] It is also possible to conceive this Declaration as applying to all nonstate actors, and not merely to companies.

This will entail negotiating and adopting a number of international instruments in due course. Such a process will of course take time, but that in itself should not be ground to delay initiating the process.

Making companies comply with human rights norms and holding them accountable for their failure to do so will require introducing some "fundamental" changes to the relevant laws and policies that concern the incorporation as well as business operations of companies.[60] These changes should be rooted in the normative assumption that even if companies are specialized social organs, they ought to be subjected to non-negotiable human rights norms. In this context, it may be worthwhile to draft Model Laws to provide states with *concrete* guidance as to what legislative and policy adjustments they should make to deal with the privatization of human rights when acting at domestic, bilateral, regional, and international levels.

Keeping in mind the fractured nature of international law, it will be vital for the Declaration to assert the normative hierarchy of human rights and human rights instruments over other areas and the instruments concerning them. The Declaration should inform the mandate of not only the UN but also other international agencies such as the International Labor Organization, the International Monetary Fund, the World Trade Organization, the World Bank, and other financial institutions such as the Asian Infrastructure Investment Bank. The arbitration tribunals operating under the bilateral investment treaties (BITs) and international financing agreements should also consider the Declaration's implications for their dispute resolution work.

In terms of the scope of the Declaration and any subsequent international instruments, they should apply to all types of business entities and not just MNCs, despite the fact that the operations of MNCs do pose more significant regulatory challenges.

The Declaration (and subsequent treaties) should conceive the possibility of employing a number of enforcement mechanisms – both state-based and non-state-based – at municipal and international levels to ensure the companies that do not comply with the agreed obligations can be held accountable in an efficient and speedy manner. In particular, the Declaration should contemplate to institutionalize the role of CSOs in enforcing and implementing human rights norms against companies. For example, a committee of CSOs in each state could be allowed to receive and deal with complaints of human rights abuses by business. Although such a committee might not have formal enforcement and compliance powers, its determinations could be posted on a designated website to be used in dynamic ways by diverse stakeholders.

In additional to recognizing the role of traditional sanctions (civil, administrative, and criminal) in ensuring corporate compliance, the Declaration should

---

60   This proposal goes beyond what the GPs contemplate, for instance, in Principles 3 and 8–10.

acknowledge the role of informal means and social (dis)incentives in enforcing human rights norms. These two tools will be especially important for victims in those situations where states are unwilling or unable to act against companies for diverse reasons.

V SUMMARY: MOVE BEYOND THE "PRESENT"

The vision put forward in this chapter about the role of states, companies, CSOs, and international law in global human rights governance admittedly contemplates moving beyond the *present*: the present that treats human rights as negotiable social expectations in terms of their application to non-state actors, the present that regards companies as specialized organs created to maximize profit subject only to non-binding human rights obligations, the present in which parent companies are legally allowed to outsource risks to their subsidiaries as a legitimate business practice, the present that confers on states an almost exclusive right to create and enforce international norms, and the present that does not fully utilize the potential of CSOs in creating as well as enforcing norms in informal, horizontal, and non-state-centric ways.

States, companies, CSOs, and international law are merely means to achieve certain ends. If a reorientation of their role and place in society becomes necessary to realize better human rights in changed circumstances, we should be willing to make the necessary adjustments, rather than seeking refuge in the unsuitable past or the inadequate present. This chapter suggests that we should move beyond the consensus narrative and confront critical issues which divide the BHR community. I also outline why and how international law should move beyond remaining a "state-centric" regulatory tool. Rather, it should harness the potential as well as power of CSOs in humanizing business.

4

Putting "Human Rights" Back into the UN Guiding Principles on Business and Human Rights: Shifting Frames and Embedding Participation Rights

Tara J. Melish

Framing is critical [to winning a public debate] because a frame, once established in the mind of the reader (or listener, viewer, etc.) leads that person almost inevitably to the conclusion desired by the framer, and it blocks consideration of other possible facts and interpretations.[1] – Framing expert, George Lakoff

There is a critical question that is too frequently obscured in discussions of the UN Guiding Principles on Business and Human Rights (GPs): Why precisely is it that the most vocal and consistent critics of the GPs are *human rights* organizations, precisely the groups that have been pushing the longest and hardest for a more effective, non-business-as-usual approach to corporate human rights abuse? Indeed, whether big or small, North- or South-based, international or local in orientation, or highly or loosely networked, human rights NGOs have consistently taken a critical posture toward the GPs. Although their openness to GP engagement has varied,[2] each has tended to see the GP framework as "regressive," a "step backward" in the protection of human rights,[3] one based on a corporate good will model that not only has proven itself ineffective over decades of trial and creative experimentation,[4] but that – most revealingly and consequentially – ignores the critical elements of a *human rights approach* to social change. Indeed, in order to render the GPs

---

[1] George Lakoff, George Lakoff Manifesto 2, www.infoamerica.org/teoria_textos/manifiesto_lakoff.pdf; see also: George Lakoff, *The All New Don't Think of an Elephant! Know Your Values and Frame the Debate* (2014).

[2] Groups that do not take a human rights approach to community-based problem-solving as the primary emphasis of their work have been more open to engaging the GPs. In this respect, I am highly sympathetic to the framing used in Chris Jochnick's contribution to this volume, while believing that it may oversuggest differences in the substance of the critical postures taken by human rights NGOs (as a category) toward the GPs. See *infra*, note 5.

[3] See, e.g., FIDH et al., "Joint Civil Society Statement on the Draft Guiding Principles on Business and Human Rights" (3 March 2011); Christopher Albin-Lackey, Human Rights Watch, "Without Rules: A Failed Approach to Corporate Accountability," in *Human Rights Watch: 2013 World Report* (2013) (recognizing GPs as "woefully inadequate" by "setting a lower bar than international human rights standards").

[4] Indeed, international efforts at corporate voluntarism in the human rights field have been vigorously pursued at the highest levels since the 1960s.

acceptable to business, and thereby promote high-level corporate and state buy-in, the very essence of a "human rights approach" to community problem-solving – the core empowerment, participation, and accountability features that make the human rights idiom effective and useful to vulnerable communities and their advocates – was systematically removed from the framework and its regulatory logic. The central challenge for human rights groups looking forward, then, is *how* to put the "human rights" back into the "business and human rights" (BHR) framework, either within the GPs themselves or in some other associated source of "law."[5]

If one listens to John Ruggie – former Special Representative to the Secretary General on Business and Human Rights (SRSG), intellectual author of the GPs, and principal promoter, defender, and publicist of those principles – one will none-theless come away with a very different answer: Human rights groups, he repeatedly suggests, resist the GPs because they are stubbornly wed to a top-down, old-school model of global governance that has little place in today's highly complex and polycentric world. Indeed, in his campaign-like global efforts to defend the GPs from challenge, and forestall increasingly coordinated efforts to supplement them with more binding and participatory mechanisms (particularly through a new human rights treaty instrument), the former SRSG has adopted a highly powerful and politically resonant frame for understanding international debate on the GPs.[6]

Aiming to move beyond the all-or-nothing "voluntary versus mandatory" frame long dominant in the field, that new frame seeks to resituate international debate along a spectrum of ideal global regulatory response types. That typological spectrum runs from "experimentalist" or "polycentric" governance regimes or regime complexes at one end (often gathered under a "new governance" heading) to rigid "command-and-control" treaty regulation on the other. Through this frame, the former SRSG is able to shift the axis of debate in a new direction while continuing to draw sharp and categorical distinctions between the GPs and the model they replaced, the UN Norms on Business and Human Rights (Norms).[7] Though

---

[5] Human rights NGOs have tended to respond to the GPs in one of two primary ways: by rejecting their utility outright for influencing human rights conditions on the ground or by recognizing their utility in limited respects while insisting on their direct supplementation with additional human rights tools, instruments, and procedures to bring them, at a minimum, back into line with the hard-fought international standards already recognized in the human rights field. This is particularly true regarding the framework human rights principles of participation, accountability, nondiscrimination/equality, empowerment, and legality of rights, known as the "PANEL" principles.

[6] John Ruggie's recent book, *Just Business: Multinational Corporations and Human Rights* (Norton 2013), is a revealing firsthand account of the campaign-like strategies of "meaning management" and staged endorsement the former SRSG has undertaken at the highest levels to promote the GPs, distance himself and his framework from human rights NGOs, and gain the backing of the business community and powerful states.

[7] As Professor Ruggie openly acknowledges, his "first official act [as SRSG] was to commit 'Normicide'" – designed to establish a "clean break" from the Norms and, consequently, open the door to constructive engagement with the business community. It was achieved by concluding in his first official report – in "deliberately undiplomatic language" – that the Norms suffered from "exaggerated legal claims" and were "engulfed by [their] own doctrinal excesses." See *Just Business, supra,*

strongly supported by human rights groups, those Norms were of course rejected by the business community and failed to win approval within the UN Human Rights Commission in 2005, giving direct rise to the SRSG's mandate and process of drafting the GPs.

The new frame operates by jointly locating the Norms and civil society calls for a comprehensive human rights treaty at one extreme end of the regulatory spectrum. They are based, the former SRSG insists, on an antiquated treaty-based regulatory model that has proven itself ineffective and ill-suited to modern global challenges. That traditional model – top-down, rigid, and highly prescriptive – presumes there is a singular "one-size-fits-all" approach to global problem-solving that every actor, everywhere, must uniformly adopt.[8] The human rights paradigm, says the former SRSG, is *based* on this rigid model, with advocates continually insisting there "ought to be a law, one single international law, which binds all business enterprises everywhere under a common set of standards protecting human rights."[9] Although human rights NGOs cling religiously to this model, the former SRSG asserts – driving him "batty," as he likes to say, with their insistence that it is the only way forward – the model represents a nonstarter approach that, in contrast to the GPs, will offer no practical relief or recourse to real people in real situations on the ground.[10]

The GPs, by contrast, are located at the opposite, happier end of the global regulatory typology. They are presented as a fresh and innovative example of a new global legal pluralism that takes a "polycentric" or "new governance" approach to global problem-solving.[11] This "new" approach appreciates and values the diversity of stakeholders that need to be constructively engaged in twenty-first-century problem-solving (including particularly businesses themselves), the plural

---

pp. 54, 158. Ruggie regularly attributes the same "excess" to human rights groups calling for more mandatory supplementation to the GPs.

[8] See, e.g., John J. Ruggie, "A UN Business and Human Rights Treaty? An Issues Brief," (28 Jan. 2014), 3–4; John Ruggie, "International Legalization in Business and Human Rights," Remarks delivered at presentation of the Harry LeRoy Jones Award of the Washington Foreign Law Society, Washington DC (11 June 2014), p. 4 ("One would think that this [top-down approach to international lawmaking, which seeks to squeeze the entire bundle of B&HR challenges into a single, all-encompassing treaty] would have lost its appeal by now, given its repeated failure to produce meaningful results").

[9] *Just Business*, p. 55. See also John Ruggie's contribution's in this volume. The charge in fact turns the "human rights paradigm" on its head.

[10] See, e.g., Ruggie Remarks, ibid., note 8, p. 6 ("From the vantage of victims, an all-encompassing [B&HR] treaty negotiation is not only a bad idea; it is a profound deception."); John G. Ruggie, Letter to Editor, "Bizarre Response by Human Rights Groups to UN Framework Plan," *Financial Times* (19 January 2011) ("Do Amnesty and the [other human rights NGOs] really urge [the GP framework's] defeat – delivering 'nothing' to victims yet again? How much longer will they ask victims to wait in the name of some abstract and elusive global regulatory regime when practical results are achievable now?").

[11] John Gerard Ruggie, "Global Governance and 'New Governance Theory': Lessons from Business and Human Rights," *Global Governance* 20 (2014), 5–17 (describing GPs as "an exercise in polycentric governance").

governance regimes they in fact respond to in their day-to-day operations (corporate, public, and civic), and creative ways for aligning interests across these distinct and insufficiently intersecting regimes. The GPs are conceived to do precisely that, Ruggie asserts, and it is for this reason they have received such widespread support and institutional uptake across stakeholder groups.

Deftly and repeatedly promoted by the former SRSG in his regular GP talking points and frequent public lectures, the frame is a highly effective strategy for promoting the GP project as the only real game in town. It creates a cognitive frame that, by placing the GPs at one ideal-type extreme and a comprehensive human rights treaty on the other, leads the listener almost inevitably to the framer's desired conclusion: the GPs are good – their supporters are reasonable, flexible, and responsive to real world outcomes; comprehensive human rights treaties are bad – their supporters are rigid, doctrinaire, divisive and shortsighted in their singular quest for a treaty-based "silver bullet" that is hopelessly outdated and nonresponsive to the complexity and polycentricity of real-world problems.[12]

Though grossly misrepresentative of the actual positions of the parties,[13] the heuristic serves the GP project well.[14] It guarantees steady business and Global North support of the GPs and GP implementation process (by framing their alternative as direct international legal regulation). It sidelines good faith calls for new treaty-based tools of accountability and participatory empowerment as extremist and regressive, blind and indifferent to the actual day-to-day needs of real people on the ground. It casts defenders of the GPs, including powerful businesses and Global North states, as the "true" defenders of human rights progress in the B&HR field. It also casts human rights NGOs (the GPs strongest and most effective critics) and the growing number of Global South states supportive of a new treaty instrument in the field as obstacles to real progress, stubborn, and myopic in their ideological

---

[12] See, e.g., John Ruggie, "Progress in Corporate Accountability" (4 February 2013) (deriding human rights calls for more mandatory supplementation of the GPs as hopelessly based on "some idealized global command-and-control regulatory regime" that "risks turning the clock back rather than moving us forward").

[13] Indeed, human rights groups are not now, nor ever have been, advocates of rigid command-and-control regulation – and no human rights treaty has ever even remotely followed this approach. To the contrary, human rights advocates have for decades been at the forefront of global efforts to incorporate greater experimentalist and new governance features into regulatory regimes, particularly around increased stakeholder voice and participation, multiple and intersecting monitoring and accountability arrangements, interpretive flexibility, and responsiveness to local community-based priorities and understandings. This is core to what the "human rights framework" demands. Meanwhile, the GPs have come under heaviest attack for their *failure* to adopt the central features of "new governance" or experimentalist regime types. See Tara J. Melish and Errol Meidinger, "Respect, Protect, Remedy and Participate: 'New Governance' Lessons for the Ruggie Framework," *The UN Guiding Principles on Business and Human Rights: Foundations and Implementation* (ed.), R. Mares (Martinus Nijhoff Publishers 2012).

[14] See Rodríguez-Garavito contribution in this volume (defending use of typology as merely a "heuristic"). As framing theory teaches, heuristics can misdirect thinking and action as much as they can direct it.

extremism and "doctrinal excess,"[15] and hence justifiably sidelined in the process of implementing the GPs and their "new regulatory dynamic." The frame thus leads, by design, not only to the general conclusion that human rights groups and other civil society NGOs *can*, even *should*, legitimately be bypassed in the GP implementation process (including in the work of the new UN Working Group tasked with its promotion), but also – most relevantly for this volume – toward proposals for moving the GPs "beyond the end of the beginning" that maintain intact the framework's elite-centred, internationalist, and voluntarist logic, while merely tinkering with details at their outer margins. Indeed, by seeking "intermediate pathways" between the two ideal regime types, such proposals lose the core of what is at stake and *actually* in contention.

It is here that my central critique of the original background contribution to this volume by César Rodríguez-Garavito rests. Although the author correctly identifies the principal deficiency of the GPs from a human rights (*and new governance/ experimentalist*) perspective[16] – that is, the framework's failure to take systematic and explicit account of the critical role played by "empowered civil society participation" in closing the massive governance gaps that pervade the field – the author's uncritical embrace of the former SRSG's frame[17] leads him to a bewilderingly impoverished set of proposals for addressing that deficiency. The chapter is thus a powerful testament to the effectiveness of the former SRSG's chosen frame. It demonstrates how that frame not only leads large numbers of listeners to the "conclusion desired by the framer" (that the GPs are the only real game in town, and hence efforts to expand their content in the form of a treaty or other regulatory instrument are either fundamentally misguided or simply impractical), but also "blocks consideration of other possible facts and interpretations,"[18] including, most critically, the *actual* reasons human rights NGOs insist that the GPs require more mandatory and expressive supplementation.

A new frame for situating international debate on the GPs is critically needed. Part I below offers what I see as a far more accurate frame. Parts II and III then use this frame to rethink answers to the two key questions identified by Rodríguez-Garavito for constructively taking the GPs "beyond the end of the beginning": How can "empowered civil society participation" effectively be incorporated into the

---

[15] See note 7 above.

[16] For an analysis of the overlap between "new governance" and "human rights" approaches to regulatory problem-solving, see Tara J. Melish, "Maximum Feasible Participation of the Poor: New Governance, New Accountability, and a 21st Century War on the Sources of Poverty," *Yale Human Rights and Development Law Journal* 13: 1 (2010).

[17] See Rodríguez-Garavito in this volume. In the original background version of his chapter, the author locates the GPs within a typology of global regulatory responses that, he asserts, runs from "treaty-based regulation" at one end of the regulatory spectrum to "voluntary standards and polycentric governance" at the other end. He then locates the GPs at the latter end, and incorrectly calls it "new governance."

[18] See note 1 above.

GPs' "dynamic logic"? And what role, if any, does a human rights treaty instrument have to play?

I SHIFTING FRAMES: COMPETING THEORIES OF SOCIAL CHANGE

If the principal competing visions of the GPs do not run along an "experimentalist versus command-and-control" spectrum, along what continuum do they run? As I see it, the core international debate on the GPs is one that straddles not two distinct governance or regulatory regimes, but rather two distinct theories of how social change or system transformation is most effectively influenced in complex, powered society. It is the fundamental divergence between these two theories of social change and, most importantly, *the respective toolsets required to advance them* that explains human rights NGOs' skepticism toward the GPs. Let me explain.

Like other UN global design projects that John Ruggie has played a leading role in developing (e.g., the Global Compact and Millennium Development Goals), the GPs are based on a particular acculturative theory of system transformation, known in international relations theory as social constructivism or sociological institutionalism. Professor Ruggie is an important intellectual progenitor of this theory.[19] Very simply stated,[20] the theory posits that individual actors in global society (states, business entities, civil society groups) act in particular ways primarily because they are socialized into certain behavioral patterns, largely by the shared norms and norm-informed practices of their self-identified global reference groups. The most effective way to modify "bad" behavioral patterns within such groups is thus to influence the shared cultural systems through which appropriate conduct is normatively defined in a given community. A particular methodology is identified to affect this normative shift. It has three core components: (1) "authoritative" adoption of a standardized international script for global uptake, (2) structured and framed in a way that will promote voluntary buy-in and formal uptake by the relevant reference groups, and (3) promotion of international processes designed to stimulate elite engagement with script norms and other reference group elites, leading to voluntary uptake, mimicry, and standardization of policy forms across the group.

Through these elite engagement processes, it is theorized, norms come to be seen as part of the reference group's self-identity. When this "tipping point" is reached, individual components of the global script become embedded and internalized as a new set of constitutive rules that define and prestructure the scope of socially

---

[19] See, e.g., J. G. Ruggie, "What Makes the World Hang Together? Neo-utilitarianism and the Social Constructivist Challenge," *International Organization* 52:4 (1998), 855–885.

[20] For a more complete description in the GP context, see Melish & Meidinger, note 13 above. For Ruggie's own description, see above.

acceptable conduct in the field.[21] The resulting taken-for-granted quality of the underlying norms is henceforth able to resolve the misaligned incentive structure and collective action problems that, in the BHR context, the former SRSG attributes to the absence of consensus regarding appropriate policy forms and outcomes. Keeping businesses and states engaged in the GP "implementation process" – understood as formal uptake practices across a widening group of actors – is thus fundamental to the project's "success." It explains the former SRSG's confident pointing to elite international (OECD, IFC, EU, AU, ASEAN, ISO) formal uptake practices as "evidence" of successful GP implementation (wholly independent of any translation into policy change on the ground).[22] It also accounts for his resistance to, even antagonism toward, civil society's insistence on more mandatory norms and other participatory levers for engaging in "accountability politics" from below, as well as the UN Working Group on BHR's steely focus on script dissemination and high-level corporate actor engagement in its international meeting spaces (rather than serving a role more akin to other Human Rights Council Special Procedures, which tend to prioritize spaces for civil society engagement).

Human rights groups, by contrast, tend to view this account of social change as simplistic, naïve, and incomplete. They insist that genuine social transformation occurs only when affected communities *themselves* have the power and voice to engage decision-making processes that affect their lives, as active subjects of law, not mere objects. From their perspective, human rights abuse occurs for one primary reason: *powerlessness*. People will continue to be abused while they lack power – power to understand, to challenge, to confront, and to engage the causes and conditions of their abuse. Critically, they must do this *themselves*, as active subjects of the law, not passive objects thereof. Indeed, any model of change based on other people – especially the very ones responsible for misconduct – doing this for them (whether out of humanitarianism or direct self-interest) is misguided at best, a status quo power play at worst. Interests are too strong, and the power of dominant groups to whitewash, elide, ignore, agenda-set, influence-peddle, and misrepresent too great.[23]

The GPs are a "step-backward" for human rights groups, then, for two related reasons. First, they fail to recognize the essential role that rights-holders *themselves*

---

[21] See, e.g., *Just Business*, pp. 166–169 (describing GPs implementation logic in terms of three phases of the "life cycle of norms" – norm emergence, norm cascade, and norm internalization – and concluding that "[a]mong the main international standard-setting bodies" and "leading multinational corporations" the first two phases are effectively complete, while the latter phase has just begun).

[22] See, e.g., *Just Business*, pp. 121–123 (triumphantly describing "swift uptake" of GPs by international standard-setting bodies); John J. Ruggie, "A UN Business and Human Rights Treaty? An Issues Brief," (28 Jan. 2014), p. 2 (same, while conceding that "no systematic assessment is available of overall results to date").

[23] For a powerful overview of the corporate sector's highly organized public relations strategies aimed at reframing the UN agenda on B&HR, see Jens Martens, "Corporate Influence on the Business and Human Rights Agenda of the United Nations" (Working Paper, Brot für die Welt/Global Policy Forum/MISEREOR, June 2014).

play in identifying (indeed defining what constitutes) abuse, its causes, and contextually appropriate mechanisms, arrangements, and procedures for preventing it in the first place. Instead, the GPs envision processes of human rights policy development and decision-making as unfolding in a primarily top-down unidirectional fashion, with corporate actors determining what is required consistent with corporate self-interest and self-identity (and isomorphic mimicry of forms). That is, driven by elite-centered ideational incentives and the idea that corporations are or should be human rights leaders as a matter of constructed self-identity, the GPs contemplate no power shift between stakeholders whatsoever. Corporations and powerful states are the active agents and norm entrepreneurs at their "dynamic" center, while rights-holders and their civil society advocates remain bystanders and onlookers, passive "beneficiaries" of outsider good will. Indeed, while corporations "should" consult with such communities, they have no obligation to nor consequence for not so doing.

It is this disregard for direct rights-holder engagement and participatory access to agenda-setting processes that leads to the second core human rights critique of the GPs: The framework's failure to offer any express *tools* or *legal resources* to affected communities such that rights-holders themselves have the *power* and *capacity* to engage the causes of their own abuse.[24] Such rights-building tools would enable communities to better understand the field-specific scope of their rights, the necessity of community-based mobilization around them, the correlate duties held by other social actors (both substantive and procedural), and how such duties may effectively be leveraged to shift the dynamics of decision-making toward the protection of human rights, in locally responsive ways. This deficiency is true both in the *inexpressiveness* of the GPs' terms (in relation to both rights and duties)[25] and in their lack of reference to any *rights of participation* or *institutional pathways* for the real-world exercise thereof. Given the massive power and information disparities that prevail in the corporate domain, such legal resources are vital for the exercise of bottom-up accountability politics by vulnerable communities.[26] It is little wonder,

---

[24] As used here, "legal resources" refer to those normative tools and institutional pathways through which affected persons and communities can know their rights, stand up to defend them when aggrieved, and actively engage in the day-to-day praxis of empowered participatory governance in matters that affect their lives. See generally Clarence J. Dias and James C.N. Paul (1985), "Developing Legal Resources for Participatory Organizations of the Rural Poor," *Third World Legal Studies* Vol. 4, Article 2.

[25] The GPs have been recognized as a primary exemplar of an "*inexpressive* international instrument" given their failure to articulate clear commitments on the part of social actors, to which other social actors can hold them to account. See Andrew K. Woods, "Inexpressive International Agreements" (unpublished manuscript on file with author).

[26] Accountability, in this regard, means that "some actors have the right to hold other actors to a set of standards, to judge whether they have fulfilled their responsibilities in light of these standards, and to impose sanctions if they determine that these responsibilities have not been met." R. W. Grant and R.O. Keohane, "Accountability and Abuses of Power in World Politics, *American Political Science Review* 99 (2005), 29.

then, that the GPs have attracted so little knowledge or buy-in by affected communities anywhere in the world. They simply lack the tools to be meaningful or relevant to local level struggles against corporate abuse.

The result is a BHR governance regime fertile with opportunities for "creative compliance" and other forms of "greenwashing" or "decoupling." That is, companies predictably take the cue to engage in highly formalistic uptake practices designed to legitimize brands and avoid exposure by activists, while failing to engage in any genuine ground-level operational change.[27] Examples abound. Such examples give direct voice to the human rights concern that ideational incentives and voluntary efforts to "know and show" will not, by themselves, meaningfully change conduct on the ground. Localized, independent, and regular checks on power and interests, backed by the credible threat of material consequences and penalty defaults (whether social, economic or legal) by those stakeholder groups most affected by corporate misconduct, are indispensable to "success."[28] To do this, however, rights-holders need to be recognized as central to the process of defining problems, envisioning solutions, setting agendas, destabilizing expectations, monitoring compliance, and incentivizing behavior. Equally critically, to ensure rights-holders can exercise those roles in fact, they need to be provided an expressive set of rights-based leverage tools for asserting their voice and socially amplifying their power.[29]

It is toward remedying these two deficiencies that NGO calls for more mandatory and expressive GP supplementation – particularly through a human rights treaty – are directed. As I read them, such calls seek three primary things: (1) more *expressive commitments* on the part of global actors that set clear principles and broad standards and goals for achievement (not rigid, one-size-fits-all rules, which, by definition, are not responsive to local needs and experiences); (2) a framework and instituted processes through which those goals can be pursued by the full range of stakeholders, including particularly those most affected by corporate misconduct; and (3) express rights of participatory engagement to enable rights-holders themselves to

[27] The GPs' limited "remedy" prong provides little meaningful relief in this context. It does not entitle affected communities to engage in problem-solving, agenda-setting, and regular monitoring of business-related human rights harms, but rather only to seek (allowable) redress once discretionary abuse has already occurred.

[28] For an important example, see the Coalition of Immokalee Workers Fair Food Program, described as "one of the great human rights success stories of our day" and "the best workplace monitoring program" in the United States. See http://ciw-online.org/fair-food-program. See also Melish, "Maximum Feasible Participation of the Poor," note 16 above (describing strategies of "new accountability" movements across Global South and North).

[29] See generally Gráinne de Búrca, Robert O. Keohane, and Charles Sabel, "New Modes of Pluralist Global Governance," NYU *Journal of International Law & Politics* 45 (2013) (concluding that "successful" experimentalist governance regimes and practices *"depend on* extensive and open participation of civil society actors in agenda setting, revision, and ongoing problem solving... *Enlarging the circle of decision-making, and keeping it accessible to new participants is a condition of success*) (emphasis added). For an application of this argument in the human rights arena, see Melish & Meidinger, note 13 above.

engage the framework on an equal basis alongside other stakeholders, including accounting for failures.

Such calls, it demands emphasis, are consistent not only with a *human rights approach* to social change (with its focus on promoting the agency, power and dignity of the socially situated rights-holder), but also with the very logic of *experimentalist governance*. Indeed, genuine experimentalist systems are recognized to be constituted by four core elements: 1) the articulation of a broad framework for setting general goals or standards in a participatory manner; (2) local units (public and private) pursuing the goals in locally appropriate ways; (3) regular reporting and peer review by a variety of stakeholders; and (4) a system for revising goals, metrics and decision-making procedures "by a widening circle of actors in response to the problems and possibilities revealed by the review process."[30] The GPs and their UN follow-on activities are neither structured nor envisioned to do *any of this*. Rather, they merely *assume* that it will be done by others – somewhere, somehow – ignoring entirely the power differentials and structural barriers that prevent it from happening in fact. To frame them as "experimentalist" and "polycentric" thus not only misapprehends what is required of such governance regimes – namely, open stakeholder access and *exercisable* rights of participation at all stages of design, monitoring, accountability, and review – but dramatically distorts the lines of debate about *what* critics find wanting in the GPs and *how* they wish to update them.

Reframing the debate is critical. By more accurately understanding international debate on the GPs as a contest between those who advocate elite-driven acculturation-based models of social influence (the former SRSG, the WG, corporate interests, many Global North states) versus those who insist on bottom-up accountability politics (affected communities, human rights NGOs),[31] the contours of where "intermediate pathways" lie becomes much clearer. Indeed, assertions to the contrary notwithstanding, human rights advocates do not reject acculturation-based strategies (like the GPs) when promoted as *one of multiple* relevant and important strategies of social influence.[32] What they "reject" in the GP framework

---

[30] Sabel and Zeitlin, "Experimentalist Governance," in D. Levi-Faur (ed.), *The Oxford Handbook of Governance* (Oxford Univ. Press 2012), 169–183; see also "New Modes of Pluralist Global Governance," note 30 above (identifying five similar components).

[31] While human rights NGOs uniformly insist on more mandatory or expressive rights of civil society participation, independent oversight, and accountability, they do differ in their willingness to speak "for" affected communities in exercising those rights. On a typological spectrum running from pure acculturation-based strategies of social influence to pure power shifting ones, then, some will locate at the extreme latter end, while others will move toward a more centered position, explaining their higher openness to GP engagement. Compare Chris Jochnick, Chapter 7, in this volume.

[32] By focusing on the operational limits of the Working Group and hence recommending the "replacement" of its current mandate with a *different*, more rights-holder centered mandate, Rodríguez-Garavito nonetheless moves oddly (and seemingly unwittingly) in this direction. The better option would be to envision *different* orchestrational bodies or sites for engaging these distinct modalities of influence, as other treaty-based human rights regimes do. See, e.g., CRPD and its Optional Protocol (creating an oversight committee with periodic reporting and individual complaints functions and, separately, a Conference of States Parties for peer-to-peer stakeholder learning). The creation of

is the virtual unitary focus on top-down acculturative dynamics, together with its promoters' dismissiveness, even antagonism, toward more rights-holder-centered and bottom-up accountability strategies. These latter strategies, human rights groups insist, are indispensable not only in themselves, but also for the very viability of norm-based acculturation processes; they serve to ensure that a "logic of consequences" spurs, incentivizes, destabilizes, and disrupts logjams in processes geared toward embedding a "logic of appropriateness."[33]

Indeed, as even acculturation-based models' most ardent defenders acknowledge, acculturative forces do not invariably increase respect for human rights; they may in fact lead to worsening and more dangerous human rights conditions on the ground.[34] Designing a human rights regime exclusively, or even primarily, around such forces is thus shortsighted and counterproductive. Rather, optimal human rights regime design requires that attention be given not only to interest discovery among elite players, but also to interest conflict and how less powerful actors seek to narrow power asymmetries through organized mechanisms of social (legal, economic, political) leverage. A "business *and human rights*" framework makes little sense without it. Human rights NGOs and affected communities should thus be expected to continue to reject the GP framework as "*the* authoritative focal point" in the B&HR field[35] – or even "authoritative" at all[36] – while rights-holder empowerment and participatory engagement are not made a more systematic institutional feature.

II EMPOWERED CIVIL SOCIETY PARTICIPATION: HOW TO GET THERE?

Consistent with the above critique, Rodríguez-Garavito rightly focuses on the need for greater attention in the GP framework to "empowered civil society participation" and the availability of institutional pathways for the exercise of countervailing power. Nevertheless, by falling for the framing convention set out by the former SRSG, his reference points become skewed and he ends up advancing proposals that bear little relationship to the actual problem diagnosed. In short, he advances two proposals for moving the GP implementation process forward: (1) pursue a treaty, but one narrowly limited to corporate responsibility for "gross" human rights

---

a separate UN Special Rapporteur on B&HR, to complement the work of the current Working Group, would be a first step in this direction.

[33] John Ruggie seems to recognize this in his early work as SRSG. See, e.g., J.G. Ruggie, "Business and Human Rights: The Evolving International Agenda," *American Journal of International Law* 101 (2007), 836. ("The Achilles heel of self-regulatory arrangements to date is their undeveloped accountability mechanisms").

[34] R. Goodman and D. Jinks, "Incomplete Internalization and Compliance with Human Rights Law: A Rejoinder to Roda Muchkat," *European Journal of International Law* 20 (2009), 443–444.

[35] The former SRSG continually presents and promotes the GPs as such.

[36] Accord Bonita Meyersfeld, Chapter 11, in this volume.

violations (and states' associated extraterritorial obligations); and (2) replace the current mandate of the UN Working Group (WG) tasked with GP orchestration with one more like other UN special procedures in the human rights field. Neither, I contend, will have any appreciable effect on shifting power to vulnerable communities.

Simply stated, the treaty proposal errs by assuming (in line with the SRSG's frame) that the "comprehensive treaty" desired by human rights NGOs is one that would rigidly codify a set of highly prescriptive rules for corporations that every business entity, everywhere, must uniformly adopt. Understood as such, the logical "intermediate pathway" between the GPs' current "dynamic logic" and civil society's preferred "treaty route" lies precisely where Ruggie and the author jointly locate it: (1) reducing the subject-matter scope of the desired command-and-control treaty (hence the former SRSG's insistence on a "precision tool"); and (2) limiting its jurisdictional application to those few "bad apples" who are uninfluence-able by the elite-driven social constructivist logic of the GPs – that is, those engaged in the "worst of the worst" violations rising to the level of international crimes (genocide, war crimes, crimes against humanity, etc.).[37] The proposal, concededly, makes perfect logical sense under one critical condition: *you buy into the frame.* If you don't, it entirely misses the mark. Indeed, by misidentifying the position of human rights NGOs (who favor a very different kind of "comprehensive treaty," I believe),[38] the proposal is entirely nonresponsive to the "countervailing power" critique. It fails to create *any* new tools of participatory empowerment or institutional engagement for the millions upon millions of communities the world over affected by negligent and abusive conduct in the business domain. The proposal instead favors a regime that states have already rejected in the Rome Statute,[39] and that will be so politicized, distracting, and selectively deployed (given the Global North's power and structural interest in protecting its own) – and so dominated by the usual narrow band of international criminal law suspects – as to be nonrelevant to local struggles and actors on the ground.

The WG proposal is similarly deficient, but for a different reason. By focusing on international "orchestration," it puts the cart before the horse. It fails to address the core reason so few affected communities know or care about the GPs in the first place and hence have *reason* to substantively engage them at all, at international *or local* levels. Indeed, if the type of "empowered civil society participation" that the human rights critique envisions is to be incorporated into the GPs' "dynamic" implementation logic, the GPs *themselves* must acknowledge it and provide some

---

[37] See, e.g., John Ruggie, Chapter 2, in this volume.   [38] See discussion below Part III.

[39] Negotiators of the Rome Statute expressly declined to extend its jurisdiction to "legal persons," like corporations, for participation or complicity in precisely the international crimes identified in the Ruggie proposal. Why states would change their positions on this so quickly is unclear to me, especially as national trends seem to be moving in the opposite direction. And if they did, why create a new instrument rather than simply amend the Rome Statute or create an optional protocol thereto?

set of locally meaningful tools to promote it and hence enable local buy-in. Without doing this, creating limited new spaces for engagement in international WG activities will serve only to increase the marginal participation of those civil society actors who are *already empowered* to participate in high-level fora like the WG, and, to a large extent, are already participating therein (albeit to a lesser degree than corporate interests).[40]

A far more basic update to the GPs and their implementation logic is required. In a 2011 piece, Errol Meidinger and I proposed one way that key participatory empowerment tools could be incorporated directly within the GP framework. We proposed incorporation of a fourth "Participate" pillar into the "Protect, Respect and Remedy" Framework (enlarging it modestly to a PRRP Framework).[41] By building express recognition of the critical role of civil society actors directly into the GP framework itself, we envisioned three distinct but closely related value-added benefits. First, it would elevate an *expressive commitment* to the participatory rights of civil society actors to the same normative platform held by state and corporate actors, thereby providing a normative base from which they could demand equal attention and participation in the implementation process. Such a platform would make it difficult for state and corporate actors to simply dismiss or sideline civil society actors, as they so frequently do, in the process of constructing national action plans, new regulations, "human rights due diligence" processes, and community "consultation" designs, consistent with their (inexpressively framed) duties under the current GPs. In so doing, it would likewise serve to complement, contextualize, and dynamize the "Remedy" pillar, making clear that affected communities are not simply post-hoc grievance holders, entitled to speak up and be heard only after harm has occurred. Rather, it would recognize unmistakably that they have critical and indispensable roles to play at *all* stages of decision and policymaking affecting their lives – including at the design stage, before harm occurs, and in continual monitoring, agenda-setting, awareness-raising, and review processes.

Second, and most instrumentally, incorporation of a fourth "participate" pillar would provide the structural foundation for the concrete elaboration of a series of cross-cutting (and expressively framed) GPs dedicated specifically to *operationalizing* a participatory role for civil society actors at each key stage of "implementation." Applicable across public law and corporate governance systems, such operational principles would recognize civil society's right to participate in, for example, the pre-award review of concession contracts; the conduct of prior impact studies; the development of National Action Plans;[42] the independent monitoring and review

---

[40]   See also contribution by Bonita Meyersfeld in this volume (noting that the GPs have been engaged by "empowered actors in empowered places").

[41]   See Melish & Meidinger, note 13 above.

[42]   For an important effort in this regard, see Danish Institute for Human Rights & International Corporate Accountability Roundtable, *National Action Plans on Business and Human Rights: A Toolkit for the Development, Implementation, and Review of State Commitments to Business and Human Rights Frameworks* (June 2014), pp. 42–44 (calling on all governments to develop NAPs and to

of corporate grievance procedures, due diligence plans, and complaint mechanisms; as well as other recognized national and international-level monitoring and accountability arrangements. They would also include key safeguards regarding access to information, transparency, and participatory accessibility, as growing numbers of treaties have done in BHR related fields, including corruption, the environment, and the workplace.[43] By expressly recognizing these cross-cutting participatory governance principles as central to the duties to "protect" and "respect" in the framework, key leverage points would be created through which civil society actors could more meaningfully insert themselves, as a matter of right, into a wide range of on-the-ground implementation processes.[44] The experimentalist character of the framework as a whole would thereby be strengthened, far more actors would be induced to engage it, and hence far larger "cumulative effects" could be generated across governance domains.[45]

Third, and again closely related, an expressive set of rights and participation-enabling duties under a fourth pillar would serve to enhance and expand sites of independent implementation oversight, especially those most accessible and normatively open to rights-holder engagement. Indeed, because the GP framework does not contemplate specific institutional mechanisms of independent compliance oversight (such as an individual complaints procedure or periodic reporting regime), a "participate" pillar would provide important normative contact points with the existing human rights architecture, including National Human Rights Institutions, UN special procedures, and human rights tribunals (national, regional, international). For such bodies, rights-holder participation, voice, agency, and access are guiding framework principles. While the former SRSG likes to reference the "implementation" capacities of international investment, banking, financial, and other "economic law" institutions, including OECD National Contact Points, these are not the kinds of procedures to which affected communities have ready access or to which they are likely to turn. Creating more contact points with national and international institutions *designed* to promote and defend the rights of the least

ensure effective participation by all relevant stakeholders through stakeholder mapping, capacity-building, and ensuring participation by disempowered or at-risk stakeholders).

[43] See, e.g., UN Convention Against Corruption, pmbl., arts. 5, 6, 10 and especially 13 ("Participation of Society"); Convention on Access to Information, Public Participation in Decision-Making and Access to Justice in Environmental Matters (Aarhus Convention) (1998); UN Convention on the Rights of Persons with Disabilities, pmbl., arts. 4.3, 33, etc. [hereinafter CRPD].

[44] A "participate" pillar would thus function in a parallel manner to the "remedy" pillar. While that pillar may formally be cast as a "duty" or "responsibility" in the framework, it is in practice regularly invoked as a *right* of civil society actors, including by the former SRSG. See, e.g., "Global Governance," note 11 above, pp. 5, 9 ("For affected individuals and groups, the GPs stipulate ways for their further empowerment to realize the *right to remedy*.") (emphasis added).

[45] In this sense, the proposal fit seamlessly into the former SRSG's emphatic articulation of the core aim of the GP framework: to close regulatory gaps by creating more effective and dynamic alignment between state, corporate and civil society governance systems, allowing *each* to mobilize more effectively to reinforce each other's strengths, address each other's weaknesses, and act as mutual balance and accountability checks. See, e.g., *Just Business*, p. 78.

powered is thus critical. This is particularly true in light of the increasing "fragmentation" of international law, and hence imperative of finding ways to promote
interpretive convergence across governance regimes,[46] while, at the same time,
helping to ensure that the GPs do not continue to fall behind evolving standards
in the human rights field.

Other longer-term methods could of course be proposed for achieving similar ends
outside the GP architecture. One good example – one I support, as detailed below – is
the adoption of an international treaty instrument expressly recognizing the participatory rights and roles of civil society in all stages of the implementation process, as
other recent human rights treaties have profitably (and without controversy) done.[47]
Our proposal was simply that the *same* expressive commitment made to "respect,"
"protect," and "remedy" should be made with respect to civil society "participation,"
recognizing it not only as a right under international law but as an indispensable
element of polycentric governance regimes. One that both state and corporate actors
have a duty/responsibility to ensure, and which, as a cross-cutting and intersectional
principle of human rights law, requires its own set of guiding principles to ensure
effective operationalization across governance systems. Without this being done, we
were confident that the issue of participation would be reduced to a side-note and
taken off the table.[48] Indeed, as the initial volume contribution itself recognizes, *the
GPs do not incorporate* civil society participation as a systematic institutional feature
in their current elaboration, stating merely and weakly that corporations should
"consult" with potentially affected communities in assessing human rights "risks"
(Principle 18). Whether they do so or not, and, most critically, how they do so, is
entirely up to their own discretion. Stated another way, within the present GP framework civil society actors are left bereft of any express normative toolset to demand their
effective participation in GP implementation processes *as a matter of right*.

It is useful to recall in this regard, the literature on expressive commitments in
international (and national) law. That literature understands expressiveness as one
of the key functions of law. It allows states and other actors to clearly and publicly
manifest a commitment to some principle above and beyond whatever obligations
are imposed. That public manifestation of commitment serves important intrinsic
and instrumental ends. Most significantly, it allows a range of social actors to hold
those who commit to account for their commitments.[49] Critically, this is true

---

[46]   Ruggie, "Global Governance," note 11 above (noting impacts of fragmentation).
[47]   CRPD, note 44 above, arts. 4.3, etc.
[48]   In the 2014 conference giving rise to this volume, Professor Ruggie objected that such a "participate"
pillar would have been a political impossibility given certain rejection by states (like China and
Russia) – and even by civil society actors themselves. This posture nonetheless seems to ignore the
large number of treaties that are regularly adopted by states with civil society "participation rights"
embedded expressly within them (see, e.g., note 44 above) as well as civil society's organized
protagonism in demanding such embedding.
[49]   See, e.g., Beth A. Simmons, *Mobilizing for Human Rights: International Law in Domestic Politics*
(Cambridge 2009). See also Robert Cialdini, *Influence: Science and Practice* (1985), pp. 92–103

regardless of whether those commitments are publicly manifested in a formally binding instrument (e.g., a treaty) or nonbinding one (the GPs). The key distinction in this regard is not necessarily between binding and nonbinding commitments, but rather between *expressive* and *inexpressive* ones.[50] Expressive commitments are sticky; they encourage a wide audience to monitor their implementation and insist on implementation. Inexpressiveness may serve short-term political ends, but also carries large opportunity costs. Most relevantly in the GP context, it removes the power of civil society actors to use principled commitments to make those commitments stick. That is, to insist on them not as a privilege granted at another party's discretion, but as a normative *right* authoritatively recognized as a principle of conduct in a human rights-respecting society.

Are there additional ways to directly incorporate such "sticky" norms into the GP framework? Certainly. For instance, civil society groups could organize and sponsor the drafting of a set of "*Supplementary* Guiding Principles" that addressed the participation and accountability issues left out of the GPs – drawing on and cross-referencing, perhaps, the UN Guiding Principles on Extreme Poverty and Human Rights, which do make participatory empowerment of affected communities a central institutional feature.[51] Such groups could then lobby states, the Working Group, and other special procedures to request the Human Rights Council to endorse the formal updating of the GPs as a short-term priority.

A different, albeit far less effective and authoritative approach would be to encourage the WG to prepare a thematic report that directly addressed the right to participate in GP implementation processes at all levels. It could invite participatory interventions by all stakeholders and focus on "best practices" that have been adopted with respect to allowing civil society participation in a wide range of processes encouraged by the GPs. An obvious downside of this approach is that the WG has already, in its first thematic report on indigenous peoples' rights, manifested a disinclination to recognize fully and robustly the participatory rights of affected stakeholders under current international law.[52] Such an approach, if pursued in isolation, could then set the participatory project backward, rather than taking it forward, even while years would pass before the WG produced any deliverable. While the WG's current membership will soon change, its institutional reluctance to robustly address participation issues is undoubtedly tied closely to the scope of its mandate, itself intimately linked with the acculturative regulatory logic of the GPs. It is unlikely, then, that the WG will significantly change its approach to this issue. Likewise, thematic reports prepared by special procedures lack authoritative standing among many stakeholders; they could not serve to authoritatively

---

(collecting research showing that people who commit and have their commitments publicized are more likely to keep their commitment, even after the publicity is over).
[50] See Woods, note 25 above.
[51] A/HRC/21/39; HRC Res. 21/11 (27 September 2012) (adopting GPs by consensus).
[52] See A/HRC/WG/12/3/1.

embed participation within the GP framework, such that it became part of the "dynamic regulatory logic" that drives it.[53]

The surest path forward, then, lies in a dual approach: the organized pursuit of a substantive updating of the GP framework with more expressive rights of participation, while simultaneously pursuing the longer-term project of negotiating a treaty instrument that would make those "soft" expressive commitments to participatory governance "hard" *for states* under international law. Indeed, as studies show, human rights commitments are "stickiest" – and hence most "mobilizable" – when those commitments have been made not only *expressively* but also through *binding* treaty law.[54] I turn to that critical longer-term proposal below.

III A BINDING TREATY: WHAT, WHY AND BINDING ON WHOM?

Calls for a treaty on business and human rights have of course been made recurrently for over half a century. On 26 June 2014, the UN Human Rights Council took an important, if preliminary, step toward that inevitable development. Responding to the coordinated proposals of over ninety states and over 500 civil society organizations, it agreed to establish an Open-Ended Working Group to consider elements of an international treaty on business and human rights. As discussions begin on what those elements should entail, one thing is clear: the heavily promoted idea that human rights groups demand a "command-and-control"-style treaty that directly binds business under international law must be left at the door. Let us be clear: No human rights treaty has *ever* followed that model, and human rights groups have never promoted it in any human rights treaty negotiation. It is inconceivable to me that they would do so in the BHR context.

Rather, the kind of BHR treaty that human rights NGOs and affected communities are most likely to support is one that – like other human rights treaties – follows an experimentalist approach and focuses on three elements: (1) defining rights in flexible but expressive terms that resonate with the lived experience of rights-holders; (2) embedding express civil society participation rights as tools of engagement throughout its structure and implementation logic, and (3) clarifying *states' duties* to take all necessary and appropriate measures to respect, protect and ensure human rights as they are impacted by corporate misconduct. In each of these respects, I suggest, the most useful and relevant model lies with the UN's most recently adopted human rights treaty: the UN Convention on the Rights of Persons with

---

[53]   See Albin-Lackey, note 3 above (recognizing problematic nature of GPs "setting a lower bar than international human rights standards" since "many companies now see the principles – incorrectly - as the world's definitive, one-stop standard for good human rights practice. *There is a risk that many companies will simply ignore standards the Guiding Principles do not echo.*") (emphasis added).

[54]   See, e. g., Simmons, note 49 above; Adam S. Chilton, "The Influence of International Human Rights Agreements on Public Opinion: An Experimental Study," *Chicago Journal of International Law* 15 (2014), 110.

Disabilities (CRPD). Below, I very briefly note the key elements thereof that are of greatest likely relevance to discussions on a new BHR Treaty.[55]

A. *Flexible, but Expressive Commitments*

First, the CRPD does not rigidly prescribe conduct, but rather incorporates a set of flexible, expressive, and experientially resonant terms designed to enable a wide range of actors to engage them as tools of leverage, mobilization, and participatory engagement in their diverse local struggles. Indeed, largely at the insistence of rights-holder groups and their civil society allies participating in the drafting process,[56] the UN Committee charged with its negotiation carefully avoided "shopping lists" and overspecification of details and standards as an agreed operational modality. It did so precisely to ensure that the Convention's text would remain relevant and vital over time, space, and context. It is thereby capable of responding to new challenges and modes of abuse as they arise, as well as the vastly different challenges faced by differently situated rights-holders and duty-bearers across the world. It also wished to avoid the negative inference that anything not expressly included in a detailed provision was intended to be excluded. Thus, broadly exemplary terms with inclusive references and a higher level of generality were consistently preferred to overly-specific, narrowly tailored ones or "lists" of abuse and standardized implementing measures. The same will undoubtedly be true of a BHR Treaty.

B. *Embedding Participation Rights*

Second, to ensure that rights-holders *can* in fact engage in processes directed at a meaningful incorporation of their rights into policies, practices and procedures that affect them, the CRPD focused on embedding rights-holder participation rights and institutional pathways for their exercise (what I call "participation nodes") throughout its text and dynamic implementation logic. "Full and effective participation [of rights-holders] and inclusion in society" was thus affirmed repeatedly as a core guiding principle of the treaty, reiterated in the Preamble, Purpose, and General Principles. The treaty likewise codified it as a central *obligation* of all States parties. The "General Obligations" clause thus commits all public actors, under a "shall" provision, to "closely consult with and actively involve persons with disabilities [PWDs].... [i]n the development and implementation of legislation

---

[55] Space constraints prevent fuller discussion and analogy between the disability and B&HR contexts. For more on the CRPD, see, e.g., Tara J. Melish, "The UN Disability Convention: Historic Process, Strong Prospects, and Why the U.S. Should Ratify," *Human Rights Brief* 14(2) (2007); Tara J. Melish, "An Eye Toward Effective Enforcement: A Technical-Comparative Approach to the CRPD Negotiations," *Human Rights and Disability Advocacy* (Sabatello and Shulze (eds.), Penn Press 2013).

[56] See Gráinne de Búrca, "The EU in the negotiation of the UN Disability Convention," *European Law Review* Vol. 35, No. 2 (2010) (hypothesizing that CRPD's highly experimentalist character was driven by the EU, but concluding driving factor was civil society NGOs and rights-holder groups).

and policies to implement the present Convention, and in other decision-making processes concerning issues" affecting their lives.[57] These same participatory rights and duties were repeated and made more operationally specific with respect to key substantive rights, monitoring arrangements, information collection and accessibility, compliance regimes, and oversight systems.

Let me note just a few provisions given their importance for a BHR treaty. First, the provision on national-level implementation and monitoring affirms unambiguously that "[c]ivil society, in particular [PWDs] and their representative organizations, *shall be involved and participate fully in the monitoring process.*"[58] Another provision specifically requires states to ensure *"effective* monitoring" by *"independent* authorities" of "all" facilities and programs designed to serve PWD, whether public and private.[59] State parties are likewise required to collect and disaggregate data for purposes of policy formulation, and to *ensure* its accessibility to PWD. At the same time, the CRPD expressly commits States to the establishment of national implementation machinery specifically tasked with responsibility over the treaty's subject matter. It is to and through these instituted processes that rights-holders can direct their collective concerns, demands, inputs and organized oversight. They include (1) a focal point or focal points within government to oversee implementation of the treaty; (2) a coordination mechanism to ensure coherence in policy and action across the public sphere; and (3) a set of independent monitoring mechanisms (like NHRIs) with competence over the treaty's effective implementation. With respect to each of these, states commit to ensure *full civil society participation,* particularly by the treaty's rights-holders themselves. The same is true of the treaty's international supervisory machinery.

Given the massive power and information disparities that pervade the BHR field, there is little doubt that the same kinds of overlapping commitments to participatory rights of access to decision-making structures and processes – at local, national and international levels – should likewise drive the logic of any new BHR treaty.

C. *Specifying* States' *Duties*

Finally, for highly instrumental and operationally pragmatic reasons, human rights treaty law has remained centered on clarifying *states' duties* to respect and ensure human rights. This is true even as human rights law is increasingly applied to every imaginable kind of private conduct. It is indeed precisely in recognition of this reality that the GPs focused on the *state (legal) duty to protect* human rights from business-related abuse. And, yet, while few dispute the general existence of this duty under international treaty law, there remains significant uncertainty about its sector-specific operational contours. Indeed, corporate actors have amassed such broad and powerful rights across legal borders that it is increasingly unclear where their

---

[57] CRPD, art. 4.3.   [58] CRPD, art. 33 (emphasis added).   [59] CRPD, art. 16.3 (emphasis added).

prerogative ends and what role public law has to define and constrain it. It is precisely here, then, in clarifying the state legal duty to respect, protect, and ensure rights to affected communities, that a "carefully constructed precision tool" is most needed.

In this regard, the former SRSG's repeated assertion that such a treaty would not "add value" is unpersuasive. It indeed misconstrues the purpose and content of all specialized treaties in the human rights domain. Such treaties do not create "new" rights, but rather serve as precision instruments in clarifying the scope and specialized content of more generally articulated rights and duties with respect to highly abusive subject areas long marginalized or ignored in national agendas and mainstream human rights procedures. Correspondingly, the most valuable role for a BHR treaty lies in more expressively articulating states' obligations under international law to regulate corporate conduct; to prevent abuse from occurring (through safeguard measures, regular oversight, monitoring, etc.); to respond to abuses when and where they occur, diligently and with a view toward guaranteeing against future violations; and to ensure civil society participation and independent mechanisms for monitoring, oversight, and dynamic regulatory response, at local, national and international levels alike.[60]

A precision instrument of this kind would indeed serve multiple *power shifting ends.* Not only would it create stronger, more precise leverage tools for rights-holders and their advocates to engage states' wrongful acts and omissions directly, but it would also address the elephant in the room: *States themselves* need new legal tools of empowerment and leverage to *be able to regulate and monitor* in the business domain. Increased legality and treaty-based specificity around state obligations thus serve to enhance opportunities for state-civil society alliances (often pursed in adversarial terms, but understood covertly as collaborative), while, at the same time, allowing states to expressively *self-bind* and hence gain legal leverage to assert themselves in their own regulatory role[61] (including in multistate or regional arrangements across the Global South). It is little surprise, then, that the principal proponents of a comprehensive treaty are Global South states and civil society organizations – precisely those with least power and fewest rights vis-à-vis the massively resourced and legally powered corporate sector.

IV LOOKING FORWARD

In his initial contribution to this volume, César Rodríguez-Garavito invites an immensely important and timely project: creative conversation and strategic thinking from a variety of global voices on the "dynamic dimension" of the GPs. In other

---

[60] Specialized human rights treaties thus virtually always include obligations clauses that are longer and more articulated than those found in general instruments.

[61] See generally Karen J. Alter, *The New Terrain of International Law: Courts, Politics, Rights* (Princeton Univ. Press 2014) (discussing state delegation of jurisdiction to international fora as a way to self-bind and hence gain power vis-à-vis other actors).

words, their "capacity to push the development of new norms and practices that might go beyond the initial content of the GPs," thereby ensuring "cumulative, step-by-step progress" in improving companies' real-world compliance with human rights standards. I salute this initiative and hope that my small contribution here will aid it in two ways. First, by encouraging a critical rethinking of the dominant frames used to promote and explain the GPs in public debate, with particular attention to the damaging ways those frames have served to sideline and marginalize the voices, roles, and strategic insights of affected communities and their human rights allies. Second, by helping to ensure that conversations moving forward remain solidly focused on identifying and promoting the tools, procedures, and resources that affected communities themselves need to participate – actively and meaning-fully – in the policy and decision-making processes that so affect their lives. If those goals are achieved, I believe, a foundation will have been built upon which we can indeed move the GP framework "beyond the end of the beginning."

5

From Guiding Principles to Interpretive Organizations: Developing a Framework for Applying the UNGPs to Disputes That Institutionalizes the Advocacy Role of Civil Society

Larry Catá Backer

The late 20th and early 21st centuries have seen a number of important trends in governance, some better known than others. Two are noteworthy in the context of developing governance structures for the detrimental human rights effects of economic activity. The first is the tendency to seek to construct integrated metagovernance[1] orders under which human behavior may be managed; the second is the movement toward the abstraction of the individual even as individual dignity rises to the top of the objectives of metagovernance. The first has produced the great international polycentric systems of human rights governance of economic activity, not the least of which is the U.N. Guiding Principles for Business and Human Rights (2011) (UNGPs), and the necessity of a unifying order to harmonize the state duty to protect and the corporate responsibility to respect human rights under that framework. It has also fostered international movements to bring governance back into the state through a system of international treaties aimed at managing the substance of domestic legal orders.[2] The second has

---

[1] Metagovernance can be understood as the governance of governance, the construction of a harmonized set of values, norms and principles underlying governance systems and drawing them together. Cf. Jan Kooiman and Seven Jentoft, "Meta Governance: Values, Norms and Principles, and the Making of Hard Choices," *Public Administration* 87(4) (2009), 818–836. The cyclicity of such efforts grounded in the urge to manage increasingly complex social life is explored in Bob Jessop, "Governance and Meta-Governance in the Face of Complexity: On the Roles of Requisite Variety, Reflexive Observation and Romantic Irony in Participatory Governance," in *Participatory Governance in Multi-Level Context* (eds.), Hubert Heinelt, Panagiotis Getimis, Grigoris Kafkalas, Randall Smith, and Erik Swyngedouw (New York: Springer, 2002).

[2] The great human rights instruments that make up the so-called International Bill of Human Rights (IBHR) provides nice example of this tendency toward state-based metagovernance. The IBHR is founded on the Universal Declaration of Human Rights. See A Universal Declaration of Human Rights, U.N. General Assembly, A/RES/3/217 (10 December 1948). The Universal Declaration of Human Rights was codified in international law through the International Covenant on Civil and Political Rights and the International Covenant on Economic, Social and Cultural Rights, both of 1966.

accelerated the development of mass movements and mass democracy that now serves as the ideological core of legitimate governance. It has also given rise to the emergence of mass collectives, representing either individuals or capital – the great multinational corporations and civil society actors – within which mass politics and mass economic activity can be undertaken. Each represents and embodies the individual who is no longer relevant as an autonomous actor within metagovernance systems. The second would transform global NGOs into the incarnation of individuals whose human rights are adversely affected by state and multinational enterprises.

This chapter considers the ramifications of these trends in the development of a necessary governance architecture for the sound implementation of the UNGPs. The chapter's thesis is this: the logic of emerging metagovernance points to the need to establish a central mechanism for the interpretation of transnational normative governance instruments and particularly the UNGPs, and the logic of emerging mass governance principles points to the need to vest representative civil society organization with the authority to bring cases and advocate before such an interpretive body. Movements to develop comprehensive treaty structures pose a threat to the establishment of a workable transnational order compatible with the realities of contemporary governance. Section 1 briefly contextualizes the issue within the formative trends of metagovernance and mass movements that characterize our age. Section 2 then considers contemporary critiques of the development of the GPs through the UN Working Group on human rights and transnational corporations and other business enterprises (WG), established in 2011 by the U.N. Human Rights Council. On that basis, it suggests the manner in which these trends ought to be applied to develop effective mechanism for the implementation of the UNGPs at the international level, taking advantage of the polycentricity at the heart of governance systems in this century. Section 3 ends with an analysis of the alternative governance framework now advanced by states and suggests the way its reactionary character detracts from the important project of operationalizing metagovernance of the human rights effects of economic activity.

I FROM LAW, STATE, AND INDIVIDUAL TO METAGOVERNANCE AND MASS POLITICS

The movement toward harmoniously conceived and operated metagovernance has ancient roots. Its modern manifestation appeared both in the construction of 19th century imperial and colonial states, and thereafter, on their collapse under the weight of the contradictions of their own formative logics, in the construction of the international system of the community of states. Indeed, the middle 20th century might be understood as marking the point of apotheosis of the state, when the state assumed internal supremacy within its territory (in dynamic relation with its population under democratic theories of governmental legitimacy) and among the community of states that retained a global monopoly of regulatory power.[3] That power was itself challenged by the most successful product of governance internationalism – globalization. It brought into the equation of power entities other than states, in a well-known process of permeability, porosity, and polycentricity that caused the current crisis of governance management, only a portion of which touches on the problem of human rights governance.[4] That crisis could be understood as such not because globalization created governance gaps, but because governance systems were no longer seamlessly and harmoniously connected (at least in theory to a complex network of public law institutions centered on the state and their international instrumentalities). The resulting anarchy challenged both the old order (represented by the U.N. system and its related bodies) and the ability of powerful governance players, mostly states but also intellectuals and elements of civil society and business, to use that power instrumentally for particular ends. Much of the work of the last thirty years among the great stakeholders of the law-state *ancien régime* has been to try to figure out how to reconstruct integrated and harmonious metagovernance, centered on law and the state, so that governance instrumentalism may again be deployed to proper ends – like human rights – under common standards.[5] Alternative conceptions including polycentric governance, are viewed as either transitional or with great suspicion as derogating from the legitimacy reinforcing structures of law and the state.

The other is the movement toward the abstraction of the individual. With its origins in Western religion, it acquired a stronger political dimension after the French and American Revolutions of the 18th century and the rise of democratic theories of governmental legitimacy. It acquired its present character during the 20th century and its tendencies toward essentialism (reducing an individual to some characteristic or other) and institutionalization/bureaucratization on the other (understanding individuals as components of collective organisms). These were given concrete expression under both fascism[6] and Marxist Leninist state organization[7] in the mid-20th century as well as theoretical grounding in both the

---

[3] How that power was exercised *in fact* divides academics and others into a variety of "camps" whose positions have fueled generations of academics, the details of which fall outside the scope of this short essay. Cf. *Fifty Key Thinkers in International Relations* (2nd edition) (eds.), Martin Griffiths, Steven C. Roach, and M. Scott Solomon (New York: Routledge 2009).

[4] Larry Catá Backer, "The Structure of Global Law: Fracture, Fluidity, Permeability, and Polycentricity," *Tilburg Law Review* Vol. 17(2) (2012), 177–199. Available at SSRN http://ssrn.com/abstract=2091456.

[5] Larry Catá Backer, "Economic Globalization Ascendant: Four Perspectives on the Emerging Ideology of the State in the New Global Order," *La Raza Law Journal* Vol. 17(1) (2006), 141–168. Available at SSRN http://ssrn.com/abstract=917417.

[6] James A. Gregor, *The Ideology of Fascism: The Rationale of Totalitarianism* (New York: Free Press, 1969).

[7] Joseph Stalin, *Problems of Leninism* (Moscow: Foreign Languages Publishing House, 1953).

biopolitics of Michel Foucault[8] and the systems theories of Niklas Luhmann[9] and Gunther Teubner.[10] The individual was subsumed within the "masses," a statistical abstraction of common characteristics and behaviors, or the necessarily undifferentiated body of system and subsystem whose collective communication determined the parameters of human behavior and collective response. The collective individual, then, necessarily required a collective personality, one that could protect the abstracted individuals it absorbed without dissolving into the masses that gave them form. This tendency has produced a tendency toward the institutionalization of mass movements, necessary perhaps under the logic of mass democracy. But it has also contributed to the development of an institutionalized civil society that stands for and leverages individual desire, the way, perhaps that corporations stand in for the "desires" of capital as aggregated in the antipode of civil society, the transnational corporation. Civil society has emerged as the form in which the masses may be individualized, and individual dignity protected. Within metagovernance structures, especially in large states and in the international arena, civil society both represents and substitutes itself for the individual, and individual will can be manifested only as an aggregated abstraction. In the absence of the group, the individual is reduced to virtually nothing in global governance (other than perhaps a bundle of rights some of which might be remedied someplace).

These movements together produce the current framework of transnational governance; just as this century heralds the end of the autonomous nation-state, so too does it mark the end of the ideal of the autonomous individual as an instrument of governance. This is an age of *collectives* working within polycentric governance systems operating in an anarchic metagovernance space. But it is also an age of resistance and of efforts to restore the status quo preglobalization. The question for this century with regard to the construction of effective governance responses to significant problems focusing on the detrimental effects of economic activity on human rights then is: how can a method of coordinating polycentric systems be created that provides ample and effective political and juridical space within which collective actors can participate, with the object of producing a measure of legal coherence in human rights governance?

The field of human rights has developed "a new governance sense" that is essentially polycentric. It implicitly rejects a rigid embrace of classical regulatory

8   Michel Foucault, trans. Graham Burchell, *Security, Territory, Population: Lectures at the Collège de France 1977–1978* (New York: Picador, 2003). See also Michel Foucault, trans. Graham Burchell, *The Birth of Biopolitics: Lectures at the Collège de France, 1978–1979* (New York: Picador, 2010).
9   Niklas Luhman, *Political Theory in the Welfare State* (New York: Walter DeGruyter, 1990); see also Dietrich Schwanitz, "Systems Theory According to Niklas Luhman—Its Environment and Conceptual Strategies," *Cultural Critique* 30 (1995), 137–170.
10 Gunther Teubner, "The Corporate Codes of Multinationals: Company Constitutions Beyond Corporate Governance and Co-Determination," in *Conflict of laws and Laws of Conflict in Europe and Beyond: Patterns of Supranational and Transnational Juridification* (ed.), Rainer Nickel (Oxford: Hart, 2009).

theory centered on law and the state, one which is based on the creation of comprehensive universal and legally binding instruments prescribing policies in a top down fashion and administered through national legal orders in favor of a strand of emerging "new governance theory" which are polycentric in character. "New governance theory rests on the premise that the state by itself cannot do all the heavy lifting required to meet most pressing societal challenges and that it therefore needs to engage other actors to leverage its capacities."[11] It rests as well on the premise that these capacities are themselves autonomous regulatory sources with substantial normative power over the communities that have adopted them. Polycentricity, then, suggests regime complexes born of the realities of power fracture in contemporary globalization in which distinct emerging governance regimes are understood as building blocks that may be arranged and orchestrated to particular ends.

But the "new governance" framework for understanding the possibilities of polycentricity itself constrains the analysis. More troubling, it leads almost inexorably back to a framework in which the state is accorded pride of place and for which law serves as a means of conforming the hierarchy of power in which the individual invariably continues to be treated as little more than a well-managed object of strumental policies effected from the top even if derived from a system that in its formal aspects appears to be drawn "from the bottom up."[12] The essence of the problem of new governance can be understood in three respects. First is the underlying premise of new governance that the object of both theory and practice is to produce not merely coordination but a stronger relationship among emerging governance systems. But polycentricity is not a shattered plate that must be put together again before one can eat off of it, an approach that expresses a nostalgia for the unity once represented by state power and an effort to recreate it by other means – a sort of "silver age" approach to governance theory seeking a return to unity and assuming that power is incomplete unless united. It seeks the undoing of polycentric space by harmonizing rather than by coordinating.[13] The second is the dependence inherent in managing and integrating polycentricity. There is a certain allure to new governance for civil society. It suggests a way in which they might leverage authority off states and enterprises. But that sort of power is always dependent, and ultimately servile. It is safe, but it is also a contingent authority, participation that is always subject to reward for "good" behavior and sanction for bad. Third, polycentricity is only efficient when systems are harmonized. The idea of

---

[11] John G. Ruggie, "Global Governance and 'New Governance Theory': Lessons From Business and Human Rights," *Global Governance* 20 (2014), 5–17.

[12] Larry Catá Backer, "On the Tension between Public and Private Governance in the Emerging Transnational Legal Order: State Ideology and Corporation in Polycentric Asymmetric Global Orders" (2012.). Available at SSRN http://ssrn.com/abstract=2038103.

[13] Larry Catá Backer, "Transnational Corporations' Outward Expression of Inward Self-Constitution: The Enforcement of Human Rights by Apple, Inc.," *Indiana Journal of Global Legal Studies* Vol. 20 (2) (2013), 805–879. Available at SSRN http://ssrn.com/abstract=2050180.

management and integration is essential for workable polycentricity under a back-
wards-looking conceptualization of new governance. It ignores the possibility of
coordination rather than integration. It is possible to suggest that polycentricity in
globalization is moving toward anarchy, rather than toward integration. The result
may also produce order but of a completely different sort, one grounded in anarchy
but within which all governance systems seek legitimacy through coordination
grounded in a unifying set of governance principles,[14] one that rejects the antic-
ontextualism premises of integrationist approaches.

"But all of that is conceptual, and conceptual arguments by themselves do not
necessarily change minds and practices, no matter how reasonable they may be.
Persuasion is much more likely to succeed if it is also experiential."[15] John Ruggie's
statement resonates powerfully in the context of framing governance for economic
actors' activities detrimental to human rights. The next section considers the possibilities of that specific enterprise.

II FROM THEORY TO THE PRACTICE OF COORDINATING HUMAN RIGHTS GOVERNANCE THROUGH THE UNGPS

The UNGPs drew on the insight of polycentricity in metagovernance and collectiv-
ity to construct a structure of managed polycentric governance among three distinct
governance systems that the authors identify as state law, corporate governance and
civil governance systems (Backer 2012c). The UNGPs start with a view of the
principal global challenge for human rights and governance: the regulation
of global business. They embrace the notion of both the existence of a governance
gap and a need to fill it. That, in turn, suggests that there is a space where there is no
governance – a governance free zone – something that is implausible.[16] The premise
itself is usefully interrogated, and in any case is belied by the logic of the UNGPs
itself. The UNGPs' three pillar framework defines three distinct governance systems
whose coordination is necessary for the objective of coherent governance of economic actors' activities detrimental to human rights. The three blocks represent (1)
the state and domestic/international law systems, (2) enterprises and social norm/
nonstate governance systems, and (3) civil society and remedial objectives through
multiple normative systems. The "idea behind the GPs is that each building block is
placed in such a way that it compensates for the weaknesses of the others and

---

[14] Larry Catá Backer, "Governance Polycentrism – Hierarchy and Order Without Government in
       Business and Human Rights Regulation," *Coalition for Peace and Ethics Working Paper* No. 1/1
       (2014). Available at SSRN: http://ssrn.com/abstract=2373734.
[15] Ruggie, "Global Governance and 'New Governance Theory': Lessons From Business and Human
       Rights," *Global Governance* 20 (2014), 5–17.
[16] Larry Catá Backer, "Economic Globalization and the Rise of Efficient Systems of Global Private Law
       Making: Wal-Mart as Global Legislator," *University of Connecticut Law Review* 39 No. 4 (2007),
       1739–1784.

exercises pressure for upward movement, or continual improvement in the protection of human rights affected by business activities."[17]

But civil society commentators also suggest that the civil society component is weak and not compensated by the remedial pillar. The solution, for the authors, is the development of a stronger institutional role for civil society by more directly empowering civil society through more robust participation within the mechanisms through which the state duty to protect and the corporate responsibility to respect are discharged. This form of empowerment envisions civil society as something like the private attorney general from U.S. legal theory[18] – as an autonomous monitoring and accountability force representing the mass of individuals in the protection of their rights as against the institutional forces of state and enterprise. "In polycentric governance terms, this entails an organization playing an 'orchestration' role by engaging the social actors involved in the regime, promoting collaborations and discussions among them and disseminating standards and practices."[19] Civil society, in effect, represents the individual in their aggregate manifestation, and their role ensures that all three major stakeholders in the human rights arena – states, corporations, and individuals – are reified in equivalent form, as aggregations of political, economic, and mass power.

Within this vision of metaharmonization represented by the UNGPs and the aggregation of abstract individuals within the institutional forms of civil society, the WG, established in 2011 by the UN Human Rights Council, serves as an orchestration mechanism overseeing this process of implementation, of placing the building blocks of the UNGPs in coherent fashion. The success of the WG appears to be mixed. Many have characterized the WG's first years by a (far too) narrow interpretation of its mandate. As a consequence, and not without substantial criticism by civil society groups, the WG focused on dissemination and implementation of the UNGPs. Critics have made a case for a skewing of focus by the WG, one that I have made in the context of the 2013 Annual Forum, toward enterprises and the state, with civil society elements relegated to an indeterminate consulting but clearly secondary role. With an eye toward the production of national action plans by European states and encouraging the development of systematic human rights due diligence, the WG missed an important opportunity. That opportunity would have been to extend the focus of its mandate to civil society, and more importantly, to the rights holders who were the objects of the UNGPs. At the same time, the singular focus on national action plans appears to have permitted enterprises to avoid the principal consequences of their autonomous responsibility to respect human rights, and in that process avoided any governance responsibility associated with their human rights due diligence regimes. Even within the limited managed polycentric space of new

---

[17] See César Rodríguez-Garavito's Chapter 1 in this volume.
[18] William B. Rubenstein, "On What a 'Private Attorney General' Is—And Why It Matters," *Vanderbilt Law Review* Vol. 57 No. 6 (2004), 2129.
[19] Rodríguez-Garavito, Chapter 1 in this volume.

governance within which the WG appears to operate according to the logic of the UN system,[20] the UNGPs' potential – of a polycentric system of collaborating institutional actors operating symmetrically within the harmonizing framework of the UNGPs – is undermined by the actual WG's operational practice and its asymmetrical implementation of the UNGPs.

One can explain away this state of affairs as a necessary consequence of the WG's need to prioritize. But a better explanation might suggest a faulty prioritization. One can suggest superior alternative priorities. The first is grounded in the establishment of mechanisms that could produce a quasi-judicial facility through the WG. The second is to delegate the role of mediator between individuals and the other mandate stakeholders to civil society. The third and most important, though, then turns on issues of power – that is to the power to constitute and discipline the civil society community within which this authority is to be exercised. This later takes two distinct forms – who gets to participate in civil society events, and who gets to count as civil society for purposes of its role within the WG framework. Each is discussed in turn.

First, the WG ought to serve or to establish a body that could serve as an authoritative source of decisions about the *application* of the UNGPs in *disputes* brought to it by states, enterprises or civil society acting as *collective representatives* of otherwise voiceless individuals. This suggests one of the most interesting, though lamentably not fully developed, possibilities that polycentric metagovernance offers the WG framework for UNGPs oversight – the missed opportunity of the WG to "consider individual cases of human rights violations in the context of business activity."[21] Rodríguez-Garavito suggest a mechanism for interpretation that "could include receiving and responding to individual submissions and complaints."[22] This suggests not only a way for enhancing the autonomous role of individuals (and their civil society advocates) within the UNGPs, but also the fundamental importance of an autonomous interpretive role for the UNGPs outside of the domestic legal orders of states or the governance orders of enterprises. It also suggests that within the third pillar lies the foundation for the authority of individuals to seek remedies for the breaches of state duty to protect or corporate responsibility to respect human rights.

But the WG missed more than that. The WG failed to grasp the opportunity to become the source of the highest and most credible and consistent interpretation of the UNGPs applied in context. *That failure to take on a quasi-judicial role*, not unlike that of the European Court of Justice in interpreting the application of European Law, in *form and effect*, though not binding in fact, has significantly diminished the importance of the WG's work and might well imperil the dynamic element of the UNGPs. The UN Development Program (UNDP) remains

---

[20]   See, e.g., Jamie Darin Prenkert and Scott J. Shackelford, "Business, Human Rights, and the Promise of Polycentricity," *Vanderbilt Journal of Transnational Law* 47 (2014), 451–500. Available www .vanderbilt.edu/wp-content/uploads/sites/78/Prenkert-Final.pdf.
[21]   Rodríguez-Garavito, Chapter 1 in this volume.   [22]   Ibid.

a framework in search of a jurisprudence. Most significant value lies in its application to concrete disputes among the critical stakeholders to the UNGP – states, business, and individuals on whose behalf civil society plays a decisive role. The principles of the UNDP can only be reified – made concrete – through the dynamic evolution and deepening of the "law" of the UNGPs' consistent application through a bottom up, case-by-case basis. And this, from the perspective of both static and dynamic evolution of the UNGPs, is fundamental – both for the WG and for those civil society elements that can play a crucial role in bringing such actions and thus adding muscle to the third pillar. To this end an interpretive facility is imperative. There is no evolution of the UNDP without a substantial body of application in which the UNGPs are manifested in the actions of its three stakeholders. This is especially the case were the WG to consider acting as an interpretive facility for National Contact Point (NCP) complaints undertaken pursuant to the OECD's Guidelines for Multinational Enterprises that have incorporated the UNGPs in substantial measure. In the absence of such a facility dedicated to the interpretation of the UNGP, it is left to the NCP to take up that project through their interpretation of chapter IV of the Multinational Guidelines, which incorporate the UNGPs.[23]

The *binding effect* of the determinations of any interpretive facility is less important than the project of producing these interpretations consistently and in the context of disputes actively contested among states, enterprises, and civil society actors before the UNGPs neutral interpreters. The production of case based glosses on the UNGPs would, of itself, and irrespective of its binding nature, produce guidance that would invariably be taken up by those bodies with substantially more authority to bind. This is not revolutionary practice but merely the application of a reality that the consistent production of glosses that produce a unified and coherent interpretation of the UNGPs will necessarily have an impact on the work of courts, intergovernmental bodies, enterprises, and civil society actors that would be influenced by, even if not made to, follow the interpretations. It is essential to build a body of interpretive glosses of the UNGP on the context of actual disputes. The work of the Ethics Council of the Norwegian Sovereign Wealth Fund Global provides an example, as does the work of the OECD National Contact Point.[24] This can be done; given the political will. And indeed, polycentricity's logic suggests that it can be done even if states are unwilling by the collaboration of enterprises and business in the creation of such a mechanism, in the way that business and civil

---

[23] See, e.g., UK National Contact Point, Initial Assessment by the UK National Contact Point for the OECD Guidelines for Multinational Enterprises (May 2014). Available www.gov.uk/government/uploads/system/uploads/attachment_data/file/315104/bis-14-854-palestinian-lawyers-complaint-against-g4s-ncp-initial-assessment.pdf.

[24] Larry Catá Backer, "Sovereign Investing and Markets-Based Transnational Rule of Law Building: The Norwegian Sovereign Wealth Fund in Global Markets," *American University International Law Review* 29(1) (2013), 1–121.

society sometimes cooperate in the construction and monitoring of supply chain CSR codes. Even "bad" decisions, decisions that are either rejected by an applying state or that may be repudiated in later decisions, would help move the construction of a coherent vision of the UNGPs as applied in the right direction, and secure an important role for civil society as the advocate for individuals otherwise less well represented in the process of fleshing out the UNGPs. In the absence of an interpretive mechanism, the UNGPs will always exist in a potential state. Without the ability of civil society to bring complaints for interpretation, the individual – the one actor who is at the heart of all of these human rights efforts – will be denied an effective collective advocate in every instance except those where states have undertaken a positive obligation to serve in that capacity, and where that obligation is backed by enforceable law.

Second, the WG's system building must include, along with national action plans, a more robust planning for the roles of enterprises and civil society in their respective fields. In place of the current asymmetrical disinvolvement of civil society, a "collaborative governance" model might serve as an antidote, one essential to the construction of any quasi-judicial facility in the WG or similar organ. This, in turn, requires building institutional mechanisms that bolster civil society in their representative capacities. Within these mechanisms, civil society would play a mediating role, as "engagers" (the "good citizen civil society organization) and "confronters" (the disruptive civil society actor).[25] Moreover, civil society is an essential element of this quasi-judicial facility for the same reason that individuals are understood as reincarnated in mass collectives with a collective authority. That authority is grounded in the embrace of a notion, implicit in the third pillar, of the autonomous rights of the individual, which states and enterprises are obliged to protect and respect, and for which remedies against both are appropriate. The protection of those individual rights against state and enterprise actors does not arise from within the corporate responsibility (and its mechanisms) or from the state duty (and its legal frameworks), but is inherent in the individual human dignity that exists outside of either. This is recognized in the framework of the UNGPs, both in the reference to the source of the corporate responsibility in the International Bill of Rights and ILO Convention (under the new governance or polycentric framework), and to the reference to the state duty in terms of its international legal obligations (under the classical framework of international law). But to be effective it may be exercised collectively. Just as the responsibility to respect human rights is vested in collectives of capital – so the remedial rights of individuals can be vested in civil society as collectives of individuals organized for the protection of their rights. But this view requires a challenge to the all too easy and now quite antiquated preglobalization logic of the law-state system.

---

[25]   Rodríguez-Garavito, Chapter 1 in this volume.

Third, the issue of who gets to participate touches on both formal and functional limits built into the WG system that makes it difficult for many civil society actors to participate. In effect, the economics of global governance, like that of the relationship among states, is grounded in economic power and territory. The costs to attend sessions, disengagement resulting from exclusion and exclusionary participation rules contribute to this state of affairs. Just as the most powerful and developed states tend to dominate international public discourse, so do the civil society "usual actors" tend to dominate civil society discourse within those contexts that seek civil society "perspective." And that pattern tends to bind large actors more closely to each other than to either weaker states or smaller NGOs; it may well be that Amnesty has more in common with the bureaucrats within the UK administrative state than they have with smaller UK NGOs in terms of interest, perspectives, modes of operation, communication intermeshing and the like.[26] In this context, efforts at reform may be as alienating as the rules they replace.[27] More difficult, perhaps, is the issue of disciplining membership in civil society. If civil society is accorded a more prominent institutional role, then who gets to count as "civil society"?[28] It is clear that the autonomy of civil society can be perverted by the creation of organizations that are mere instrumentalities of states and enterprises. That should be troubling. What might be in order are more robust rules, or a more aggressive interrogation of the premises underling the structures under which the WG operates.

III THE REACTIONARY TURN: THE WITHERED PROMISE OF A TREATY REGIME AS A GOVERNANCE ALTERNATIVE

Yet this complex construct offered as a coherent response to the complexities of emerging governance premises may well be undone by the allure of the forms of *ancien régime* systems, whose forms offer the outward form of stability and cohesion, but which can deliver neither. One of the most interesting of these formal, gesture-based alternatives currently on offer touching on the GP and WG enterprise is the

---

[26] Cf. Backer, "Economic Globalization Ascendant," p. 6.

[27] Cf. Conectas Direitos Humanos, Dejusticia and Justiça Global, Working Group on the Issue of Human Rights and Transnational Corporations and Other Business Enterprises: A Review of the First Two-and-a-Half Years of Work (25 November 2013). Available http://conectas.org/arquivos/editor/files/6_Dej_Con_JG_WG2years_Nov2013.pdf. "Worse, if the international community uses Global North civil society as the means through which this cram down is to be effected, the resulting colonialism becomes social and cultural–and polycentric–one in which the governance preferences of international civil society, global donors, and foundations, will be leveraged, and disguised as capacity building, substantially and unnecessarily narrow, the choices for Global South states in fashioning their compliance with their Pillar one duties." Larry Catá Backer, "On the Problem of the State in the State Duty to Protect Human Rights–Fostering National Action Plans as a Means of Refocusing the State Duty on the Business of the State Itself," *Law at the End of the Day*, 10 May 2014. Available: http://lcbackerblog.blogspot.com/2014/05/on-problem-of-state-in-state-duty-to.html.

[28] Considered in Larry Catá Backer, "Fractured Territories and Abstracted Terrains: The Problem of Representation and Human Rights Governance Regimes Within and Beyond the State," 23(1) *Indiana Journal of Global Legal Studies* (2016), 61–94.

substitution of the polycentrism of the UNGPs with a comprehensive treaty on business and human rights. The arguments against this approach are well understood. First treaty making has very high transaction costs. Second, such efforts require substantial state support. Third, treaty making is particularly burdensome for smaller organizations (and states) that seek to participate, and their voices are likely to carry less weight (even as they might bear the brunt of the burdens of the obligations created and waivers permitted). Fourth, a treaty might augment the scope of the state duty and corporate power in bad ways – that is in ways that are detrimental to civil society and perhaps to the individuals who are the objects of all this activity.

All of these drawbacks augment the case for complementarity, for the use of targeted treaty making, rather than the rejection of treaty making as part of the arsenal of managing business and human rights. But the arguments for complementary treaty making (in this case focused on a treaty covering gross human rights violations of enterprises) are more troubling for the enterprise of polycentricity. There is a sense of an Enlightenment master clockmaker view of human rights institutionalism which, deliberately or not, appears to be deployed in the service of an instrumental metamachinery whose parts work together toward a unified single end.

Four principal arguments are typically offered up in support of treaty complementarity, three are elegant and elegantly countered. The last is more subtle and troubling. First it serves to elaborate an integrated approach to the UNGPs construction of "three estate" governance – by states, enterprises and civil society as the new bodies of a human rights "estates general." Second, it might improve alignment with the edifice of public international law. It might also be subsumed thereunder. Third, it is an example of principled pragmatism in the spirit of that animating the GP project itself that could unleash polycentric and experimental regulation embedded in the GPs. The fourth reason suggests treaty utility proceeding from its power to establish extraterritorial obligations for states to close a structural regulatory gap – by unleashing the particularized interests of states against enterprises operating within the territories of other states unable or unwilling to conform to the desires of the intervening state. Extraterritoriality has always troubled me, and ought to be a source of worry for people from the Global South.[29] Of course the answer to the worry about the neocolonialism and developed state imperialism inherent in regimes of extraterritoriality is usually couched in "Third World Approaches to International Law" (TWAIL) terms.[30] But even the idea that extraterritoriality is

---

[29]   Larry Catá Backer, "At the 2nd U.N. Forum on Business and Human Rights–Reflections," in Bilchitz and Deva (eds.), *Human Rights Obligations of Business: Beyond the Corporate Responsibility to Respect? Law at the End of the Day* (1 December 2013). Available http://lcbackerblog.blogspot.co.il /2013/12/at-2nd-un-forum-on-business-and-human.html.

[30]   Sara L. Seck, "Transnational Business and Environmental Harm: A TWAIL Analysis of Home State Obligations," *Law Trade & Development* Vol. 3 No. 1 (2011), 164–202.

a process rather than a politically driven force – that is that intervening states would be applying international law, rather than their own, abroad, still ought to be troubling. States can only apply the international law through their own subjective interpretation of it – the interpretation issue. Second, international law applied through states is limited to those portions of those items of international law that have been domesticated and subject to such reservations – the partial international law issue. Extraterritoriality also creates a new regulatory gap, between empowered states and the passive states into which power is projected.[31]

The value of extraterritoriality in the business and human rights regulatory tool kit ought to be reconsidered. It might be more effective, for example, to set up an international body with the authority to hear cases involving states in weak or absent governance. But even this is tricky. The application of this jurisdictional standard to states against which more powerful states might wish to affect suggests one of the ways such extraterritoriality schemes can quickly become undermined in the service of the interests of the states with the power to use it. More useful, perhaps, would be the development of a fact-finding facility at the international level that might apply the UNGPs to particular complaints and whose findings, while not binding on states, could be used as "facts" applicable to local litigation. In the end, extraterritoriality exposes a preference for global players for binding "law" to arc the course of business enterprise and human rights back to its beginning. It is certainly true that *within* the law-state system, instructions that are not commands have no formal force and are subordinate to lawfully enacted commands. But *outside* the state system, what may not be binding through states may well be binding within enterprises and other governance communities adopting them. This self-binding makes them no less binding; it just shifts the source of binding power.[32]

IV CONCLUSION

The contradictions and conflicts surrounding the development of the UNGPs evidence the power and temptations of the great normative institutional forces that affect the governance projects of transnational society in the early 21st century. They show both the strength of the drive for order and rationality even within emerging polycentric orders beyond the state, and the necessary transformation of the individual within this polycentric universe from singular being to disembodied abstraction made flesh in the body of civil society. But the search for *unifying* order misdirects the project of creating a coherent system of business and human rights compatible with global governance norms. It is in that respect that one can understand the profound ways in which the WG may be missing opportunities. Two of

---

[31] Backer, "Economic Globalization Ascendant," p. 6.
[32] Larry Catá Backer, "Multinational Corporations as Objects and Sources of Transnational Regulation," *ILSA Journal of International & Comparative Law* 14 (2008), 499–523.

which are worthy of serious development. The first is a facility for delivering interpretations of the GPs whether or not deemed binding by state or enterprise instrumentalities. The second touches on the creation of an institutional framework for providing a means of hearing specific complaints brought from individuals through representative civil society for determination of the application of the GPs in context. Both require the strengthening of the remedial pillar to deepen its interpretation as an autonomous source of process and governance inclusion for the power of individuals, now represented by a civil society sector that is neither dependent on state nor enterprises, as a subject rather than as an object of GP governance.

6

A Treaty on Business and Human Rights?

A Recurring Debate in a New Governance Landscape

Claret Vargas

INTRODUCTION

It seems impossible to discuss the future of the business and human rights field in general, and of on the UN Guiding Principles (GPs) in particular, without also considering the ongoing negotiations at the United Nations (UN) level on a treaty on the human rights obligations of transnational corporations. Arising from the UN Human Rights Council's decision to launch the "elaboration of an internationally, legally binding instrument on transnational corporations and other business enterprises with respect to human rights,"[1] the treaty process has reignited the debate between hard-law and soft-law approaches that, as Rodríguez-Garavito explains in the opening chapter of this volume, has marked the contemporary business and human rights (BHR) field since its beginnings in the 1970s.[2]

The origins of the GPs and the treaty process are intertwined, and the movement toward the treaty was, in large part, a forum for the direct expression of discontent with aspects of the GPs, particularly by grassroots organizations, NGOs and several Global South States concerned with implementation.[3] Now that the Open Ended Working Group established by the Council for that purpose has begun its work, there has been some concern that states and businesses are reportedly stalling on their implementation of the GPs on the argument that one must wait and see what happens with the treaty process.[4] The dominant discourse about the treaty process

---

[1] UN Doc. A/HR/26/L.22/ Rev.1 (25 June 2014).

[2] In Chapter 1 in this volume, Rodríguez-Garavito provides an in-depth review of the history of the most recent effort to develop a treaty on business and human rights. A repetition of this history is thus unnecessary. See pages 17–22 in this volume.

[3] See, e.g., Asia Pacific Forum on Women, Law and Development (APWLD), "Shaping the treaty on business and human rights: views from Asia and the Pacific," http://apwld.org/shaping-the-treaty-on-business-and-human-rights-views-from-asia-and-the-pacific/; Treaty Alliance Joint Statement, "Enhance the International Legal Framework to Protect Human Rights from Corporate Abuse," available at http://www.treatymovement.com/statement.

[4] E.g., intervention by M. Mdwaba, noting that there are states and businesses "hanging on to technicalities" to postpone implementation of GPs. Closing panel, 18 November 2015. *United Nations Forum on Business and Human Rights* (16–18 November 2015) (authors' field notes)

and its interaction with the GPs, however, has been one of mutual strengthening and complementarity.[5] As both processes are likely to continue in earnest, it is important to consider what treaties can bring, what evidence there is to support assumptions about the power of treaties, in addition to the already existing discussion about the political, legal, theoretical, and pragmatic arguments for or against a treaty.[6]

While the debate about the content of the GPs versus the content of a potential treaty has given greater attention to the static dimension of these instruments, I build on Rodríguez-Garavito's argument in Chapter 1 of this volume and take a dynamic focus, one aimed at understanding the substantive goals of the treaty process and assessing the likelihood that a treaty would actually achieve them. Guided by a concern about implementation and actual impact on the ground, I examine how those goals are likely to be achieved by a treaty as well as by the GPs implementation process, and what needs to be done to ensure that both processes reinforce human rights norms, clarify state obligations, empower affected communities, and activate mechanisms to foreclose impunity by business actors. Because of space constraints, this chapter does not propose or discuss in detail the specific content that the treaty should have.[7]

In this chapter, I begin by defining the key concerns that animate the support for a binding treaty by some of its key proponents. I then examine the debate about the

---

[5] See, e.g., Claire Methven O'Brien, Amol Mehra, Sara Blackwell, and Cathrine Bloch Poulsen-Hansen, "National Action Plans: Current Status and Future Prospects for a New Business and Human Rights Governance Tool," *Business and Human Rights Journal*, 1 (2016), 118. International Commission of Jurists, *Needs and Options for a New International Instrument in the Field of Business and Human Rights.* (2014), available at http://icj.wpengine.netdna-cdn.com/wp-content/uploads/2014/06/NeedsandOptionsinternationalinst_ICJReportFinalelecvers.compressed.pdf. ("This report assumes therefore that any future international instrument in this field will coexist and mutually reinforce the Guiding Principles").

[6] See Deva, Melish, Rodríguez-Garavito, and Ruggie in this volume (Chapters 3, 4, 1, and 2, respectively). See also Olivier De Schutter, "The Challenge of Imposing Human Rights Norms on Corporate Actors," in Olivier De Schutter (ed.), *Transnational Corporations and Human Rights* (Oxford: Hart Publishing, 2006); Olivier De Schutter, "Towards a New Treaty on Business and Human Rights," *Business and Human Rights Journal* 1 (2015) (proposing four options for treaty design that could lead to more effective compliance with human rights norms); Surya Deva and David Bilchitz (eds.), *Human Rights Obligations of Business: Beyond the Corporate Responsibility to Respect?* (Cambridge: Cambridge UP); Bilchitz, David, "The Necessity for a Business and Human Rights Treaty," (30 November 2014). Available at SSRN http://ssrn.com/abstract=2562760; Ruggie, John, "Quo Vadis? Unsolicited Advice to Business and Human Rights Treaty Sponsors," (2014). Available at http://www.ihrb.org/commentary/quo-vadis-unsolicited-advice-business.html; Bernaz, Nadia, "Multilateral Agreement on Investment: Time to Awaken the Beast? – A contribution to the 'Business and Human Rights Treaty' Debate," (2014), available at http://rightsasusual.com/?p=756.

[7] Contributions regarding the options for an eventual treaty include Anita Ramasastry and Douglass Cassel, "White Paper: Options for a Treaty on Business and Human Rights," *Notre Dame Journal of International & Comparative Law* 6.1 (2015); Olivier De Schutter, "Towards a New Treaty on Business and Human Rights," *Business and Human Rights Journal*, 1 (2015); International Commission of Jurists, *Needs and Options for a New International Instrument in the Field of Business and Human Rights* (2014), available at http://icj.wpengine.netdna-cdn.com/wp-content/uploads/2014/06/NeedsandOptionsinternationalinst_ICJReportFinalelecvers.compressed.pdf.

treaty in three steps: First, I ask whether there is evidence that a binding instrument will help address these key concerns, including closing the implementation gap and addressing impunity effectively. I review the literature on existing and comparable human rights treaties, and suggest that the binding nature of a human rights instrument does not necessarily increase the likelihood of implementation. Instead, I highlight the factors that have been identified as likely to improve implementation and analyze how and whether those factors exist in GP implementation processes.

Second, having analyzed the factors in binding and nonbinding treaties that can improve implementation, I argue that, for purposes of practical implementation, it is more helpful to view these two types of instruments as located in a continuum of more or less likely to be implemented, rather than as part of a binary of hard and soft law instruments.

Third, in the spirit of improving the likelihood of implementation, I present case studies and draw from my theoretical analysis to make recommendations for a more effective implementation of BHR norm and suggest that these recommendations are equally important for the treaty process as they are for the GPs implementation process.

THE KEY CONCERNS AND GOALS OF TREATY PROPONENTS

The voluntary nature of the GPs has been a lightning rod for many of the civil society organizations and NGOs that coalesced, first, around attempting to strengthen the GPs[8] and, later to demanding and pushing forth a binding treaty process. The roots of the current treaty process are tightly interwoven with discontent over lack of implementation of existing norms, and express the fear that the GPs would enable more impunity, or at least do little to change the current state of implementation of human rights norms. The experience with corporate social responsibility[9] surely informed NGOs' and affected communities' deep suspicion of the interest of business in an effective implementation of human rights norms in the midst of their operations, and it provided a tangible preview of ways in which corporations can

---

[8] See, e.g., FIDH, "Joint Civil Society Statement," (available at www.fidh.org/en/issues/globalisation-human-rights/business-and-human-rights/Joint-Civil-Society-Statement-on,9066 and on file with author) critiquing the GPs' failure to incorporate authoritative interpretations of human rights law and cautioning about a softening of the language of State obligations to regulate corporations.

[9] See, e.g., Fiaschi, et al. "To Abuse or Not to Abuse. This is the Question: On Whether CSR Influences Human Rights Abuses of Large Multinational Corporations (1990–2006)," *Laboratory of Economics and Management Working Paper Series* (2011), available at http://business-humanrights.org/sites/default/files/media/documents/to-abuse-or-not-to-abuse-fiaschi-guiliani-macchi-murano-perrone-jun -2011.pdf. The study finds that the adoption of CSR principles decreased direct abuses, but increased indirect human rights violations, suggesting that "CSR experience may lead to a higher degree of sophistication in the way in which human rights abuses are concealed." (10). See also Anita Ramasastry, "Corporate Social Responsibility Versus Business and Human Rights: Bridging the Gap Between Responsibility and Accountability," *Journal of Human Rights* 14:2 (2015) (contrasting CSR and BHR and their distinct narratives and intents).

maneuver their way into seeming to respect human rights while violating them or aiding and abetting their violations.

Communities' interventions on the international stage regularly remark on impunity, lack of access to justice and the implementation gap between state obligations under international norms and the realities on the ground. For example, the Treaty Movement Joint Statement of 2013, calling for a binding treaty, refers to lack of access to justice, remedy and reparations as a key concern animating its call for a treaty.[10] Other statements by organizations and communities reflect similar concerns and highlight the need to devise solutions to the chronic lack of access to justice and remedies.[11] Corporate impunity was also at the center of the 2015 ESCR-Net Peoples' Forum on Human Rights and Business, held in Nairobi, Kenya, where participants shared their own stories of direct experience with corporate impunity and expressed particular concern with the corporate capture of state institutions, which compounds the obstacles to building rights-respecting regimes.

The recurrent concerns that advocates, communities, and NGOs express when they voice their support for a binding treaty can be summarized as: effective implementation of human rights protections in the business context, access to justice, and ending corporate impunity. There is concern with regard to states' unwillingness to regulate corporations domestically and extraterritorially and provide victims with adequate access to justice and remedies.

BINDING HUMAN RIGHTS TREATIES AND THE IMPLEMENTATION GAP: LIMITS AND POSSIBILITIES FOR BETTER COMPLIANCE

Treaty proponents have argued that implementation gaps will not be bridged by the GPs and can only be closed through a binding instrument. At the root of this argument are assumptions about the ways in which binding and nonbinding instruments operate. A simplified version of the assumptions is that binding instruments are part of hard law and carry legal consequences for their breach, while nonbinding instruments are "soft law" and they do not; there are, therefore, fewer ways to incentivize or force compliance with nonbinding instruments. To test these assumptions, I ask whether a binding human rights treaty can make the work of closing the

---

[10] Treaty Alliance, "Joint Statement: Call for an international legally binding instrument on human rights, transnational corporations and other business enterprises," (2013). Available at www.treatymovement.com/statement-2013. The statement also calls for the treaty to "provide monitoring and compliance mechanisms" and "provide for protections" for victims, whistleblowers, and human rights defenders.

[11] See, e.g., FIDH Intervention, Panel VII "Building National and international mechanisms for access to remedy, including international judicial cooperation, with respect to human rights violations by TNCs and other business enterprises." OEWG, Resolution A/HRC/26/9. First session (6–10 July 2015). See also APWLD "Shaping the treaty on business and human rights: views from Asia and the Pacific," note 5 above.

implementation gap easier and/or more likely and, if so, I ask what role the binding nature of the treaty plays in this process.

First, I consider whether human rights treaty ratification improves human rights conditions and, if so, by what mechanisms. Some studies on the effects of human rights treaties have found no correlation between a state's ratification of a treaty and an improvement of human rights practices in the country. Hafner-Burton and Tsusui,[12] for example, find no change or a slight increase in violations of human rights norms after a state has ratified a relevant human rights treaty. Most large N quantitative analyses on the topic reach similar conclusions, but there is some disagreement. Christopher Fariss, for example, identifies and corrects for the greater strictness in accountability standards that commonly used human rights reports acquire over time, as human rights become more entrenched. Having identified and corrected for these changes, he found a positive correlation between ratification and improved human rights conditions.[13] The debate is still ongoing.

Although the literature represented here by Hafner-Burton and Tsusui (2005)[14] and the line of inquiry exemplified by Fariss come to opposing conclusions regarding the correlation of treaties and improved human rights conditions, they share an understanding of the complementary importance of civil society advocacy and demands for human rights norms implementation.[15] On the one hand, the studies that identify a negative or nonexistent correlation between treaty ratification and human rights conditions also observe a "paradoxical" effect of treaties on the legitimacy of human rights norms. That is, even if states ratify human rights treaties without the intention or capacity to implement them, they still legitimize the international norms enshrined in these instruments. Thus, they empower civil society demands for their implementation. Studies that identify a positive correlation between treaty ratification and improved human rights conditions (e.g., Fariss) also support the notion that human rights norms gain increasing legitimacy through the ratification process. In turn, this greater legitimacy empowers civil society to demand implementation.

Thus, recent studies on the effectiveness of human rights treaties arrive to opposing conclusions regarding the correlation between treaty ratification and improved

---

[12] Emilie Hafner-Burton and Kiyoteru Tsutsui, "Human Rights in a Globalizing World: The Paradox of Empty Promises," *American Journal of Sociology* 110.5 (2005).

[13] Fariss, Christopher J., "Respect for Human Rights Has Improved Over Time: Modeling the Changing Standard of Accountability," *American Political Science Review* 108(2) (2014), 297–318, at 312.

[14] See also Hathaway, "Do Human Rights Treaties Make a Difference?" *Yale Law Journal* 111 (2002), 1935–2042. Neumayer. "Do international Human Rights Agreements Improve Respect for Human Rights?" *Journal of Conflict Resolution* 49.6 (2005) (treaty ratification is more likely to improve human rights conditions where States have strong civil society with links to international NGOs or strong democratic institutions). But see Goodman and Jinks, "Measuring the Effects of Human Rights Treaties," *European Journal of International Law* 14 (2003) (challenging Hathaway's methodology).

[15] Fariss observes that human rights advocates gain more access to information and broaden the scope of their reporting in the context of increased acceptance of human rights norms enshrined in treaties such as the CAT. Fariss (2016) 21–22.

human rights conditions. However, both support the proposition that human rights norms are increasingly legitimized in part because of international treaties. As this increased legitimation takes hold, civil society has more tools and opportunities to apply pressure on states to force compliance. Both lines of inquiry lead to the conclusion that positive results are not as likely in states where civil society does not have conditions for sustained advocacy, including mechanisms to hold governments accountable at the domestic level and connections to the international networks to enhance and amplify their advocacy.

Other analyses of norms legitimation and the process for states to internalize and comply with international human rights norms engage with the work of nonstate actors (including advocates and international human rights organizations) and have mapped out the process by which international norms acquire sufficient legitimacy to compromise the domestic and international legitimacy of noncompliant states.[16] These studies also trace the mutually reinforcing connection that domestic advocacy has with international human rights norms as they acquire more and more legitimacy, and the ways in which internalization of these norms is aided when the state participates repeatedly in the transnational legal process.

The crucial ingredient that a treaty adds to the implementation effort, then, is the increased legitimation of an international norm and the increased costs that this legitimacy creates for noncompliant states. This legitimation process has a discernible effect on the power of civil society to hold states accountable for failures in implementing human rights protections.

The research here does not, however, make claims regarding the comparative advantage that a binding treaty might have over other instruments, including the GPs. While it is safe to suspect that a treaty would add to the effects that the GPs could have with regard to the legitimation of relevant norms, we should inquire into the processes by which treaties have been observed to legitimize international norms and ask whether similar processes exist for nonbinding instruments such as the GPs.

Legitimating International Norms: A Task for Binding and Nonbinding Instruments

In this section, I explore the process of legitimation of human rights norms and argue that it is not only, or particularly achievable through binding instruments and claim that some of the conditions for legitimation of the relevant norms are already present in the GPs and can be further strengthened.

---

[16] See Finnemore and Sikkink, "Norm Dynamics and Political Change," *International Organization* 52 (1998), 903; Goodman and Jinks. *Socializing States: Promoting Human Rights Through International Law* (Oxford UP, 2013); Gränzer, "Changing Discourse: Transnational Advocacy Networks in Tunisia and Morocco," in *The Power of Human Rights* (eds.), Risse, Ropp, and Sikkink (1999), 109–133. But see Hafner-Burton, et al. "International Human Rights Law and the Politics of Legitimation: Repressive States and Human Rights Treaties," *International Sociology* 23 (2008), 124–125.

In an examination of the debate about hierarchy of norms in international law, Dinah Shelton explains that there is significance to the nature of the agreement, but cautions that there should not be too easy a dismissal of "soft law" or nonbinding agreements:

> An examination of practice demonstrates that the mode of adoption [of agreements] does matter and that states consciously choose the form of texts to distinguish those that are legally binding from those that are not. Nonetheless, normative statements contained in nonbinding texts can generate a political impact equal at times to that of legally binding instruments and can give rise to customary international law through state practice.[17]

Thus, although binding agreements are the most obvious conduits for norm legitimation, the process by which both binding and nonbinding instruments have a political impact and/or generate customary international law can be the same. The usual indicators of a norm being customary international law are not dependent on whether the norm emerged from a binding or a nonbinding instrument.[18] Moreover, as I showed previously, what promotes effective implementation of norms is not whether the norm is ultimately formally binding or not (whether under customary law or based on treaty ratification), but rather whether the norm is legitimized to the point of enabling civil society advocates to call their states to account for failing to comply with these norms.

There is, of course, an important signalling effect that treaty ratification accomplishes. Simmons characterizes it as "making of an explicit, public, and lawlike promise by public authorities to act within particular boundaries in their relationships with individual persons."[19] Ratification of human rights treaties also often includes a "precommitment" to hear claims of noncompliance with the treaty's terms and creates an ability to "sharpen the focus on particular accepted and proscribed behaviors."[20] These commitments and promises "help define the size of the expectations gap when governments fail to live up to [the treaty's] provisions."[21] The effects of treaty ratification that Simmons highlights result in an improved ability of domestic and even international stakeholders to demand compliance.

In the BHR context, we should consider whether the GPs' stated aim to create an "authoritative focal point around which the expectations and behavior of the relevant actors can converge"[22] can result in a similar signalling and gap-exposing

---

[17] Shelton, "Normative Hierarchy in International Law." *American Journal of International Law*, 100 (2006), 292–293. See also Ratner, "Does International Law Matter in Preventing Ethnic Conflict?" *New York University Journal of International Law & Politics* 32 (2000), 668 ("Soft law and the relevance (or irrelevance) of different degrees of normativity deserve a full place in theories of compliance.")
[18] See Higgins, *Problems and Process: International Law and How We Use It* (1994), 17–39.
[19] Simmons, *Mobilizing for Human Rights: International Law in Domestic Politics*, Cambridge University Press (2009), 4, 7.
[20] Ibid., p. 14   [21] Ibid.   [22] Ruggie (2013), p. 78.

effects, complete with the attendant empowerment of domestic advocates to call
their states to account for failures to close the implementation gap.

There are, to be sure, noncompliance signals that states send when they prefer
a nonbinding versus a binding agreement. For example, with regard to the Universal
Declaration of Human Rights, Simmons notes that the strong push for this document to be nonbinding was a sign of the lack of commitment to enforce its terms,
and this was underscored by "the weakness of the declaration, and its lack of
enforcement and institutionalization."[23] In other words, it contained all the trap-
pings of a symbolic gesture for human rights alongside a strong practical set of
omissions against their enforcement. However, binding agreements can also be
toothless and easy to disregard. Indeed, as Shelton points out, "soft-law" is also to
be found in binding treaty clauses.[24] The key, then, may not be in the binding or
nonbinding nature of the agreement, but rather in the capacity of the agreement
to trigger the positive effects that scholars identify with human rights treaties.[25]

RETHINKING THE BINDING VERSUS NONBINDING DIVIDE

The line between binding and nonbinding instruments is blurred and does not track
easily with the division between soft and hard law. A recent example of a nonbinding
agreement that accomplishes effects similar to those of binding treaties is that
of the Guiding Principles on Internal Displacement[26] (hereinafter, "GPsID").
The GPsID aimed to "consolidate and restate existing international human rights
and humanitarian law relevant to internal displacement."[27] They were unanimously
approved for dissemination by the UN General Assembly in 2001. Since their
approval, they were adopted explicitly by "States with some of the largest populations
of IDPs," including Uganda, Sri Lanka, and Colombia and were cited in UN and
US statements condemning Sudan's forcible displacement of persons.[28] Entwiskle
examines the dissemination and adoption of norms regarding IDPs after the adoption of the GPsID through the lens of the "norm life-cycle"[29] and argues that the

---

[23] Simmons (2009), p. 56 n.34.
[24] Shelton (2000) p. 323, citing, as an example, article 2(1) of the International Covenant on Economic,
      Social and Cultural Rights, Dec. 16, 1966, 993 UNTS 3.
[25] See Justine Nolan "Responsibility to Respect: Soft Law or Non-Law?" in *Human Rights Obligations of
      Business Beyond the Corporate Responsibility to Respect?* (eds.), Surya Deva and David Bilchitz
      (Cambridge: Cambridge UP, 2013), 159–160.
[26] U.N. Econ. & Soc. Council [ECOSOC], Comm'n on Human Rights, "Guiding Principles on Internal
      Displacement: Report of the Representative of the Secretary-General, Mr. Francis M. Deng, Submitted
      Pursuant to Commission Resolution 1997/39." U.N. Doc. E/CN.4/1998/53/Add.2 (11 February 1998)
      (prepared by Francis M. Deng)
[27] United Nations. Office for the Coordination of Humanitarian Affairs. Internal Displacement Unit.
      No Refuge: The Challenge of Internal Displacement. (2003) p. 30.
[28] Entwisle, "Tracing Cascades: The Normative Development of the U.N. Guiding Principles on
      Internal Displacement," *Georgetown Immigration Law Journal* 19 (2005), 374–375.
[29] Finnemore, and Sikkink, "Norm Dynamics and Political Change," *International Organization* 52
      (1998).

"tipping point" for norm formation was a series on nonbinding but strong norm-affirming events:[30] the creation and unanimous adoption of the GPsID, as well as the formation of the Internal displacement Division within the UNHCR, and statements and actions of support for the compliance with the norms in the GPsID by state and nonstate actors. These events "symbolized the international community's recognition of the need for norms on internal displacement."[31]

Part of what made the GPsID capable of triggering a norm cascade regarding IDPs was that their content was widely recognized as being drawn from already existing international legal norms and state obligations already assumed under existing binding treaties. Thus, although they were not binding treaties, they played an important role in signalling: the "close relationship between the [GPsID] and existing international law allows [them] to serve an indicative function – when a party fails to respect the nonbinding Guiding Principles, the party typically violates binding international law as well."[32]

The experience of the GPsIDs should be instructive for the BHR space. Like the GPsIDs, the GPs (on business and human rights) have been presented as collecting and providing an authoritative focus for already existing obligations in international law.[33] Like the GPsIDs, the GPs on Business and Human Rights have also received institutional support in the creation of the WG, have been explicitly adopted by States through National Action Plans (despite well documented silences and failures in these processes), and have been cited as authoritative by regional rights courts,[34] among other supranational bodies.

While the GPs could be viewed as effective precursors to a binding treaty,[35] the GPs are also an international instrument that, in its own right, can activate the factors that lead to better implementation. These factors include the legitimation of BHR norms achieved by casting the GPs as an "authoritative focal point" of obligations that already exist in international law, including binding human rights treaties; expressions of state commitment to GPs; focused definition of the obligations of the states and, thus, an exposure of the implementation gap; reliance by international human rights bodies on the GPs to define the contours of state failures to comply with existing binding treaties.

Additional norm-affirming factors include the creation of the WG and the institutional support for the implementation of the GPs in the UN, as well as its

---

[30] For a definition of a "norm-affirming event" see Ellen Lutz and Kathryn Sikkink, "International Human Rights Law and Practice in Latin America," *International Organization* 54 (2000), 655.

[31] Entwisle (2005), p. 379.

[32] Gross, "Improvement with Impunity: Development-Induced Displacement and the Guiding Principle 6(2)(c) Proportionality Test Applied to the Merowe Dam Project in Sudan," *American University International Law Review*, 24 (2008), 385–386.

[33] See Ruggie, *Just Business* (2013), pp. 82, 106.

[34] *Case of the Kaliña and Lokono Peoples v. Suriname.* Judgment, Merits, Reparations and Costs. Inter-Am. C.H.R. Ser. C No. 309 (November 25, 2015), ¶¶ 223–226.

[35] See Shelton (2006), p. 321.

production of guiding documents for states to produce norm-affirming documents such as National Action Plans. All these factors can work to empower civil society to demand better compliance with human rights norms.

Another key tool for compliance of human rights treaties is the universal periodic review process. It has been critiqued for a number of shortcomings – including states' failure to provide information or to participate in the process, lack of expertise in the committee, failure to provide detailed recommendations and noncompliance with recommendations.[36] Studies that focus on the effect on human rights conditions show that there is still an improvement in compliance for states that participate in these processes.[37]

Self-reporting has been found to activate mechanisms of socialization, information access, improvement and dissemination, and domestic mobilization, among others.[38] Activists have called for effective implementation mechanisms in a future BHR treaty,[39] but the GPs can also use existing and effective periodic review processes. Such mechanisms have been used for nonbinding instruments, particularly with respect to environmental agreements.[40] One way for the GPs to have these mechanisms is for the UN to incorporate "private sector impacts into the Universal Periodic Review process."[41] In addition to providing more information and opportunities for communities and advocates to use the periodic review processes for corporate accountability campaigns, these developments could also allow civil society to make the implementation gap much more visible, and accelerate the cycle of information, capacity-building, and implementation that Dai describes.

---

[36] For a review of the literature on the shortcomings and failures of periodic review mechanisms, see Cosette Creamer and Beth Simmons, "Do Self-Reporting Regimes Matter? Evidence from the Convention Against Torture." (16 February 2016). Boston Univ. School of Law, Public Law Research Paper No. 15–55. Available at: http://ssrn.com/abstract=2697730, p. 4–5 (citing Alston and Crawford, 2000; Bayefsky, 2001 (system is inadequate and in crisis); Hafner-Burton 2013: 102 (lack of requisite expertise by committee members); McQuigg 2011 (failure of states to take heed of recommendations); Hampson, 2007; Schöpp-Shilling, 2007 (widespread nonreporting and late reporting)). See also Creamer and Simmons, "Ratification, Reporting and Rights: Quality of Participation in the Convention against Torture," *Human Rights Quarterly*, 37 (3) (2015).

[37] See Xinyuan Dai, *The Conditional Effects of International Human Rights Institutions, Human Rights Quarterly* 36.3 (2014), 569–589; see also Creamer and Simmons (2016).

[38] Creamer and Simmons (2016); Dai (2014); Nguyen "Unpacking Treaty Practice: The Differential Information Power of Monitoring Mechanisms." Paper presented at the *9th Annual Conference on the Political Economy of International Organizations*, available at http://wp.peio.me/the-9th-annual-conference/program-and-papers-2016.

[39] Treaty Alliance Joint Statement "Enhance the International Legal Framework to Protect Human Rights from Corporate Abuse." Available at www.treatymovement.com/statement (calling for a number of key provisions in the treaty, including an independent monitoring mechanism)

[40] Shelton, "Normative Hierarchy in International Law," *American Journal of International Law* (2006), 319.

[41] Jungk, *Letter of Resignation presented to the UNHCR, Mandate of the Working Group on the issue of human rights and transnational corporations and other business enterprises* (7 March 2016). Available at https://business-humanrights.org/sites/default/files/documents/Margaret_Jungk_HRC_resignation .pdf.

With a focus on the implementation gap, human rights instruments are better viewed not as belonging to one of two polarities – binding or nonbinding – but rather as part of a continuum, with those agreements with the fewest factors that can improve implementation of human rights norms at one end of the spectrum and those with more such factors at the other.

GLOBAL GOVERNANCE RETOOLED: EFFECTIVENESS OF HUMAN RIGHTS COMMITMENTS IN A POWER IMBALANCED WORLD

In the long history of weak political will and entrenched business interests at the expense of human rights, the emergence of the Guiding Principles and the treaty process may be simply another wave. But if they are to bring real change, both processes should invest more seriously into the design of enforcement mechanisms. Moreover, rather than mere compliance, it is important to consider effectiveness, as defined by David Victor: "The extent to which the commitment has actually influenced behavior in a way that advances the goals that inspired the commitment."[42]

This focus on effectiveness leads us back to the key concerns of communities and advocates, as well as their critiques of the GPs and the most recent meeting of the OEWG regarding the treaty process. They have expressed concern about the absence of their voices in the development of mechanisms and norms, and have expressed their well-reasoned expectation that this flawed process will lead to ineffective agreements and continued impunity for violations of their rights.[43]

As Rodríguez Garavito chronicles, the WG had to be coaxed into correcting its blind spots with regard to affected communities' representation and participation at the annual Forum on Business and Human Rights.[44] Indeed, the experience of successful implementation campaigns and the limited sample of exemplary cases that WG brought to the 2015 Forum on Business and Human Rights both point to a simple fact: affected communities and their advocates are indispensable in the design of the most effective implementation and monitoring mechanisms.

A successful example of effective implementation of the GPs was presented at the 2015 Forum on BHR is the Fair Food Program (FFP). It is worth exploring in detail

---

[42] Victor, David and Raustiala, Kal, *The Implementation and Effectiveness of International Environmental Agreements* (1998), 661.

[43] See "African Civil Society Seeking a Treaty to Stop Corporate Abuse and Provide Real Remedies for Affected People" (23 November 2015), available at: http://business-humanrights.org/en/african-civil-society-groups-seeking-treaty-to-stop-corporate-abuse-and-provide-real-remedies-for-affected-people; "Indigenous Peoples Caucus Statement to the 4th UN Forum on Business and Human Rights," (20 November 2015), available at http://iva.aippnet.org/statement-of-the-indigenous-peoples-caucus-on-business-and-human-rights-conducted-on-15th-of-november-in-geneva-switzerland/.

[44] See Rodríguez-Garavito, "Business and Human Rights: Beyond the End of the Beginning," Chapter 1 in this volume, 21–22 and notes 52–53.

because it gets at the power imbalance question from a mechanism-design perspective. The FFP is an initiative of the Coalition of Immokalee Workers (CIW) for "worker driven social responsibility." This initiative provides effective remedies to agricultural workers in 90% of the tomato industry in Florida. I present the FFP program as it was described by the CIW representative at the 2015 BHR Forum:[45]

1. A worker drafted code of conduct that includes violations that are not covered by existing law and that are not known by experts outside of the industry.
2. Worker-to-worker education about the code "so that workers can be informed frontline monitors of their own rights."
3. A 24-hour complaint line "so that the abuses that workers experience can be quickly and effectively solved."
4. In-depth audits on participating farms that "complement the education and complaint process and uncover abuses that workers may not be able to see themselves."
5. Market consequences for violators of the code "established through binding agreements between the CIW and the brands, whereby companies . . . agree to only purchase from growers who are in good standing with the Fair Food Program, as determined by the Fair Food Program"

The thrust of this initiative is that enforcement is driven by workers themselves "the very humans whose human rights are in question, and so the stakeholders with the most compelling and abiding interest in seeing those rights protected" and "backed by market consequences" so that employers know that the failure to comply includes real market consequences. This process has also created an "army" of monitors (workers educated both on their rights and on the workings of the FFP) and this, in turn, makes enforcement more widespread. The evidence of the success of this initiative is significant. Since 2011, the Fair Food Program claims, the following violations have been eliminated: "forced labor, sexual assault and violence toward workers in Florida's tomato industry." They have also eliminated many of the worst actors from the industry and have received complaints about and resolved over 1200 other violations (such as wage theft and safety violations).

Importantly, brands working with the FFP have asked for its expansion to other areas of agricultural production. One of the companies that now supports the FFP (Compass Group) noted that they joined the program initially out of fear for the disruption of their college business (they provide food in many college campuses) combined with a consideration that the premium that they were asked to pay

---

45 Intervention by Greg Asbed, "Multi-stakeholder action across 'Protect, Respect and Remedy' – Addressing Specific Impacts," 18 November 2015, Session II. *2015 United Nations Forum on Business and Human Rights* (16–18 November 2015). Author's field notes.

was minimal: 1 cent per pound of tomatoes. Presenting alongside the FFP representative at the BHR forum, the executive from Compass noted that their site visits showed them compelling conditions and that it resulted in them making the requirements for the growers from whom they purchase tomatoes under the FFP even more stringent. This may be because of the lack of cost to making these requirements more stringent for brands purchasing the tomatoes (they would be paying the 1 cent premium regardless) and the recognition that they could bolster their reputation even further. That is, once the purchasers had internalized the cost of participating in the FFP program, they became (a) invested in making the program work well and (b) interested in improving it as long as it cost them no additional money. The fact that the monitoring and enforcement is worker-driven seemed to have given the FFP the ability to be flexible (in a single direction, that of additional requirements).

As Compass agreed to join this program and became invested in it, it became a mediator between the CIW and the growers. Having accepted to pay 1 cent per pound of tomatoes, Compass objected to the growers' refusal to pass on that 1 cent directly to workers, as the initially designed FFP program called for. They invited the growers to sit down with Compass at Compass offices along with CIW workers. This was the first time that growers had sat down to talk to CIW. Compass explained that it wanted compliance with the FFP design, including passing on the 1 cent premium that Compass would pay directly to workers. It also explained that it would give all its business to the growers willing to step out of the Florida Growers coalition refusing to pass on the premiums to workers and comply with the FFP initiative. Compass also expressed its willingness to boycott Florida Growers if no one was willing to comply, and they would use every plate of food they served (8 million plates per day) as an opportunity to explain to customers why they had no tomatoes to offer. Growers ultimately accepted to comply with the FFP's plan for the 1 cent tomato premium.

Recruiting one industry to put pressure on its supply chain is a known model, but it is not always successful. Some of the failures of initiatives to improve human rights conditions by engaging purchasers to demand more from their suppliers simply do not view affected communities and local NGOs as key sources of information. In the case of the Kimberley Process, for example, a participant at the 2015 BHR Forum expressed frustration about the way in which information is sought and acquired. He noted that in his work as investigative journalist and human rights advocate in Angola allowed him to speak to the EU parliament about Angola's extensive record of human rights abuses in the diamond industry, but when it came to the Commission charged with investigating allegations of human rights violations by Angola, the Commission sought no information from him or from affected peoples. Rather, it sought information from the state. More importantly, even when information about conditions on the ground does make its way to relevant decision makers in the Kimberley Process, victims and advocates are not consulted about "what can be done to engage further with the partners."[46] This last comment is especially telling because it reveals a problem that cannot be solved by fact-finding investigations. Affected communities should not only be sources of information about what violations occur, they should be consulted about the ways in which the system can be improved. They are not.

The case of CIW is unique in that it created both a worker-drafted code and a series of enforcement mechanisms itself. Thus, it got Compass Group invested in an already existing and already designed enforcement program. This seemed to have opened the doors for Compass to engage with the *purpose* of the FFP program. It is in the design of the FFP, then, that we should focus. In contrasting failed initiatives to FFP, many of them from CSR, the FFP representative asked: "What are the interests of the architects of the two different models?" He explained: "When it's a corporate-driven social responsibility, the interest is not primarily human rights, the interest is public relations. Human rights cause a problem in public relations for corporations and they need to find a way to resolve the public relations problems."[47] As a result, he explained, corporations design solutions aimed at resolving the public relations problem without necessarily resolving the underlying human rights problem. When a solution is designed by workers, on the other hand, it is designed by the only stakeholders "with a primary interest in resolving human rights violations in the workplace." he adds that this interest is coupled with "knowledge of violations that no expert has."

The key takeaway from the successful model of the FFP is the participation of the affected stakeholders in the design of the monitoring and enforcement mechanism, and in the operation of the enforcement mechanism. While the specific FFP model may not be replicable outside the workers' rights context, the model of putting the victims of violations at the center of the knowledge construction and *design* of the accountability and complaint mechanisms and, indeed, in charge of keeping those mechanisms updated and well oiled, is a lesson with implications that go beyond the agricultural and workers' rights fields.

Not coincidentally, other relatively successful accounts that were presented throughout the 2015 BHR forum had these same characteristics, though they were presented in separate panels. For example, Aurelio Chino Dahua and Wendy Pineda presented on a Peruvian Amazonian Quechua community's efforts to step in the place of the State to collect data about oil companies' specific impacts on their land, water, and health. The initiative to take control of technical environmental monitoring tasks came from the community and they were able to supplement the state's failure to collect data about conditions on the ground in order to negotiate

---

46   Intervention by Rafael Marques de Morais, speaker at "Leadership Panel I: Framing the Issues: Progress, Access to Remedy and Other Remaining Challenges," 17 November 2015. *High Level Opening Plenary, United Nations Forum on Business and Human Rights* (16–18 November 2015). Author's field notes.

47   Intervention by Greg Asbed. Author's field notes. See note 45 above.

better compliance by companies with domestic laws. The high level of technical accuracy in data collection in that case also lowered communication and trust barriers with companies, increased their willingness to engage in dialogue, and put communities at the table in discussions with companies.[48]

Another example of effective mechanisms that have benefited from community participation in the design of the mechanism was presented by Lorena Terrazas Arnez, Red Pazinde (Bolivia).[49] Terrazas Arnez detailed how socio-environmental monitoring mechanisms (including binding consultation processes) were created with the participation of and enforced by Capitanías of the indigenous Guaraní peoples in one of the largest gas and oil exploitation regions of Bolivia. Notably, the proposal to create a corps of Guaraní monitors and to build their capacity to perform monitoring that included not only affectations on the environment, but also effects on cultural patrimony, came from the communities themselves. Moreover, communities are empowered to engage companies in direct dialogue and to check companies' technical findings against the community's own.

The lessons from FFP and other experiences in enforcement mechanisms designed with the direct participation of the affected communities should be further systematized and taken up at all levels. The WGs should do so as they engage with states and ask how affected communities were involved in the development of National Action Plans and in specific NAP implementation mechanisms, for example. Treaty proponents should focus on creating the framework to enable similarly effective implementation mechanisms. It is a lesson that should be incorporated into the reporting requirements about corporate impact that Margaret Jungk suggested. And it is a lesson that NGOs, advocates and communities should also welcome: how often, after all, do we ask to be included in the *design* of the solution?

CONCLUSION

The goals and concerns of communities and NGOs in BHR are related to closing the implementation gap and ending corporate impunity; though they are often expressed through the language of the "binding versus nonbinding" divide. The GPs and their focus on consensus no doubt helped to bring these concerns

---

[48] Aurelio Chino Dahua, (FEDIQUEP, Quechua Federation of the Upper Pastaza, Peru) and Wendy Pineda (AIDESEP, Interethnic Assoc. for the Development of the Peruvian Rainforest) "Community-Based Social & Environmental Monitoring; FPIC process." Panel, *Company commitments and community-led initiatives: making meaningful community engagement a best practice* (18 November 2015). *United Nations Forum on Business and Human Rights* (16–18 November 2015). Author's field notes.

[49] Lorena Terrazas Arnez, "Experiencias de monitoreo socioambiental en el consejo de capitanes guaraníes de Chuquisaca" *Parallel Session, Recognizing Indigenous Peoples' Rights to Land, Territories and Resources, and Challenges in their Access to Mechanisms for Redress.* (16 November 2016) *United Nations Forum on Business and Human Rights* (16–18 November 2015). Author's field notes.

afloat with greater force, for they contained language that communities experienced with corporate and state abuses identified as useful to skirt responsibility. The treaty process, likewise, has been criticized for limiting its scope to transnational corporations.[50]

In this chapter, I drew from empirical studies on the effectiveness of treaties and implementation mechanisms to suggest that binding human rights treaties have only had an effect in improved human rights conditions when they are part of a process that enables civil society mobilization and other forms of pressure to force states to comply with international human rights norms. I identified legitimation of norms and follow-up mechanisms as results and components of binding treaties that seem to have a positive effect on state compliance. I further argue that these tools are not exclusive to binding treaties and that the binding-nonbinding divide is less helpful than viewing international instruments as part of a continuum, in which those with the most access to tools to facilitate implementation on one end, and those with the least at the other end.

Finally, I argue that a BHR instrument – whether the GPs or an eventual BHR treaty – is more likely to have an impact on implementation if there is sufficient attention on the proper design of implementation mechanisms. Even within the space of implementation mechanisms, I argue that there is a generalized failure to engage with affected communities as knowledge producers and codesigners of their own implementation mechanisms. I present examples of successful implementation using such an approach and argue that rather than calling upon corporations to develop mechanisms to benefit communities' enjoyment of their rights, states must find ways to involve in the design process the stakeholders most directly interested in having this mechanism succeed. If nothing else, the lessons from the weak performance of treaties should be that norms alone will not result in change, and that we need to think creatively and critically about who is in the room when the solutions are being created.

---

[50] See, e.g., "Indigenous Peoples Caucus Statement to the 4th UN Forum on Business and Human Rights," "The Indigenous Peoples recommend a legally-binding treaty applicable to all transnational, national and sub-national business enterprises. This treaty should cover all violations of human rights (not merely grave violations). Furthermore, the treaty drafting process should be inclusive and participatory for all States, civil society and Indigenous Peoples." Available at: http://iva.aippnet.org /statement-of-the-indigenous-peoples-caucus-on-business-and-human-rights-conducted-on-15th-of-november-in-geneva-switzerland; Lopez and Shea (2016) 114 (reporting that while most NGOs at the First OEWG meeting expressed concern that the scope of the treaty was limited to transnational corporations, most States who spoke on the issue defended the limit of scope to transnational corporations).

PART II

The Practice of Business and Human Rights

Advocacy and Regulatory Strategies

7

Shifting Power on Business and Human Rights: States, Corporations and Civil Society in Global Governance

Chris Jochnick

From the birth of the corporate form, companies have been embroiled in abuses and scandals. Struggles against corporate crimes have been led by abolitionists, anticolonialists, workers, unions, consumer advocates, community groups, social movements, and environmentalists, among others. It is only in recent years, that the human rights movement has joined the fray. The UN endorsement of the Guiding Principles on Business and Human Rights (the GPs)[1] marks the *arrival* of "business and human rights" and begs a question – what do human rights bring to the long-standing struggle against corporate abuse?

Many often conflate the pursuit of human rights with work at the global level around international human rights instruments and treaty bodies. Viewed through that prism, the GPs and the related UN Working Group to promote the GPs (the WG) represent a significant step forward, with eyes to a more binding treaty and responsive body. But the real power of human rights lies in their ability to affect the day-to-day circumstances and capacities of people on the ground. Viewed from that perspective, there is still a long way to go and the starting point must be more directly tied to shifting those power dynamics that lie at the root of abuses.

BACKGROUND

For three decades, the international community has worked to develop global human rights regulations for corporations. That effort saw its peak in the drafting of the "UN Norms on the Responsibilities of Transnational Corporations and Other Business Enterprises with Regard to Human Rights" (the Norms).[2] The moment

---

[1] See: www.ohchr.org/Documents/Publications/GuidingPrinciplesBusinessHR_EN.pdf. The history of the process leading up to the passage of the GPs is described in John Gerard Ruggie, *Just Business: Multinational Corporations and Human Rights* (New York: Norton, 2013). A rich literature has emerged around business and human rights. See e.g., Radu Mares (ed.), *Business and Human Rights at a Crossroads: The Legacy of John Ruggie* (Leiden: Martinus Nijhoff, 2011); Surya Deva and David Bilchitz (eds.), *Human Rights Obligations of Business Beyond the Corporate Responsibility to Respect?* (Cambridge: Cambridge University Press, 2013).

[2] UN ESCOR, 55th sess., 22nd mtg., Agenda Item 4, UN Doc E/CN.4/Sub.2/2003/12/Rev.2 (13 August 2003).

was short-lived; within a few months of their emergence, the UN Human Rights Commission summarily dispatched the Norms in favor of a more modest goal – a global consensus around business and human rights. Six years later, the UN Secretary General's Special Representative John Ruggie succeeded in delivering on that goal with the unanimous endorsement of the GPs by the UN Human Rights Council.[3]

In considering the contribution of human rights to the struggle against corporate abuse, it's important to clarify what we mean by human rights. Mainstream human rights practice, as developed and led by western organizations like Amnesty International, Human Rights Watch, the International Commission of Jurists, and traditionally supported by Western foundations like the Ford Foundation and the Open Society Institute, has focused on formal, apolitical reporting on violations (primarily civil and political rights), lobbying Western governments and engaging the global human rights architecture – international legal instruments and human rights bodies.[4] This "top-down" approach is not out to question the basic balance of global power or the role of business in society, but instead focuses on egregious abuses of individual human rights. The approach has been critiqued for marginalizing local actors and social movements, downplaying socioeconomic issues, and ignoring questions of politics and power.[5]

By contrast, other groups have forged a bottom-up approach to human rights characterized by grassroots and political activism, broad and flexible deployment of human rights rhetoric, and empowerment of local stakeholders and movements.[6] This approach questions markets and corporations at a more profound level, is instrumentalist about human rights, and focuses more intently on asymmetries of power. This approach tends to operate on the margins of mainstream human rights institutions and to receive little support from traditional human rights donors.[7] The approach is critiqued for diluting the legitimacy of human rights and for a lack of pragmatism/realism.[8] Stephen Hopgood helpfully

---

[3]   UN document A/HRC/17/31 (21 March 2011).

[4]   See e.g., Makau wa Mutua, "The Ideology of Human Rights," *Virginia Journal of International Law* 36 (1996).

[5]   See e.g., Tony Evans, "Human Rights Law as Power/Knowledge," *Human Rights Quarterly* 27 (August 2005); David Kennedy, *The Dark Sides of Virtue: Reassessing International Humanitarianism* (New Jersey: Princeton University Press, 2004); Caroline Bettinger-Lopez, et al., "Redefining Human Rights Lawyering Through the Lens of Critical Theory: Lessons for Pedagogy and Practice," *Georgetown Journal on Poverty Law and Policy* 18 (2011).

[6]   See e.g., Neil Stammers, "Social Movements and the Social Construction of Human Rights," *Human Rights Quarterly* 21 (November 1999); Balakrishnan Rajagopal, "International Law and Social Movements: Challenges of Theorizing Resistance," *Columbia Journal of Transnational Law* 41 (2003). Much of the development community, including groups like Oxfam, have adopted a so-called "rights-based approach" which aligns more closely with this bottom-up approach to human rights. See David Cohen, Rosa de la Vega, and Gabrielle Watson, *Advocacy for Social Justice: A Global Action and Reflection Guide* (Connecticut: Kumarian Press, 2001).

[7]   For a survey of human rights funding see http://humanrights.foundationcenter.org/issues/

[8]   See e.g., Aryeh Nieir, "Social and Economic Rights: a Critique," *Human Rights Brief* 13 (2006).

labels these two approaches "Human Rights" (top-down) and *"human rights"* (bottom-up).[9]

While these are gross generalizations, the distinction between Human Rights and *human rights* helps to distinguish between responses to Ruggie's mandate, the GPs and the WG. Put crudely, those with a Human Rights perspective were likely to recognize the legal shortcomings in the Norms (even while sympathizing with them), to engage with Ruggie's mandate enthusiastically, to argue for a more robust interpretation of human rights law and to want to see the WG tackle victim complaints.[10] Those with a *human rights* perspective were likely to have had little capacity or interest in engaging with Ruggie's mandate, to stonewall and critique "regional consultations" by Ruggie and the WG, to question the level of influence/participation of corporations in the GPs process, and to view the GPs and WG as regressive.[11]

Ruggie approached his mandate without any particular allegiance to either human rights camp. On the one hand, he did not share the Human Rights fixation on the global human rights architecture. Notwithstanding (or more likely because of) his deep roots in the UN, he was skeptical about the potential of a UN process to deliver a far-reaching or binding regulatory instrument. He dismissed the Norms as an ideological overreach and took pains to distinguish his more modest approach of "principled pragmatism."[12] On the other hand, as a "pragmatist," he was not out to question the global balance of power, but took as his starting point the need to bring governments and business leaders along. As he states, "[t]he GPs had to be carefully calibrated: pushing the envelope but not out of reach."[13]

Ruggie's approach delivered significantly for the Human Rights camp. He brought an unprecedented energy and profile to a UN process around business and human rights, he grounded the GPs largely in human rights instruments, and he won the unanimous endorsement of the UN Human Rights Council for a document identifying human rights responsibilities for corporations. For the Human Rights-minded, his failure to affirm a legal "duty" for corporations and to interpret rights more robustly are outweighed by the progress achieved and despite lacking a grievance-resolving role, the WG can still play a useful role by legitimizing and disseminating the GPs.

Ruggie delivered much less to the *human rights* camp. He went to lengths to engage with groups from all corners, but his final document reflected a very top-down framing. In his effort to win industry support, Ruggie was careful not to

[9]   See e.g., Stephen Hopgood, *The Endtimes of Human Rights* (New York: Cornell University, 2013).
[10] The International Corporate Accountability Network (ICAR) and its strong work around the GPs reflects a Human Rights perspective (see generally at: http://accountabilityroundtable.org/); as compared with the more skeptical distance maintained by ESCR-Net (see e.g., commentary on the first UN Forum on Business and Human Rights at http://www.escr-net.org/node/365081).
[11] An exchange between Earthrights International and Ruggie early in the process underscores some of the *human rights* camp's concerns www.earthrights.org/legal/ominous-outlook-un-norms.
[12] Ruggie, *Just Business*, pp. 47–55.   [13] Ibid., p. 107.

impinge significantly upon the prerogatives and necessities of businesses and instead he appealed directly to business self-interest and familiar corporate processes – risk management, due diligence, etc. The GPs fundamentally reaffirm (by not questioning) the central role of multinational corporations (MNCs) in developing countries. By contrast, the GPs say little about the rights and role of civil society groups or stakeholders. Stakeholders appear in the GPs as instruments of companies – e.g., to provide insights (help manage risk) – or as victims deserving of remedies. Nothing in the GPs recognizes the critical role to be played by civil society and stakeholders as protagonists or watchdogs.[14] Likewise, the WG – as one more distant, politically constrained, UN body – offers little support to a bottom-up approach.

WHY IT MATTERS

Underlying much of the distinction between Human Rights and *human rights* is a perspective on power. A Human Rights approach can live with power asymmetries as long as rights are *formally* recognized; a *human rights* approach believes that human rights are not compatible with gross power asymmetries, and sees human rights as one of many flexible means toward empowerment. A Human Rights approach, almost by definition, caters to more powerful actors in the belief that a coalition of these actors can be moved to do the right thing on human rights.[15] That approach may make sense where targeted rights (e.g., liberal or civil and political rights) align with the interests of powerful governments and market actors, and some pressure from above can tip the balance.

By contrast, *human rights* proponents believe that power asymmetries are too great, that alignment is too superficial, to the point that the only way to get real traction on human rights is by undermining the legitimacy of traditional powerful actors and bringing new sources of power (e.g., workers, consumers, communities and their civil society representatives) to the fore. They believe that it is only through the constant protagonism of these stakeholders that human rights can be realized and guaranteed. These stakeholders provide the essential bulwark to resist violations and ensure respect for human rights over the long term.

As Hopgood and others point out, the Human Rights approach made most sense in a uni- or bipolar world where the rhetoric of rights (narrowly conceived) could effectively bring powerful pressure from the United States (and other actors) to bear on recalcitrant governments.[16] The importance of a *human rights* approach becomes increasingly evident considering how power has grown more diffuse

---

[14] See Chapter 1 by Rodríguez-Garavito in this volume. See also Tara J. Melish and Errol Meidinger "Protect, Respect, Remedy and Participate: 'New Governance' Lessons for the Ruggie Framework" Buffalo Legal Studies Research Paper No. 2012–019.

[15] See Chris Jochnick, "Confronting the Impunity of Non-State Actors: New Fields for the Promotion of Human Rights," *Human Rights Quarterly* 21 (1999).

[16] Hopgood, *Endtimes*, pp. 1–23.

(between states and between the state and other actors), new powerful actors have emerged (non-Western governments and corporations) who are less amenable to Western-dominated rights rhetoric and as rights are more progressively interpreted to challenge the status quo (e.g., economic and social rights and real accountability for corporations). Such an approach better meets the need for more flexibility around rights interpretation, the ability to reach a wider range of targets (institutions and corporations) and the capacity to mobilize a broader coalition of protagonists/ advocates to pressure violators.

While the two approaches can be synergistic, there are tensions, particularly related to the allocation of resources and engagement with formal institutions. Given the scarcity of resources (e.g., funding and time) for corporate accountability/business-human rights work, prioritizing one approach will almost certainly come at the expense of another; to date, resources have been heavily skewed to Human Rights at the expense of *human rights*. A Human Rights approach also risks legitimizing institutions, processes and frameworks (courts, international bodies, laws) that marginalize or compete with more progressive, grassroots voices and visions.[17]

Ruggie's first report to the UN Council[18] went far toward establishing the case for a *human rights* approach. In it he diagnosed a mounting "governance gap" created by the vast and growing power of MNCs, backed by thousands of investment agreements and the support of powerful elites at home and in host states, that far outmatch weak and often corrupt host governments. Soft law efforts (e.g., multistakeholder initiatives and voluntary commitments) and other "gap-filling" efforts were only touching a fraction of companies and not getting to the root of the governance problem. Ruggie's hardheaded diagnostic of power imbalances cried out for an equally hardheaded call for more radical approaches to corporate accountability.

Ruggie critics have long shared this diagnostic and rightfully lamented the glossing over of power imbalances in the final outcome of his work – the GPs. They emphasize the need for building "countervailing power" and more "empowered participation," as Rodríguez-Garavito puts it in Chapter 1 of this volume. But too much of the business and human rights "energy" falls back into the same formal, top-

---

[17] An extensive literature describes these risks, particularly in a domestic setting. See e.g., Gerarld Rosenberg, *Hollow Hope: Can Courts Bring About Social Change* (Chicago: University of Chicago Press, 1991); Gerald Lopez, *Rebellious Lawyering: One Chicano's Vision of Progressive Law Practice (New Perspectives on Law, Culture, and Society)* (Westview Press, 1992); Stuart Scheingold, *The Politics of Rights: Lawyers; Public Policy and Political Change* (Ann Arbor: University of Michigan Press, 2010). A Human Rights approach runs the same risk, as well described in David Kennedy, "The International Human Rights Movement: Part of the Problem?" *European Human Rights Law Review* 3 (2001), 254; and Lucie E. White, "To Learn and Teach: Lessons from Driefontein on Lawyering and Power," *Wisconsin Law Review* 699 (1988).

[18] See the Interim Report of the Special Representative of the Secretary General on the Issue of Human Rights and Transnational Corporations and Other Business Enterprises. E/CN.4/2006/97, http://www1.umn.edu/humanrts/business/RuggieReport2006.html

down models embodied by the GPs and the WG. Two popular initiatives[19] illustrate this: (a) the push to make the WG's mandate more victim-empowering (e.g., receive grievances, focus on victims' issues) and (b) the movement for a narrow business and human rights treaty focused on gross human rights violations.[20]

With their focus on UN instruments and processes, these initiatives are unlikely to affect power in any meaningful way. International human rights treaties and treaty bodies have a woeful record of vindicating rights and holding states accountable.[21] These bodies are only able to respond to a tiny fraction of the human rights victims of the limited number of state parties under their respective remits. That challenge is made exponentially more difficult when pitted against the vast range of human rights issues facing workers, communities and consumers affected by 80,000 MNCs and their hundreds of thousands of subsidiaries. Neither the WG nor some speculative business and human rights treaty body can hope to even scratch the surface on violations.

Likewise, even putting aside the tremendous political hurdles,[22] it is hard to see how a new treaty focused on corporate human rights violations will result in any significant shift in power.[23] In order to reach any kind of consensus a treaty will necessarily require a narrowing in rights, and possibly actors,[24] making it less relevant to broader constituencies. The process of developing the treaty and any eventual engagement with the treaty body will shift influence and resources to a narrow group of elite actors – diplomats and northern human rights experts – marginalizing grassroots struggles and influence.

International human rights instruments and bodies do of course have the potential to affect meaningful change; but that potential lies not in vindicating rights or directly empowering victims. Rather, it lies with their ability to influence other legal and political regimes and institutions (at the top)[25] and to change individual consciousness and mobilize collective pressure (at the bottom).[26] In this case, the GPs have actually gone far toward providing the political consensus and legal legitimacy

---

[19] As elaborated on in Chapter 1 by Rodríguez-Garavito of this volume.

[20] See the Global Movement for a Binding Treaty at http://www.treatymovement.com/

[21] Joel Trachtman, "Who Cares About International Human Rights? The Supply and Demand of International Human Rights Law," *NYU Journal of International Law and Politics* 44 (2012); Oona Hathaway, "Do Human Rights Treaties Make a Difference?" *The Yale Law Journal* 111 (2002); Eric A. Posner, "Human Welfare, Not Human Rights," *Columbia Law Review* 108 (2008).

[22] Well described in Chapter 2 by Ruggie in this volume and in a series of blogs at www.ihrb.org /commentary/staff/business-and-human-rights-treaty-smart-strategies.html.

[23] A treaty focused more broadly on the basics of empowerment with respect to business and human rights – transparency, participation, effective oversight, etc. – might offer a more promising approach.

[24] Treaty sponsors have already narrowed the focus to just transnational corporations, see at http:// business-humanrights.org/en/binding-treaty

[25] See Jamie Darin Prenkert and Scott Shackelford, *Vanderbilt Journal of Transnational Law* 47 (2014) and Chapters 2 and 4 by Ruggie and Melish respectively in this volume.

[26] See, e.g., Simmons, B. A., *Mobilizing for Human Rights: International Law in Domestic Politics* (Cambridge: Cambridge University Press, 2009); Merry, S.A., "Transnational Human Rights and Local Activism: Mapping the Middle," *American Anthropologist* 108 (2005); Thomas Risse, Stephen

to drive both processes. As Ruggie and others point out, the GPs have already influenced a range of other legal regimes and that process is now moving from the global to the domestic sphere via national action plans.[27] Likewise, the fact that the GPs enjoy the imprimatur (unanimous "endorsement") of the most authoritative human rights body has as much power as any treaty to raise awareness, change individual perspectives and mobilize action.[28]

Both the WG and treaty proposals will require significant deployment of scarce resources, without any real prospect of changing the status quo.[29] No treaty or global institution can substitute for effective national legal regimes and those regimes require local political mobilization.[30] Policymakers create a problem by searching for shortcuts through formal global legal processes, rather than in focusing on messier, informal, political efforts to build actual "countervailing power." As the former Chair of the UN Committee on Economic, Social and Cultural Rights and former Chair of all UN human rights committees, Philip Alston, states in arguing against a similar UN body initiative: "The central problem with the [World Court for Human Rights] proposal is not its economic or political feasibility or its pie-in-the-sky idealism. It is that by giving such prominence to a court, the proposal vastly overstates the role that can and should be played by judicial mechanisms, downplays the immense groundwork that needs to be undertaken before such a mechanism could be helpful, [. . .] and distracts attention from far more pressing and important issues."[31]

SHIFTING POWER MORE DELIBERATELY

Real progress on business and human rights must start with a realistic assessment of the state of the field, and focus on opportunities to shift power – either by empowering advocates (movements, civil society groups and networks) or

C. Ropp, and Kathryn Sikkink (eds.), *The Power of Human Rights: International Norms and Domestic Change* (Cambridge: Cambridge University Press, 1999).

[27] See Ruggie, Chapter 2, in this volume.

[28] Few people beyond a handful of international lawyers makes any real distinction between the relative authoritativeness of UN instruments for purposes of raising awareness or mobilizing action around human rights violations.

[29] That said, there is no question that the treaty proposal has raised the profile and injected much needed energy into the business and human rights space and forced governments to take notice. That on its own represents a significant accomplishment.

[30] It is a telling irony that the Ecuadorian government is leading the charge for a global treaty on business and human rights while simultaneously weakening domestic oversight of corporations, politicizing the courts, actively undermining the OAS human rights system and closing down human rights organizations. See e.g., Luis Pasara, "Judicial Independence in Ecuador's Judicial Reform Process," Due Process of Law Foundation; Dejusticia; Instituto de Defensa Legal (2014); www.hrw.org/world-report/2014/country-chapters/ecuador; http://www.theguardian.com/world/2013/mar/26/ecuador-chinese-oil-bids-amazon.

[31] Philip Alston, "Against a World Court," NYU School of Law, *Public Law Research Paper* No. 13–71 (2014).

strengthening institutional support for corporate accountability (normative, political, judicial). Spaces where business interests prevail should be engaged sparingly. Formal institutions (courts, human rights institutions, government oversight bodies) are attractive targets, but offer few good prospects to vindicate rights in the short- and medium-term. Mainstream corporate curiosity about human rights will spur dialogue, best practice guides, risk management protocols, narrow stakeholder engagement, voluntary reporting, etc.; however, given the costs of engagement and the prevailing power imbalances in those opportunities, they offer limited potential for shifting power.

Better opportunities lie with those spaces where countervailing power is already ascendant or easily prompted – social movements, social media, civil society networks, popular opinion against corporate power, progressive investor groups and business leaders, consumer concerns, multistakeholder bodies with legitimate civil society participation, transparency initiatives, global fora on rights and development. Institutional and corporate commitments to human rights should be engaged and leveraged opportunistically to strengthen accountability and build legitimacy around business and human rights.

Strategies should be pursued that lean toward *human rights* – a more explicit focus on grassroots mobilization, flexible deployment of rights and opportunistic engagement with both informal and formal processes. Better prospects lie with initiatives to spark public and media awareness as well as pressure around corporate abuses.[32] Some examples of these potential strategies include: strengthening budding stakeholder and civil society networks,[33] providing tools and space for affected groups to publicize violations and engage companies directly,[34] building on technology and investor pressure to promote more transparency and accountability, hardening BHR norms through national human rights bodies and human rights policies,[35] broadening the BHR consensus through new global soft law,[36] seizing on the most promising, egregious cases to build progressive jurisprudence and tapping

---

[32] The Business and Human Rights Resource Centre (BHRRC), for example, offers an easy platform to publicize cases and to pressure companies to respond, http://business-humanrights.org/Home

[33] Tara J. Melish and Errol Meidinger describe various "bottom-up" approaches to corporate accountability in "Protect, Respect, Remedy and Participate: 'New Governance' Lessons for the Ruggie Framework," in *The UN Guiding Principles on Business and Human Rights: Foundations and Implementation* (ed.), Radu Mares (Martinus Nijhoff Publishers, 2012).

[34] The community-based human rights impact assessment initiative provides one such tool http://policy-practice.oxfamamerica.org/work/private-sector-engagement/community-based-human-rights-impact-assessment-initiative/.

[35] See ICAR project to promote national action plans http://business-humanrights.org/en/un-guiding-principles/implementation-tools-examples/implementation-by-governments/by-type-of-initiative/national-action-plans/icar-dihr-national-action-plans-project.

[36] The obstacles in establishing a treaty on business and human rights should not preclude other opportunities to reaffirm the GPs and to develop business and human rights principles through other emergent international instruments – at the global and regional levels.

the power of influential strategic allies (including investor and corporate leaders) to support any of these efforts.

Human rights have the potential to shape peoples' perceptions, to change power dynamics, to address governance gaps, to build real corporate accountability; but they also pose the risk of diverting legitimate protests, narrowing visions and reinforcing corporate power. The GPs consensus offers a new legal perspective and the promise of new tools. It remains our challenge to identify and seize on those new opportunities that offer the most transformative potential.

8

Always in All Ways: Ensuring Business Respect for Human Rights

Amol Mehra[1]

All·businesses impact human rights. In many instances, these impacts can be positive, for example, where a business invests in providing clean and potable water to a community in which it operates. In other instances, however, business activity can infringe on or violate the human rights of individuals and, at times, entire communities.

Just as there are numerous forms of corporate structure, there are also variations in business operation. Businesses differ significantly in size and scope, ranging from small, local sole proprietorships to large, multinational corporations and their subsidiaries. Complex global supply chains and contractual relationships often connect these enterprises, posing a challenge in discerning ownership and control.

In addition to this diversity in corporate form and structure, the complexity of human rights risks and impacts demands attention. Under international law, human rights range from economic, social, and cultural to civil, political, and labor rights. Additionally they include a host of human rights instruments that cover children's rights, the rights of persons with disabilities and women's rights more specifically.[2] The challenge of addressing businesses' impact on these rights is significant.

Given this layered complexity, this chapter argues that, in order to promote human rights vis-à-vis corporate activity, advocates (those seeking to ensure business respect for human rights) must continue to apply pressure on companies and governments both creatively and systematically. Advocates must be creative in developing new models to ensure business respect for human rights, which includes extending precedents or models that are already in place and concern

[1] The author would like to thank Nicole Vander Meulen, Katie Shay, and Sara Blackwell for their assistance with this chapter. The chapter was formulated and provided in the author's personal capacity and does not reflect the views of the International Corporate Accountability ("ICAR") or its Members.
[2] See generally International Covenant on Civil and Political Rights, G.A. Res. 2200A (XXI), U.N. Doc. A/6316 (1966); International Covenant on Economic, Social and Cultural Rights, G.A. Res. 2200A (XXI), U.N. Doc A/6316 (1966); Convention on the Rights of the Child, G.A. Res. 1386 (XIV), U.N. Doc. A/4354 (1959); Convention on the Rights of Disabled Persons, G.A. Res. 3447 (XXX), U.N. Doc. A/10034 (1975); Convention on the Elimination of All Forms of Discrimination against Women, G.A. Res. 24/180, U.N. Doc. A/34/46 (1979).

other harms, sectors, or regions. Advocates must also systematically apply pressure to the full set of legal and policy levers in place that regulate, incentivize, or otherwise set the conditions for corporate behavior. This includes levers that go beyond sanctioning harmful behavior to incentivize respect for human rights through the condition of a benefit (e.g., through procurement preferences). To apply this pressure effectively requires viewing the business and human rights landscape as much more diverse and comprehensive than efforts at the United Nations have done. Such efforts at the United Nations have included the United Nations Guiding Principles on Business and Human Rights (GPs), the United Nations Working Group (Working Group) on the issue of human rights and transnational corporations and other business enterprises, and the recent effort to develop an "open-ended intergovernmental working group on a legally binding instrument on transnational corporations and other business enterprises with respect to human rights."[3]

This chapter contends that, while work on business and human rights at the United Nations is both necessary and helpful, it should not distract from opportunities to achieve business respect for human rights through efforts in other fora, from the national to the international level. Both preventive and remedial measures must be built for meaningful protection to be delivered. Ultimately, those seeking to address the complexities of the business and human rights agenda with the goal of ensuring business respect for human rights need to engage always, and in all ways.

Section I gives an overview of the efforts at the UN to advance the business and human rights agenda, with commentary and suggestions to move beyond a myopic view of business and human rights through the sole lens of the UN. This section addresses the GPs, the Working Group, and provides commentary on the implications of the adoption of a resolution and process to, through an intergovernmental working group, develop the form and content of a potential treaty on business and human rights. In Section II, this chapter explains that there are a number of different levers available at the international, regional, and national levels for shifting corporate practice with respect to human rights, and that these levers must be utilized while continuing to explore new ones. Section III argues that both preventative and remedial measures must be built, seeking to reconcile the tension between policy developments in capitals from the impacts on the ground for those affected by corporate activity. Only with a systems-wide approach to addressing the myriad challenges, with a clear understanding of the various opportunities to enhance human rights protections through both preventive and remedial measures, can advocates ensure the promotion of human rights vis-à-vis business activity.

---

[3]   United Nations Human Rights Council, *Elaboration of an international legally binding instrument on transnational corporations and other business enterprises with respect to human rights*, U.N. Doc. A/HRC/26/L.22/Rev.1 (June 2014).

I THE BUSINESS AND HUMAN RIGHTS AGENDA
AT THE UN HUMAN RIGHTS COUNCIL

In the international arena, the United Nations Human Rights Council led the development of the United Nations Guiding Principles on Business and Human Rights (GPs).[4] This authoritative framework was the result of many years of work by the then Special Representative to the Secretary General, Professor John Ruggie.

Professor Ruggie's mandate and final product have been met with some controversy. Advocates criticized the voluntary nature of the UNGPs, and noted that existing governance gaps would require clear regulatory responses.[5] Further, advocates raised concerns about the prioritization of nonjudicial remedial measures as opposed to a clear call to create and strengthen judicial remedial mechanisms.[6] Regardless of these criticisms, governments endorsed the UNGPs fully, and some even committed to examine and publicly commit to taking steps toward implementation measures.[7]

Since endorsement, however, states have generally failed to implement the UNGPs fully even when engaging in National Action Plan (NAPs) processes. To date, some forty states have started or released NAPs on business and human rights. A review by the International Corporate Accountability Roundtable (ICAR) and the European Coalition for Corporate Justice (ECCJ) of existing NAPs has revealed significant shortcomings in both process and content.[8] Furthermore, some States have implemented regressive measures, erecting barriers to the enjoyment of human rights, and shielding businesses from responsibility for human rights harms. For instance, with regard to the critical remedial measures needed to provide accountability and redress for harms, some major governments have erected barriers to claimants or otherwise hindered their quest for justice. For example, the United

---

[4] Special Representative of the Secretary-General on the Issue of Human Rights and Transnational Corporations and Other Business Enterprises, *Guiding Principles on Business and Human Rights: Implementing the United Nations "Protect, Respect and Remedy" Framework*, U.N. Doc. A/HRC/17/31 (21 March 2011) (by John Ruggie).

[5] Joint Civil Society Statement on the draft Guiding Principles on Business and Human Rights International Federation for Human Rights (January 2011) www.fidh.org/IMG/pdf/Joint_CSO_Statement_on_GPs.pdf.

[6] Ibid.

[7] H.R.C. Res. 17/4 U.N. Doc. A/HRC/RES/17/4 (6 July 2011) www.business-humanrights.org/media/documents/un-human-rights-council-resolution-re-human-rights-transnational-corps-eng-6-jul-2011 .pdf. The International Corporate Accountability Roundtable and Danish Institute for Human Rights provide a list of developments toward business and human rights frameworks in their report on national action plans. The International Corporate Accountability Roundtable, and The Danish Institute for Human Rights, "National Action Plans on Business and Human Rights: A Toolkit for the Development, Implementation, and Review of State Commitments to Business and Human Rights Frameworks," pp. 64–68, http://accountabilityroundtable.org/wp-content/uploads/2014/06/DIHR-ICAR-National-Action-Plans-NAPs-Report3.pdf.

[8] The International Corporate Accountability Roundtable and the European Coalition for Corporate Justice, "Assessments of Existing National Action Plans (NAPs) on Business and Human Rights," http://icar.ngo/wp-content/uploads/2015/11/ICAR-ECCJ-Assessments-of-Existing-NAPs-2015-Update.pdf

States (a chief proponent of the GPs) has significantly limited the potential for victims of corporate harm to seek redress in U.S. courts where the harmful conduct occurred outside of the United States.[9] Further, in the United Kingdom (the first country to launch a NAP), the Legal Aid, Sentencing and Punishment of Offenders Act 2012 has gone into effect. This Act reduces the potential legal fees that lawyers can receive for bringing human rights claims and requires such fees to be paid out of the claimant's damages rather than by the opposing party.[10] Thus, two of the countries that led the charge for the development and endorsement of the UNGPs have adopted legislation that frustrates the GPs' purpose.

After Professor Ruggie's mandate ended, the UN created a Working Group on the issue of human rights and transnational corporations and other business enterprises (Working Group). This five-member group was tasked with, inter alia, disseminating the UNGPs and assisting in their implementation across stakeholder groups.[11] The Working Group began to develop a strategy, building off of its mandate that focused on three general work streams: global dissemination, promoting implementation, and embedding the UNGPs in global governance frameworks.[12]

Now, many years after the creation of the Working Group, some are of the opinion that the Working Group has failed to achieve meaningful results. In a critique reviewing the first two and a half years of the Working Group, civil society groups noted the absence of a clear and public work plan, the restrictive interpretation of the mandate, failures to address alleged violations, regressive application of international human rights law, and failure to include victims in their events and dialogues.[13]

It is within this landscape that some advocacy groups began to push for the development of an international treaty to address the impacts of corporations on human rights. The treaty push stems from the position that governance gaps can only be addressed effectively through the elaboration, uptake, and enforcement of binding international standards and commitments.[14]

In June 2014, Ecuador, South Africa, and other governments tabled a resolution at the United Nations Human Rights Council establishing an intergovernmental

[9] The International Corporate Accountability Roundtable, CORE, and The European Coalition for Corporate Justice, "The Third Pillar: Access to Judicial Remedies for Human Rights Violations by Transnational Business," p. 28, http://accountabilityroundtable.org/wp-content/uploads/2013/02/The-Third-Pillar.pdf.

[10] Ibid., p. 10. [11] Ibid.

[12] Rep. of the Working Group on the Issue of Human Rights and Transnational Corporations and Other Business Enterprises, 20th Sess., ¶ 63, U.N. Doc. A/HRC/20/29 (Apr. 10, 2012).Paragraph 63, pg. 15, www.ohchr.org/Documents/Issues/Business/A.HRC.20.29_AEV.pdf.

[13] DeJusticia, Connectas, and JusticaGlobal, "Working Group on the Issue of Human Rights and Transnational Corporations and Other Business Enterprises: A Review of the First Two-and-a-Half Years of Work," http://conectas.org/arquivos/editor/files/6_Dej_Con_JG_WG2years_Nov2013.pdf.

[14] See, e.g., "Joint Statement: Call for an international legally binding instrument on human rights, transnational corporations and other business enterprises," accessed 18 July 2014, www.treatymovement.com/statement.

process to elaborate the form and content of such a treaty. In the same month, the resolution was adopted by a vote of twenty countries in favor, fourteen against, and thirteen abstentions.[15]

A. *Building Beyond the GPs and the Working Group*

The GPs are not a ceiling, but a floor from which to build both up and out. Advocates must build "up" from the GPs to continue to clarify the ways in which States can and should engage in their duty to protect, and the ways in which corporations can and should engage in their responsibility to respect. Building "up" requires stakeholders to hone in on particular sectors or particular harms and provide more substance to the meaning of respect for human rights by corporate actors and the protection of human rights by States in particular contexts. While the UNGPs provide a good starting point for this discussion, they should not be the sole focal point.

The GPs are a framework to build "out" because remaining gaps – including, as Ruggie notes, the governance gaps of globalization that could warrant legal coverage, including around gross human rights abuses, or even the extraterritorial application of law – could be further developed. Here, for example, the Maastricht Principles could be looked to a source to further develop guidance for States on the need and means of extraterritorial application of human rights protections, particularly around business activity.[16]

The Working Group itself is constrained in that it is a political body set up to respond to a political imperative through a consensual approach. The Working Group is subject to funding constraints driven by often political decisions, with members appointed based on a political process and a mandate honed through political negotiation. These layers of political interplay raise the following question: should advancements in corporate accountability hinge on such political mechanisms? This is not to say advocates should ignore the Working Group and its work. Rather, advocates should not overemphasize the Working Group's capacity and should continue to explore the full range of opportunities to push the business and human rights agenda forward.

Ultimately, although the GPs may have helped build a common floor for a large number of issues, there is still much to be done to close gaps in protection and strengthen standards in areas where human rights are not already addressed. For efforts in this area to yield meaningful change in terms of human rights promotion, they cannot be restricted solely to the Working Group.

---

[15] UN Document A/HRC/26/L.22/Rev. 1 (24 June 2014).
[16] The ETO Consortium, "Maastricht Principles on Extraterritorial Obligations of States in the Area of Economic, Social and Cultural Rights," www.etoconsortium.org/en/main-navigation/library/maastricht-principles/.

B. Assessing the Potential of an Intergovernmental Process

As mentioned above, the establishment of an intergovernmental process toward a binding international instrument on business and human rights was met with mixed responses from civil society. Human Rights Watch, for example, recognized the need to establish mandatory standards at the international level, but maintained that doing so through an intergovernmental group and only focusing on the activities of transnational corporations was problematic.[17] ESCR-Net, a leading civil society supporter of the process, circulated a similar position statement, noting that the process should not just focus on transnational corporations.[18]

The problem with an explicit focus on transnational corporations is that human rights harms are not limited to these actors. In fact, the vast majority of corporations around the world would not be covered by such an approach, as, often, it is domestic and local businesses that are in direct engagement with their surrounding communities and therefore have the potential to cause or contribute to human rights violations.

More problematically, the development of normative consensus at the international level carries as a prerequisite that State practice be so well established as to render international agreement a possibility. Unfortunately, this is simply not yet the case on the issue of business and human rights. While state practice is in the process of developing through the various levers outlined above, there remains much progress to be made within national jurisdictions. Moreover, there is a tremendous danger of slowing momentum due to an intergovernmental process in Geneva, where lengthy negotiations on both procedural and substantive grounds can distract from action.

Even on the issue of extraterritoriality, where some States already have domestic regulations that apply abroad to prohibit human rights harms, the reality is that this practice needs to be further developed at the State level before it can be pushed internationally. For example, in the context of trafficking, the U.S. Trafficking Victims Protection Act has clear extraterritorial application.[19] Yet recent efforts in U.S. courts, including the U.S. Supreme Court, have made the reach of other human rights laws narrower, most notably by applying the "presumption against extraterritoriality" to the Alien Tort Statute.[20] The risk here is that, by pushing too

---

[17] Arvind Ganesan, Human Rights Watch, "Dispatch: A Treaty to End Human Rights Abuses?" www
.hrw.org/news/2014/07/01/dispatches-treaty-end-corporate-abuses.

[18] ESCR-Net, "Joint Statement: Call for an international legally binding instrument on human rights, transnational corporations and other business enterprises," www.treatymovement.com/joint-statement-binding-international-instrument.

[19] 22 USC 7101, Sec 223.

[20] *Kiobel v. Royal Dutch Petroleum*, 133 S. Ct. 1659 (2013). The presumption against extraterritoriality means that unless Congress explicitly has drafted a statute to apply outside of the United States, courts should assume that it does not. *Morrison v. National Australia Bank*, 561 U.S. 247 (2010).

soon for an international consensus on these issues without expanding State practice first, advocates may export dangerous models, interpretations, or precedents. For analogues, we need only look to the anticorruption space, where, once State practice was finally solid enough to establish international normative consensus, the UN Convention Against Corruption was adopted.[21] Therefore, regardless of how compelling the argument is that where states prohibit harm from occurring domestically, including by corporate actors, they similarly should prohibit their corporations from causing the same harm outside of their territorial boundaries, the reality is that this idea needs to be embedded domestically before international consensus can be built.

Critiques of the process aside, the fact is that the treaty process now exists. It will add another lever to the various ones detailed above; however, just as the GPs and the Working Group should not be seen as the only levers to trigger, this intergovernmental process must also not be seen in this way.

II THE BUSINESS AND HUMAN RIGHTS AGENDA OUTSIDE OF THE UN HUMAN RIGHTS COUNCIL

Outside of the work being done at the Human Rights Council, there is a plethora of other standards at the international, regional, and national levels that advocates must continue to use creatively and systematically to embed respect for human rights in business practice.

A. *International*

At the international level, increased attention could be placed on the OECD and the "proactive agenda." The proactive agenda works through a multistakeholder process to provide enhanced guidance on identifying and responding to risks of adverse impacts in particular product lines, regions, sectors, or industries.[22] Currently, three proactive agenda items are being developed: due diligence in the financial sector, stakeholder engagement and due diligence in the extractive sector, and responsible investment in agricultural supply chains.[23] Because they enhance specificity and provide clear guidance on particular sectors, such processes are a critical means to enhance discussion around businesses' responsibility to respect human rights. Further, because of their multistakeholder development and buy-in they offer regulators significant comfort. For example, in the context of conflict minerals reporting requirements, the U.S. legislation and implementing regulation

---

[21] Convention Against Corruption, G.A. Res. 58/4, U.N. Doc A/RES/58/4 (31 October 2003).
[22] OECD Guidelines for Multinational Enterprises, "Proactive Agenda," accessed 18 July 2014, http://mneguidelines.oecd.org/proactiveagenda.htm.
[23] Ibid.

clearly points to the OECD Five Step Due Diligence Guidance for Responsible Supply Chains of Minerals from Conflict-Affected and High-Risk Areas.[24] This Due Diligence Guidance was itself developed as a proactive agenda topic, and companies continue to support the Guidance for both their own and their suppliers' processes.[25]

International multistakeholder initiatives have also emerged to build standards as well as monitoring and implementation measures around human rights for companies in particular sectors. Such initiatives are another ripe opportunity for advocates to engage. For instance, the International Code of Conduct for Private Security Providers and the related International Code of Conduct for Private Security Providers' Association have been developed to address human rights and humanitarian law issues in the private security sector through certification, monitoring, and reporting functions.[26] In the information and communications technologies sector, the Global Network Initiative was launched to build multistakeholder principals and accountability around privacy and freedom of expression.[27]

B. Regional

At the regional level, the African Commission on Human and Peoples' Rights has developed a Special Mechanism through the Working Group on Extractive Industries, Environment and Human Rights Violations. This mechanism serves to examine the extractive industries' impact in Africa and to formulate recommendations and proposals on appropriate measures and activities to prevent rights violations.[28] The Council of Europe, a body including twenty-eight member states of the European Union, has been developing a nonbinding instrument at the European level since 2013, which may include good practice guides to addressing gaps in implementation of the GPs.[29]

---

[24] OECD Guidelines for Multinational Enterprises, "OECD Due Diligence Guidance for Responsible Supply Chains of Minerals from Conflict-Affected and High-Risk Areas," last accessed 18 July 2014, http://mneguidelines.oecd.org/mining.htm.

[25] See, for example, Ford Motor Company, "Conflict Minerals," last accessed 18 July 2014, https://corporate.ford.com/microsites/sustainability-report-2014-15/supply-conflict-reporting.html.

[26] International Code of Conduct Association, "Mandate," last accessed 18 July 2014, www.icoca.ch/en/mandate.

[27] Global Network Initiative, "About Us," last accessed 18 July 2014, http://globalnetworkinitiative.org/about/index.php.

[28] African Commission on Human and Peoples' Rights, "Working Group on Extractive Industries, Environment and Human Rights Violations," last accessed 18 July 2014, www.achpr.org/mechanisms/extractive-industries/.

[29] Council of Europe, "Corporate Social Responsibility in the Field of Human Rights," last accessed 18 July 2014, www.coe.int/t/dghl/standardsetting/hrpolicy/Other_Committees/HR_and_Business/Default_en.asp.

The European Commission (EC) is another regional arena where critical advocacy attention could also yield significant gains. On 14 April 2014, the plenary of the European Parliament adopted the directive on disclosure of nonfinancial and diversity information by large companies and groups.[30] Companies under this directive would need to disclose information on policies, risks, and outcomes with respect to human rights, among other issues.[31] There has been some criticism of this approach by some civil society groups, but the movement toward mandatory reporting on human rights is a trend that ought to be supported and expanded beyond the European region.

One particularly interesting development lies with the World Federation of Stock Exchanges (WFE), which has developed a Sustainability Working Group. This Sustainability Working Group is comprised of representatives from an array of global stock exchanges and has a mandate to build consensus on environmental, social, and governance data.[32] If the EC requirements are ultimately strong enough to satisfy advocates, one could next envisage advocacy campaigns at the WFE to ensure sharing of information and seeking to harmonize such disclosure practices across stock exchanges. Subsequently, advocates in other jurisdictions could point to these efforts and seek to marry requirements across exchanges. Such harmonization would be in the interest of businesses worldwide, as conflicting requirements in jurisdictions lead to inefficiencies in internal processes and external communications. It would also respect regulatory interests, as reforms in one jurisdiction would show that sufficient interest from stakeholders to introduce such changes domestically exists. Finally, it would meet advocates' interests, as good practice is promoted across jurisdictions and ultimately results in an increase in the number levers of accountability that exist.

C. National

At the national level, advocates can push to expand areas where governments have indicated willingness to regulate. For instance, in the United States, procurement reforms put in place by the Obama administration have focused on extending protections from slavery and trafficking and recently, protecting around discrimination against sexual orientation.[33] Such protections essentially require that contractors commit

---

[30]   European Commission, "Non-Financial Reporting," last accessed 18 July 2014, http://ec.europa.eu/internal_market/accounting/non-financial_reporting/index_en.htm.

[31]   Ibid.

[32]   World Federation of Exchanges, "WFE Launches Sustainability Working Group," last accessed 18 July 2014, www.world-exchanges.org/home/index.php/news/world-exchange-news/wfe-launches-sustainability-working-group.

[33]   Zachary A. Goldfarb and Juliet Eilperin, "Obama to Sign Order Barring U.S. Contractors from Job Bias Based on Sexual Orientation," *Washington Post*, 16 June 2014, accessed 18 July 2014, www.washingtonpost.com/politics/obama-to-sign-order-prohibiting-contractors-from-discriminating-against-lgbt-people/2014/06/16/4a83726c-f573-11e3-a606-946fd632f9f1_story.html.

to eliminating such abuses in their operations and develop due diligence plans to ensure this result. The trafficking Executive Order even applies to a contractor's supply chain.[34] Procurement reforms could be extended to other human rights issues, or even holistically across a group of harms and through a sector-based approach.[35]

Further, new disclosure and reporting obligations could be applied to sectors or regions where harms are concentrated. Disclosure models are being created in various jurisdictions, including in countries like Brazil, where stock market listing requirements also seek to obtain information on sustainability criteria, including social and governance issues.[36] In Bangladesh, following the devastating events of the Rana Plaza factory collapse, new amendments to the Labour Act of 2006 were adopted, including ILO Conventions 87 and 98 on freedoms of association and collective bargaining, respectively.[37] In the United States, the government has passed legislation and enacted implementing regulations pertaining to conflict minerals sourcing. The conflict minerals disclosure requirements require publicly listed companies to report on their policies and processes around the sourcing of tin, tantalum, tungsten, and gold from the Democratic Republic of Congo and surrounding areas.[38] Such policies could be replicated or expanded to include other conflict minerals from other conflict-affected areas, including, for example, jade and rubies from Burma.[39]

These national advancements help drive the dialogue on business and human rights from principles to practice. They ensure that respect for human rights is of legally binding consequence, and they circumvent reliance on the voluntary uptake of the UNGPs or the work of the Working Group to achieve their result. They use other levers for action in various arenas, and they seek to build on proven areas of success.

---

[34] Executive Order – Strengthening Protections Against Human Trafficking In Persons In Federal Contracts, 25 September 2012, accessed 20 July 2014, www.whitehouse.gov/the-press-office/2012/09/25/executive-order-strengthening-protections-against-trafficking-persons-fe.

[35] "Government Procurement Interim Briefing," International Corporate Accountability Roundtable, December 2013, accessed 20 July 2014, http://accountabilityroundtable.org/analysis/government-procurement-project-summary-of-forthcoming-report/.

[36] "Brazilian Stock Exchange Urges Sustainability Reporting," *Environmental Leader*, 10 January 2012, accessed 18 July 2014, www.environmentalleader.com/2012/01/10/brazilian-stock-exchange-urges-sustainability-reporting/.

[37] "Revised Bangladesh Labour Law 'Falls Short' of International Standards – UN Agency," *UN News Centre*, 22 July 2013, accessed 18 July 2014, www.un.org/apps/news/story.asp?NewsID=45470#.U6bsJ_SwLrQ.

[38] See Section 1502 of Dodd-Frank. Dodd-Frank Wall Street Reform and Consumer Protection Act, Pub. L. No. 111–203, 124 Stat. 2213.

[39] Dan McDougal, "The curse of the blood rubies: Inside Burma's brutal gem trade," *The Daily Mail*, 18 September 2010, accessed 18 July 2014, www.dailymail.co.uk/home/moslive/article-1312382/The-curse-blood-rubies-Inside-Burmas-brutal-gem-trade.html. U.S. Campaign for Burma, "Sectors to Watch," last accessed 18 July 2014, http://uscampaignforburma.org/sectors-to-watch.html.

III BUILDING PREVENTATIVE MEASURES ALONG WITH REMEDIAL MEASURES

Tension can exist between efforts to enhance preventative measures through law and regulation and those that seek to build avenues for remedy once harm has already occurred. How, for example, does an OECD process improve the conditions for those directly affected by the corporate activity on the ground? How would a company reporting policy and practice on human rights make the situation better for those ultimately aggrieved? How does an intergovernmental treaty affect a community negatively impacted by corporate activity prior to the treaty's enactment? The answers to these questions are critical, and deserve elaboration and explanation no matter what lever is at play. To answer them fully, one must separate gains that can be achieved in preventative ways from those that ultimately build redress for harm. The two aims are distinct, but related.

On the preventative end, it is precisely improved corporate practice that will enable a company to detect and address a potential violation before it occurs. As applied, for instance, clear regulatory measures around company reporting on human rights build internal policies and practices that can help prevent human rights harms from occurring in the first place. The same can be said for efforts around procurement reform. When governments begin to award contracts to companies that have systems and processes in place to monitor and detect potential human rights violations, they are ultimately engaging in their duty to protect human rights in a way that helps prevent abuses from occurring. Again, skeptics need only examine due diligence obligations in the anticorruption arena to see the tremendous impact that regulatory and enforcement structures around these issues can have in shifting corporate practice and the prevalence of the harm they are targeted at addressing.

Regardless, this does not mean that attention should be taken away from remedial measures. The truth is that there can be no right without a remedy. Consistent pressure must be applied to ensure that governments eliminate barriers to remedy in this context and specifically ensure that legal avenues of accountability are open for claimants to vindicate the violation of their rights. Part of this effort will require understanding the particular challenges of litigating against corporations, including, for example, jurisdictional limitations. Outside of these legal questions, however, critical work needs to be done to strengthen the capacity of all countries to hear cases against companies for human rights violations. This will involve strategic litigation aimed at building and reinforcing precedent, along with more basic efforts such as capacity-building on business and human rights for prosecutors and judiciaries.

Where the two relate, and where remedial measures have clear preventive benefits as well, is through the means by which public attention can be brought to cases and instances of abuse. This is particularly true in the context of economic globalization; whereby corporate actors may be held accountable even for impacts localized to specific individuals or communities. For example, an extractive company's impacts on a rural community in Colombia could result in similar harms that are suffered by a community impacted by the same company in Ghana. Remedial measures adopted in Colombia could have the real value of shifting the company's operations, and thus either preventing or mitigating abuses in their operations in Ghana. In other words, remedial measures could ensure prevention of similar harms not only to a specific community but also to those other communities potentially or actually affected by the corporation's activities.

IV CONCLUSION

The landscape of activity in the business and human rights arena is quite expansive and extends well beyond the GPs. This is not to say that the process in building the GPs, and their subsequent endorsement by governments, has not been critical to the deepening of the commitment by both governments and corporations to engage in their respective duties and responsibilities to respect human rights. Rather, it is to say that no clear causal relationship exists. Likewise, the development of standards at the international, regional, and national levels should not be too wedded to the GPs and the follow-on processes at the Human Rights Council. While the treaty process underway in Geneva resonates in terms of the quest to end impunity, there are some significant practical challenges that need to be squarely addressed before such a political process can add real value. Nonetheless, there are a number of alternative frameworks that advocates must continue to consider under creative and systematic approaches to drive the business and human rights agenda forward. Ultimately, there is no silver bullet in the quest to end corporate impunity or even to build respect for human rights in practice. Instead, advocates for a robust agenda on business and human rights must continue to use a spectrum of legal and policy levers that exist, can be extended, or can be created.

9

What Next for Business and Human Rights?

A Social Movement Approach

Louis Bickford

The international human rights movement is at an exciting moment in its history and, within that movement, a focus on business and human rights is emerging as one of the major areas of activity, interest, inquiry, and action.[1] This chapter argues that business and human rights – as a field within the broader movement – will likely become increasingly more important and influential in the future, ultimately leading to significant changes in the behavior of businesses. Moreover, key constituencies and actors involved in social justice movements and beyond (such as the communications media and academia) will increasingly understand businesses as influential nonstate actors that are implicated in the violation of (and in some cases the realization of) human rights. This is not, of course, inevitable. Choices made by key actors now will determine whether the field becomes stronger or weaker and, in turn, whether the field actually changes the behavior of business in terms of human rights over time. This chapter seeks to support and reinforce efforts to deepen the field.

In order to develop this argument, the chapter uses the tools developed by social movement theory – frame, political opportunity, and organization (also related to resource mobilization) – to demonstrate that business and human rights is at an auspicious moment in its development as a field, poised to have real impact on changing behavior and protecting human rights. Because the chapter has its origins in a workshop to discuss the Rodríguez-Garavito core chapter – a workshop at which John Ruggie was also an invited participant – the chapter draws disproportionally on both the Rodríguez-Garavito chapter and on Ruggie's written work, including his book, *Just Business*.

---

[1] See, among many others, Victor E. Abramovich and Paula Rodriguez Patrinós, "Hecho en América Latina: experiencias de activismo en derechos humanos" (Argentina: Ford Foundation, 2011); Aryeh Neier, *The International Human Rights Movement* (New Jersey: Princeton University Press, 2012); Jo Becker, *Campaigning for Justice: Human Rights Advocacy in Practice* (California: Stanford University, 2012).

SOCIAL MOVEMENT THEORY

Businesses, as nonstate actors, can and do commit a diversity of rights abuses.[2] At the same time, the states that ostensibly govern the territories in which businesses operate, whether home states or host states, can fail to protect their citizens and noncitizens from violations of rights or, seen slightly differently, can fail to fully realize the rights of people and groups under their jurisdiction.

Human rights violations, in turn, lead inevitably to discontent, frustration, and anger. Although grievance of this sort is often widespread, the emergence of successful organized action that seeks to change conditions is not automatic. There are three fundamental conditions for collective action (ideally leading to change) to emerge from grievance: (1) a coherent frame that names the problem(s) and suggests some kind of a theory for solving those problems; (2) political opportunity structures that allow for participation and the possibility of influencing change; and (3) the organization of key actors, such as NGOs, that have both individual capacity and network strength to take advantage of political opportunity structures. These groups must be able to mobilize resources (funding, expertise, skills) and channel these resources toward the realization of their mission and goals.[3]

All three of these conditions are basically met – in varying degrees – within the field of business and human rights, which makes it a field poised to move to a significantly more vital level.

Frame

This section argues that the business and human rights field has a strong, coherent, and resonant frame, articulated by international and national norms and the result of decades of work by a wide variety of actors, including human rights defenders, environmental and labor activists, and exceptional business and political leaders. This has led to what Tarrow calls "global framing." He defines this idea as "the use of external symbols to orient local or national claims" and explains that this can "dignify, generalize, and energize activists whose claims are predominantly local, linking them symbolically to people they have never met and to causes that are distantly related to their own."[4]

---

[2]   Generally, see the excellent reporting work on the Business and Human Rights Resource center www .business-humanrights.org/ (accessed 1 August 2014). Also, John Ruggie, using data from NGOs and other sources, describes the array of rights that can be trampled on by multinational enterprises in his book. See John Ruggie, *Just Business: Multinational Corporations and Human Rights* (New York: W.W. Norton & Company, 2013), 20–29.

[3]   See, generally Sidney Tarrow, *The New Transnational Activism* (Cambridge: Cambridge University Press, 2005). Also see Jee Kim, "Behind the Curtain: One Theory of Social Change," 23 June 2014, www.fordfoundation.org/ideas/equals-change-blog/posts/behind-the-curtain-one-theory-of-social-change/ (accessed 17 February 2017).

[4]   Sidney Tarrow, *The New Transnational Activism* (Cambridge: Cambridge University Press, 2005), 60.

One way that a frame is constructed is for activists to identify and draw on relevant norms, standards, and international law and deploy these as "external symbols." These norms must, of course, exist. And indeed many human rights advocates have, over the years, sought to strengthen and bolster international norms as a fundamental strategy, for example, by using strategic litigation and legal mechanisms in regional human rights systems, such as the Inter-American Human Rights System, or by working with United Nations agencies to develop norms and standards.

In this sense, the Special Representative of the Secretary-General (SRSG) for Business and Human Rights' mandate and the Guiding Principles (GPs) have been an important step forward in terms of frame coherence, providing a basic outline for states and businesses that includes three components: protect, respect, and remedy. These are, of course, *minimal* requirements and, as such, leave many unsatisfied. Indeed, many NGOs have been critical that, in their view, the GPs do not go far enough in creating clear expectations, not to mention the development of international law, governing the behavior of businesses.[5]

The GPs, moreover, are not the only instrument that clarifies expectations on states and businesses. They both build on and contribute to additional norms. The expanding normative universe in this field includes the Organization for Economic Cooperation and Development's Guidelines on Multinational Enterprises; sections of the 2011 Maastricht Principles on Extraterritorial Obligations of States in the area of Economic, Social, and Cultural Rights; and components of national laws, such as section 1504 of the Dodd-Frank financial overhaul bill in the USA, which requires extractive industries to publish payments made to foreign governments.[6]

Combined, these various instruments help create normative coherence around business and human rights. In other words, these developments make it difficult for governments or businesses to credibly make the argument that businesses are not duty-bearers as nonstate actors under international human rights norms or that governments do not have clear obligations to protect people from abuses committed by businesses. And, from the perspective of rights-holders (and their advocates), they make it equally difficult to argue that there is no clear set of minimal demands for realizing rights in the face of violations by businesses. We can say with some confidence that in addition to the anger and indignation toward businesses as human rights violators that has existed at least since the tragedy in Bhopal in 1984, there are now a set of norms and standards that are fundamentally clear and in their most basic form are captured in the Guiding Principles and other documents. Moreover, the work of the SRSG in disseminating the GPs and developing

---

[5] See Surya Deva and David Bilchitz (eds.), *Human Rights Obligations of Business Beyond the Corporate Responsibility to Respect?* (Cambridge: Cambridge University Press, 2013).

[6] Chris Albin-Lackey, "Without Rules: A Failed Approach to Corporate Accountability," *Human Rights Watch World Report* (2013), 29–40.

conversations about them in important forums – complemented by the existence of the Working Group – has helped to consolidate these norms, and I argue that the process has plausibly generated a "shift in the dynamic of the business and human rights debate, from deep polarization among stakeholder groups in 2005 to a greater shared understanding of business and human rights challenges."[7]

More recently, efforts to develop a binding international treaty – including the Human Rights Council's resolution to initiate a process to do so – will likely contribute to the further strengthening a global frame for business and human rights, although negotiations about a treaty may possibly have the opposite effect: that of muddying the waters.[8]

In sum, international norms and standards that undergird the field of "business and human rights" have generated a set of fairly coherent "external symbols" that human rights advocates can use in developing a global frame. Certainly actors could strengthen these international standards. For example, states developing national actions plans, as discussed below, could serve as a possible next step in strengthening norms and making them real on the ground (and in this sense, one can argue preferable normative strategy than putting more energy into international norm-building, such as through the proposed treaty process). After decades of work building norms and standards in this area, energies are necessarily shifting – and should shift – toward implementing these norms.

In any case, if indeed the norms represent a coherent basis for a global frame, the next question is whether relevant actors (such as NGOs and human rights leaders) in fact deploy these external symbols to animate social action. The short answer is yes. Organizations such as the Business and Human Rights Resource Center (UK), Global Witness (UK), Human Rights Watch (USA), the Center for Economic and Social Rights (USA), and Forum-Asia (Thailand), among others, are all deeply aware of the power of these norms to frame their programs and activities in the business and human rights field and use them regularly in their work.[9]

Still, certainly what the field needs in this regard is further diffusion of that frame.[10] At a minimum, this would entail further generating a global conversation

---

[7] See Mandate of the Special Representative of the Secretary-General (SRSG) on the Issue of Human Rights and Transnational Corporations and other Business Enterprises, *Recommendations on Follow-Up to the Mandate*, 11 February 2011, http://business-humanrights.org/sites/default/files/media/documents/ruggie/ruggie-special-mandate-follow-up-11-feb-2011.pdf.

[8] The debate about a binding treaty takes many forms. One excellent critical analysis of the treaty process is Mark Taylor, "A Business and Human Rights Treaty? Why Activists Should Be Worried," 4 June 2014, www.ihrb.org/commentary/board/business-and-human-rights-treaty-why-activists-should-be-worried.html (accessed 1 August 2014).

[9] Chris Albin-Lackey, "Without Rules: A Failed Approach to Corporate Accountability," *Human Rights Watch World Report* (2013), 29–40; "Who Will Be Accountable? Human Rights and the Post-2015 Development and Agenda," Center for Economic and Social Rights 2013, www.cesr.org/article.php?id=1482.

[10] A related idea is captured in some of Ruggie's "strategic pathways," such as "creating a minimum common knowledge base."

about the GPs, developing an accepted narrative that the GPs represent something real (and are not just an empty set of international standards) and are accessible and realistic to people's lives. Civil society –not just NGOs but also universities and the communications media – are well suited to perform this task. At a maximum, social movement actors can build on counter-hegemonic discursive tactics and thereby make healthy contributions to fortifying the frame. For example, Justiça Global in Brazil is challenging the dominant and generally accepted discourse about Vale, the Brazilian extractives giant. That dominant discourse highlights Vale as a strong Global South industry leader at the center of vibrant south-south economic relations. However Justiça Global seeks to paint Vale in a different light, as a multinational corporation not much different than its counterparts in the Global North. Whether explicitly or not, Justiça Global can draw on the emerging business and human rights frame in its attempts to shift this discourse to discredit Vale and heighten its reputational risk. These efforts therefore can ostensibly lead to changes in behavior through better company-level policy.

In terms of the proposal to develop a binding treaty, we do not yet know whether this will result in a clearer and more widely diffused frame. Certainly, with a successful treaty, this would be the case. In a different field, international justice, the Rome Statute, for example, is analogous. By the time the Rome Statute entered into force it clarified, for the world, the exact definition of crimes against humanity and provided a clearly articulated set of expectations on states and individuals during conflict. At its best, the proposal to establish a binding treaty on business and human rights would accomplish a similarly powerful result.

Political Opportunity Structures

Political opportunity structure involves "dimensions of the political environment that provide incentives for people to undertake collective action by affecting their expectations for success or failure."[11] These include "the opening up of institutional access, shifts in political alignments, the presence or absence of influential allies, and the prospect of repression or facilitation."[12] In the area of business and human rights, political opportunity structures might include, on the international level: the office of the High Commissioner for Human Rights (OHCHR), the Special Procedures of the OHCHR, such as those that deal with violations committed by businesses; the Human Rights Council; the Universal Period Review (UPR) process; treaty monitoring bodies; regional systems (such as the Inter-American Human Rights System and the African Commission on People's and Human Rights); state-level offices such as ministries of foreign affairs or development agencies that seek to

[11] Sidney G. Tarrow, *Power in Movement* (New York: Cambridge University Press, 2011), 85.
[12] Sidney G. Tarrow, *The New Transnational Activism* (New York: Cambridge University Press, 2005), 23.

influence the behavior of (or *in*) other states. On the national level, these institutions would include: courts, legislatures, policy making bodies, administrative agencies, and National Human Rights Institutions (NHRIs).

The Working Group (WG) on Business and Human Rights has created a key political opportunity structure in this field, since it potentially offers a way for civil society actors to engage with the GPs. In Chapter 1, Rodríguez-Garavito zeroes in on the Working Group as an emerging opportunity structure for engagement of civil society. The language in the chapter is that of "orchestration" through which the Working Group is "supposed to 'ratchet up' internalization of and compliance with human rights standards. The WG is one of the orchestration mechanisms of the GPs." Seen through the lens of civil society participation in the chapter, the WG falls short in its ability (or even its political will) to orchestrate in ways that are likely to bring in diverse forms of civil society participation. Additional and related questions – such as "who counts" in civil society – also raise challenges to the potential of the WG to be a true entryway into the process. Although the focus in this chapter seems to be limited to the Working Group as one of the "orchestrators" for this process, both the GPs themselves and Ruggie in his book point to a large number of possible orchestrators, including NHRIs, nonjudicial, and administrative bodies and other state mechanisms. Scholars and activists should also assess these. It seems like the real goal here should be to both broaden participation with existing orchestrators, and also to increase the number of entry points and opportunity structures that allow for participation. The chapter's specific critiques and recommendations in terms of access to, and participation in, the WG can make a significant difference in terms of strengthening the process through an emphasis on the voice of victims, and the practical contributions that civil society can bring to these processes. Three south-based NGOs (Conectas, Dejusticia, and Justiça Global) echo many of these critiques in another publication.[13]

Scholars and activists can also apply the question of political opportunity structures to the institutional structures that would emerge mostly at the national level under the "remedy" pillar, although this is the least developed area in terms of civil society engagement of the GPs.[14] That said, the GPs do suggest the possibility of opportunity structures: "As part of their duty to protect against business-related human rights abuse, States must take appropriate steps to ensure, through judicial, administrative, legislative or other appropriate means, that when such abuses occur within their territory and/or jurisdiction those affected have access to effective

---

[13] Conectas, Dejusticia, and Justica Global, "Working Group on the Issue of Human Rights and Transnational Corporations and Other Business Enterprises: a Review of the First Two-and-a-half Years of Work," 25 November 2013, http://business-humanrights.org/en/pdf-working-group-on-the-issue-of-human-rights-and-transnational-corporations-and-other-business-enterprises-a-review-of-the-first-two-and-a-half-years-of-work.

[14] See ""The Third Pillar: Access to Judicial Remedies for Human Rights Violations by Transnational Business," 4 December 2013, by the International Corporate Accountability Roundtable (ICAR) CORE, and the European Coalition for Corporate Justice (ECCJ).

remedy." This opens up an enormous set of possibilities for developing engagement pathways for civil society engagement around "the exercise of accountability politics by civil society."

Organized Action

What do NGOs need in order to engage most effectively with new and emerging political opportunity structures, entryways for engagement, and orchestrators, such as the Working Group? How can NGOs help build frame resonance globally and in specific societies? The answer lies in what the Rodríguez-Garavito Chapter calls "countervailing power," which I interpret, at its core, as the ability of strong civil society actors to engage or confront state and business actors in the development of the field of business and human rights.[15]

One set of actors in this equation are international human rights NGOs (IHRNGOs). Here I find worth noting that the IHRNGO's definition as a genre/type of organization is in flux. Whereas ten years ago it would have been obvious that this term referred to, for example, Human Rights Watch, Amnesty International, and the Lawyers Committee for Human Rights (now Human Rights First). Today, scholars and activists can arguably apply this category to some of the work (i.e., the work that is primarily focused on nonnational constituencies) of organizations such as the Kenyan Human Rights Commission (KHRC) or the Centro de Estudios Legales y Sociales (CELS), both traditionally "national" organizations that are increasingly working beyond their own borders in one way or another.[16] I argue that the definition of this organizational type is changing as a result of globalization, increasing geopolitical multipolarity, the existence of strong *national* NGOs in various countries around the world that can/should/will have increasing clout internationally, and indeed to the complicated dynamics of multinational enterprises in terms of home/host countries, global supply chains, etc.

In the field of business and human rights, an emerging set of IHRNGOs are taking on these questions using varied strategies and tactics. These include, among many others, organizations such as the Business and Human Rights Resource Center (BHRRC), Center for Economic and Social Rights (CESR), Conectas, Dejusticia,

---

[15] One useful (analogous) analysis of how international norms can be made real involves violence against women. The research shows that international norms and standards around violence against women tend to make a difference in the adoption of policy in contexts where strong feminist movements also exist. See Mala Htun and Laurel Weldon, "The Civic Origins of Progressive Policy Change: Combating Violence against Women in Global Perspective, 1975–2005," *American Political Science Review* 106 (2012), 548–569.

[16] A sharp conceptual distinction between "national" and "international" organizations has been at the core of Ford Foundation strategy for supporting the human rights movement since in 1973. This distinction now seems increasingly blurred. See William Korey, *Taking on the World's Repressive Regimes: The Ford Foundation's Human Rights Policies and Practices* (New York: Palgrave Macmillan, 2007), 67.

International Network for Economic, Social, and Cultural Rights (ESCR-Net), International Federation for Human Rights (FIDH), Asian Forum for Human Rights and Development (Forum-Asia), Global Witness, Justiça Global, and Human Rights Watch. These and other IHRNGOs lead as *network actors* (i.e., actors who have influence within global or regional networks) and can help contribute to *agenda setting* in international arenas (i.e., by using the GPs as reference points to bring this framework to the appropriate international forums).[17]

Rodríguez-Garavito clearly appreciates the potential of civil society as "an essential source of pressure for compliance with existing standards and cumulative regulatory progress." Moreover, the Chapter begins to get at a nuanced analysis of the different forms of civil society engagement and how different categories of action-types ("engagers," "multipliers," "confronters") may play off each other in complementary ways, and indeed that some forms of action, such as confrontation, might be required to create the pressure and countervailing power necessary to further carry out the GPs. Given power asymmetries, in fact, this kind of sociological analysis of organized civil society actors and their strategies seems essential to prescriptions that might guide how to best harness the energy from civil society. Understanding how these dynamics work is an essential task. For example, some multinational enterprises likely consider reputational risk (although certainly not all) and therefore the threat of significant damage to their public images matters. This would suggest that civil society efforts to make abuse visible is a viable strategy to push toward greater compliance by companies, at least with their obligation to "respect." With the GPs and WG in place, furthermore, civil society (NGOs, universities, the press) will play an important and diverse role in contributing to complex policy formation at the national/local level in both home and host countries. This may include the design of regulatory frameworks, the formation of public policy involving contracts, trade, labor and environmental law, and the establishment of a set of mechanisms for effective redress.

CONCLUSION

At this stage in the development of the business and human rights field, the field seems poised to move to its next level of impact. How will it get there? This chapter proposes that there are three different ways to focus on field-building. Drawing on a different but related literature – social movement theory – the chapter proposes

---

[17] See Murdie's definition for network actor. Amanda Murdie, "The Ties That Bind: A Network Analysis of Human Rights International Nongovernmental Organizations," *British Journal of Political Science* 44 (2013). Also, see Carpenter's definition for agenda setting. Charli Carpenter, Anna Tomaskovic-Devey, and Kyle Brownlie, "Agenda-Setting in Transnational Networks: Findings from Consultations with Human Security Practitioners," (National Science Foundation, 2009); Jutta Joachim, *Agenda setting, the UN, and NGOs: Gender Violence and Reproductive Rights* (Washington, D.C.: Georgetown University Press, 2007).

that we consider framing, political opportunities, and organization of actors as the three primary components of field-building.

All three of these components are more or less in place in the business and human rights field. Perhaps the most well developed is the frame. Given the existing normative documents, including the GPs, social movement actors have plenty of material to work with in order to demand compliance, raise a ruckus, create naming-and-shaming strategies, document and publicize abuse, and develop dozens of other strategies to hold both businesses and governments accountable. In short, the chapter argues that the frame is in good shape. Spending precious time and energy on deepening the frame would divert this energy from other, possibly more important, areas of work.

For example, putting energy into the treaty process (and then building the necessary infrastructure to create a viable opportunity for engagement) will inevitably come up against the massive challenges that currently undermine many existing efforts including unenforceability and the lack of participation of key states, especially home country states. This could undermine the possibility of creating new pathways to serious engagement and divert focus of civil society, paradoxically, *away* from compliance, at least in the short-term. This tension, of course, arises in the development of any new international instrument. However, increasingly robust scholarship on compliance gaps has created a different context. As Emilie Hafner-Burton puts it, the evidence suggests that international human rights law tends to protect human beings "in the settings where the worst human rights abuse is least likely to occur … [D]espite that evidence, much of today's policy efforts focus on creating more international treaties."[18]

In the second area of focus – political opportunity structure – this chapter agrees with Rodríguez-Garavito that there are significant weaknesses with the Working Group, as currently constituted. Indeed, other opportunity structures might provide more viable alternatives for pursuing claims against businesses or governments in this field.

This chapter sees the most room for development in the third area of focus: organized action. Consistent with Rodríguez-Garavito, the chapter agrees with the importance of bolstering "the countervailing power of affected communities and civil society organizations."

Indeed, civil society has an enormous role to play in all three GP pillars – holding states accountable, keeping business faithful to its obligation to protect, as well as developing and implementing remedy strategies for victims and others.[19]

---

[18] Emilie Hafner-Burton, *Making Human Rights a Reality* (New Jersey: Princeton University Press, 2013), 4.

[19] The importance of civil society actors does not always come through clearly in accounts of the development of the SRSG mandate and the subsequent development of the Guiding Principles, including in John Ruggie's important book, *Just Business*. On the one hand, Ruggie seems to agree that at least two decades of activism – including naming-and-shaming, legal actions, boycotts and campaigns, multiple forms of protest, shareholder activism, etc. – were vital in creating the context for

IHRNGOs, as part of global civil society, can help achieve this goal. Practically speaking, they can improve the field by diffusing the frame and making it resonate through a variety of strategies and tactics, some of which involve communication, narrative, story-telling, documentation of abuse, and legal action. NGOs can also take advantage of existing opportunity structures, including the Working Group, which participants should improve to facilitate civil society/NGO participation. Moreover, IHRNGOs can consciously seek to strengthen advocacy networks and other forms of international organizing in order to enhance their ability to play the role of a countervailing power.

the mandate and the work that has been done since. Indeed, there has been a "long history of efforts to hold corporations accountable" (29). That said, although the book often refers to "human rights advocates" and mentions individuals like Ken Saro-Wiwa or uses terms like "civil unrest"(e.g., in Ogoniland), it could paint a more vibrant picture of the role that victims' associations, national civil society organizations, lawyers, protest organizers, international NGOs, and other civil society actors have played in defining *business and human rights* as a frame that has led to reaction and adaptation – and a willingness to work toward the Guiding Principles – on the side of business and state actors and how these same kinds of civil society actors might now contribute. On the contrary, human rights advocates appear more frequently as part of divisive debates leading to ostensibly necessary "normi-cide" (30).

10

Regulatory Environment on Business and Human Rights: Paths at the International Level and Ideas about the Roles for Civil Society Groups

Juana Kweitel[1]

We are facing a key moment in the advocacy for a more effective regulatory environment on business and human rights. The adoption of a resolution at the Human Rights Council (HRC) in June 2014 establishing an "open-ended intergovernmental group for the negotiation of a legally binding instrument"[2] could potentially constitute a turning point.

In this chapter, I share some ideas about the future of the business and human rights agenda. The First Section discusses the normative and institutional trends at the international sphere, including both the discussions surrounding the future treaty and the role of the UN Working Group on Business and Human Rights (WG). The second section considers the roles of civil society groups and analyzes how to improve their capacities to strengthen collective action.

I PATHS AT THE INTERNATIONAL LEVEL

1 *The Proposal of a Treaty*

Many human rights advocates with a critical stance toward the Guiding Principles (GPs) equate them to a voluntary norm, such as the widespread codes of conduct and industries' voluntary standards. Based on the premise that "soft law" and voluntarism are ineffective to change corporate behavior, critics propose to solve the weaknesses of the GPs with a binding treaty. To my mind, this is a misguided reading of the GPs.

The GPs reframe the discussion on the human rights duties of States and corporations by building on existing international law. The GPs do not create new

---

[1] I would like to thank my colleague Caio Borges for discussing some of the ideas in this chapter. Any possible mistakes are mine.

[2] Resolution A/HRC/26/L.22/Rev.1. Adopted in the 26th Session of the Human Rights Council (HRC), on 25 June 2014.

obligations.[3] While they cannot be regarded as a voluntary standard, the framework lacks a consistent mechanism for enforcement.

Civil society organizations (CSOs) revived discussion on a binding legal instrument due to both the absence of a GP enforcement mechanism and the weaknesses of the WG responsible for their implementation. However, this is where consensus ends, as different players have distinct opinions on the treaty's structure, content, and proper functioning, all of which continue to be undefined. I will now briefly discuss the two distinct proposals set forth by Rodríguez-Garavito (Chapter 1 in this volume) and by Ecuador in its 2014 proposal for a treaty that sparked the current debate at the UN level.

1a. The Limitation to Gross Human Rights Violations

In Chapter 1, Rodríguez-Garavito considers the possibility of a binding treaty addressing specific violations of human rights by corporations. Among several other options for the treaty, he considers a binding agreement regarding corporate involvement in gross human rights violations and extraterritorial jurisdiction. This option converges with the former Special Representative of the Secretary-General on human rights and transnational corporations and other business enterprises' (SRSG) publicly stated proposal for an instrument addressing the "worst human rights abuses" committed by legal persons. Nevertheless, those advocating for a legally binding instrument encompassing only corporations' most "egregious human rights abuses" have so far fallen short of presenting convincing arguments for such a narrow approach.[4]

In a 2008 survey, the SRSG showed that the list of human rights violations committed by companies encompasses the full spectrum of internationally recognized human rights.[5] Can violations of social and economic rights be considered "gross human rights abuses"? If so, under what circumstances?

The very concept of "gross human rights abuses" is still unclear and undetermined. In its Interpretive Guide[6] the Office of the High Commissioner for Human Rights (OHCHR), while recognizing that "there is no uniform definition of gross human rights violations in international law," expressly includes in this category

---

[3]　John Ruggie, *Just Business: Multinational Corporations and Human Rights* (New York: W.W. Norton & Company, 2013), 124. "The GPs constitute a normative platform and high-level policy prescriptions for strengthening the protection of human rights against corporate related harm."

[4]　As highlighted below, Ecuador did not replicate this restricted view in its resolution for a new international instrument on transnational corporations and other business enterprises. The future document's breadth will therefore encompass all human rights violations, unless the sponsors and States in general decide to follow a different path in the course of the drafting process.

[5]　Ruggie, *Just Business*, p. 20.

[6]　OHCHR, The Corporate Responsibility to Respect Human Rights: An Interpretive Guide (2012) (HR/PUB/12/02).

genocide, slavery, and slavery-like practices, summary or arbitrary executions, torture, enforced disappearances, arbitrary and prolonged detention, and systematic discrimination. The OHCHR states that violations of social, economic, and cultural rights can fall under the category of gross human rights abuses if "they are grave and systematic," such as "violations taking place on a large scale or targeted at particular population groups."[7]

As one can see, this guidance is still vague and generic. For example, in the context of Latin America, despite the seriousness of the first set of gross human rights abuses in the region (forced disappearances, slave-like labor, etc.), violations to traditional and indigenous peoples' right to land and to the right to self-determination, are as challenging and grave as the former. Would the OHCHR, the WG, or other relevant international bodies consider these contextually specific violations of the right to land and self-determination (and other rights, such as physical and mental integrity, right to health, etc.) as "gross human rights abuses"?

1b. The Ecuador Proposal: The Establishment of the Open-Ended Intergovernmental Working Group

On 25 June, 2014, the HRC adopted a resolution establishing an open-ended intergovernmental working group on transnational corporations and other business enterprises with respect to human rights, with the mandate to "elaborate an international legally binding instrument to regulate, in international human rights law, the activities of transnational corporations."[8]

Regarding the scope of such a new treaty, the resolution limits it in a footnote of a preamble clause by clarifying that "other business enterprises," "denotes all business enterprises that have a transnational character in their operational activities, and does not apply to local business registered in terms of relevant domestic law."

---

[7] This conceptual approach to "gross human rights abuses," despite its lack of precision, is guiding the work of the OHCHR in its study on more effective domestic law remedies to gross human rights abuses. In the report commissioned from the OHCHR to serve as a framing paper for the study, Jennifer Zerk refrains from further seeking a definition to "gross human rights abuses." As highlighted by Flavio Siqueira in a Conectas' internal briefing, it is worth noting that the "remedies" section of the GPs (Principles 25 to 31) does not specify that their scope is limited only to gross human rights violations. No provision or commentary contained therein places priority on remedies for gross violations. In fact, any action toward the realization of the right to remedy should be based on commentary to Principle 12, which states that "business enterprises can have an impact on virtually the entire spectrum of internationally recognized human rights" and, therefore, their "responsibility to respect applies to all rights." In this sense, all internationally recognized human rights must be realized through effective remedies, and not only the most egregious violations. See Jennifer Zerk, "Corporate Liability for Gross Human Rights Abuses: Towards a fairer and more effective system of domestic law remedies," report for OHCHR (2014), www.ohchr.org/Documents/Issues/Business/DomesticLawRemedies/Two-pagesummaryMainStudyConsultationProcess.pdf. www.ohchr.org/Documents/Issues/Business/DomesticLawRemedies/StudyDomesticeLawRemedies.pdf.

[8] See note 1 above.

Importantly, the resolution does not restrict the mandate of the open-ended intergovernmental group to gross human rights violations.

There are still several questions and indeterminacies surrounding this process, but also some certainties. I group the "open questions" into three different realms.

First, the scope and functioning of the future treaty is still unclear. Will it apply to all human rights and to all economic sectors? How will the monitoring mechanism function? Will the process result in another treaty body? Could it take the form of an amendment or protocol to another treaty? If so, which one?

Secondly, considering that the treaty addresses transnational corporations and "all business enterprises with a transnational character,"[9] to what extent will it influence conditions if the main "home countries" of those companies decide not to ratify the treaty? Surprisingly, China voted in favor of the resolution.[10]

Thirdly, it is not clear how the adoption of this resolution will affect the implementation of the GPs. Since the HRC did not adopt the resolution by consensus, will the disagreements among States affect the ongoing processes of the GPs' implementation? Will the treaty process weaken the GPs?

On the side of certainties, leaving aside the somewhat dogmatic discussion on the need (or not) for a new binding instrument aimed at regulating the conduct of corporations, there is no doubt that this resolution brought fresh air to Geneva. The coalition of more than 500 organizations campaigning for the resolution's adoption helped nontraditional players to participate in processes for the first time in Geneva.

Seasoned players who have over the years accumulated indispensable knowledge on the issue of business and human rights and on the bargaining practices of Geneva (both public and behind-the-doors) were side by side with newcomers. Moreover, even without the full support of some of the largest and most influential international human rights NGOs (e.g., Amnesty International and Human Rights Watch), the resolution passed. We should celebrate the fact that Geneva can still be a source of surprises.

Ironically, the polarization between the Northern and Southern delegations, with the majority of the Northern countries openly (and quite aggressively) opposing the treaty resolution, gave traction to the treaty process. In their oral interventions, the EU and the United States publicly stated that they would not participate in the proposed intergovernmental working group.[11]

---

[9] For a critique of the term "business enterprises with a transnational character," see John Ruggie, "Quo Vadis? Unsolicited Advice to Business and Human Rights Treaty Sponsors," 9 September 2014, www .ihrb.org/commentary/quo-vadis-unsolicited-advice-business.html.

[10] In its vote, China positioned itself as being in favor of pursuing dialogue and cooperation to implement the GPs and to ensure their actual effects, highlighted the disparities among the countries in terms of economic development, judicial systems and their historical and cultural backgrounds, noted that the formulation of a new treaty is a complex issue, and underlined the importance of gradual consensus building. In Ruggie's opinion, the conditions and caveats made by the country are evidences that their support should not "be taken for granted." See note 9 above.

[11] See oral statements at http://webtv.un.org/meetings-events/human-rights-council/regular-sessions/ 26th-session/watch/ahrc26l.22rev.1-vote-item3-37th-meeting-26th-regular-session-human-rights-coun cil/3643474570001#full-text.

The future contours of this negotiation are still hard to foresee. In a sense, the June 2014 session of the Council created a stark division among states, those in favor of the "Ecuador resolution" and those supporting the "Norway resolution" (although truthfully the voting results did not exactly mirror such a division, as the latter was adopted unanimously and the former had thirteen abstentions and fourteen votes against it). The divisive setting in which states find themselves leads me to question whether or not such a division will also be reflected among civil society actors. Despite the significant support of hundreds of organizations for the new treaty, plenty of others (from the South and the North alike) are still hesitant, unsure whether the instrument will address violations occurring on the ground.

One concern raised by some civil society organizations about the treaty process relates to the meaningful participation of those which are not based in or do not have representations in Geneva. How should they keep track of the negotiations? How can civil society actors construct a coalition that can share information efficiently? How can those participating remotely ensure that the intergovernmental group appropriately hears their voice in the Palais des Nations? In this respect, I agree with Rodríguez-Garavito's argument in Chapter 1 on the risks that an exclusive focus on a treaty can bring.

2 *The Shortcomings of the UN Working Group*

Frustration with the work of the WG since its inception has also fueled substantive support to the treaty initiative. In 2013, three Latin American CSOs, Dejusticia (Colombia), Conectas (Brazil), and Justiça Global (Brazil) launched the "Observatory of the WG." The Observatory aims to analyze the WG's most important reports, question its restrictive interpretation of its own mandate, and participate in the available dialogue sessions. The Observatory's activities have rendered a clear vision of the crucial shortcomings of the Group. In a summary of the first two and a half years of work we stated that:

> The WG has given priority to some of its functions to the detriment of others, losing its original function as a "special mechanism of the Human Rights Council." The focus given to "best practices" and to the dissemination of the Guiding Principles (hereafter, the GPs) tends to ignore the main feature of the issue it is supposed to deal with: the asymmetric power relations between victims and enterprises. By refraining from adopting an explicitly provictims approach, the WG contributes little to changing the regrettable situation we live in today.[12]

---

[12] Conectas, Dejusticia, and Justica Global, "Working Group on the Issue of Human Rights and Transnational Corporations and Other Business Enterprises: a Review of the First Two-and-a-half Years of Work," 25 November 2013, http://conectas.org/arquivos/editor/files/6_Dej_Con _JG_WG2years_Nov2013.pdf.

Thus, we concluded that "the mechanism should establish a clear, transparent, and consistent working plan designed to address specific issues" and that "it should avail itself of all the prerogatives it has been entrusted with in its original mandate. Considering the limited resources, the WG should prioritize initiatives aimed at strengthening the protection of the victims of human rights abuses committed by businesses enterprises."

We made it very clear that in our vision "the mechanism should analyze communications regarding cases, and request information from States and companies. In doing so, the WG should incorporate the highest human rights standards available in its work."[13]

Subsequent to the release of that document, other important shortcomings have become clearer to civil society. Specifically, the WG must clarify the following three features in order to become a truly robust and effective human rights protection mechanism: 1) Membership, 2) Transparency, and 3) Company Engagement Criteria.

I argue these three topics are closely associated with the fact that "for the first time in the UN human rights protection system, it deals with the role of private actors in human rights abuses."[14] The issue's unique nature brings additional challenges.

1. **Membership**: While members of the group need to understand the corporate world, they must ensure that other stakeholders do not perceive their views and attitudes as lenient or blatantly subordinate to corporate interests. On this particular (and sensitive) topic, the WG has ignored some important issues and possible solutions. The selection process for the present members of the group suffered from two vulnerabilities:

   a) **Specialists with a more critical perspective of the GPs were excluded**. I noted through our close following of the WG members selection process that candidates who presented a critical view of the GPs were excluded after the interviews phase. Thus, this obvious "bar" curbed any possibility of creating a WG with the capacity to hold internal discussions based on a diversity of opinions and worldviews. This deliberated process resulted in

---

[13] The exchange of letters between Conectas and Amnesty International and the WG is reported in the chapter (22). It is interesting to remember that the WG never sent the answer to the letter to us, but rather sent it directly to the B&HR Resource Center for dissemination. In its first report, the WG said that it would not investigate cases of human rights violations. This might be a mistaken interpretation of the legacy of the SRGS mandate. In *Just Business*, Professor Ruggie explains how he convinced foreign ministries not to mandate him to have a role on adjudicating specific adversarial situations (146). "I felt that I had a grasp of the problems, I wanted to focus all energies on developing effective ways of addressing them, not identifying even more variations on their manifestations."

[14] See Conectas, Dejusticia, and Justica Global, "Working Group on the Issue of Human Rights and Transnational Corporations and Other Business Enterprises: a Review of the First Two-and-a-half Years of Work," 25 November 2013, http://conectas.org/arquivos/editor/files/6_Dej_Con_JG_WG2years_Nov2013.pdf.

a group that lacked a critical perspective toward the GPs. Moreover, some internal dissent would have benefited the WG by serving as a tool to bring back human rights organizations to dialogue with the WG.

b) **No clear rule concerning the impartiality, legitimacy, and independence of the WG's members has been adopted.** The WG's composition is not as diverse as it could be; it has a bias toward members with a corporate background. I worry that the WG has made no effort to set up specific rules disciplining previous or posterior engagements of its members.[15] This oversight – the lack of a clear framework for the appointment of WG members and rules to deal with potential conflicts of interests, such as "cooling off" periods – has served to augment the distrust of civil society on the WG.

Members could have addressed both issues in the June 2014 session of the Human Rights Council, but unfortunately they did not.

2. **Transparency**: The WG's funding has also generated distrust. Civil society actors have seriously questioned who is supporting what. Is it acceptable that companies pay for the WG activities? Should there be a rule for exclusion of certain industrial sectors, or certain companies? How should the WG disclose this information? The WG has been slow and confusing in answering these questions, further generating distrust about its independence from the corporate sector.[16]

3. **Company Engagement Criteria**: NGOs have severely criticized the organization of the Annual Forum on Business and Human Rights. They have cited the Forum's methodology and the limited participation of victims as some of the most serious issues at stake. However, another issue is an even more serious source of concern: the lack of clarity in the selection of companies that can be invited as speakers. On the one hand, companies, especially the largest ones that operate in multiple countries, face challenges that they need to address and the frank discussion of some issues could lead to solutions. On the other hand, the WG should establish some limits. The WG should not invite companies whose conduct is the target of consistent human rights violations denouncements to showcase their practices as "positive examples."

There were several problematic examples during the 2013 Forum. Organizations questioned the participation of Total, Repsol, Microsoft, Unilever, and Nestle. In analyzing the 2013 Forum, Tricia Feeney from Raid noted that:

---

[15] See, for example, the rule of the Compliance Advisor Ombudsman (CAO) of the International Finance Corporation (IFC): "CAO professional staff contracts restrict staff members from obtaining employment with IFC or Multilateral Investment Guarantee Agency (MIGA) for two years after they end their engagement with CAO." I am sure many other examples are available; the problem was a lack of willingness to address the issue of independence.

[16] A list of activities and partners is available at www.ohchr.org/Documents/Issues/Business/WGActivitiesAndEngagement.pdf.

In a particularly insensitive move, one of the few speaking slots has been given to Barrick Gold, a mining company that is currently engaged in a highly controversial remediation programme for women who were raped by its security personnel at the Porgera Mine in Papua, New Guinea. The OHCHR should be careful not to allow this event to be used by companies seeking to enhance their reputations otherwise the Forum risks turning into a cut-price version of Davos.[17]

In 2014, in an open letter to HRC members, a group of CSOs[18] requested that the WG address these and other issues, but ultimately the HRC took almost no action as the discussion over the treaty eclipsed the advocacy efforts to improve the WG.

The CSOs raised four main points in the letter[19]:

1) The WG should address with more depth and consistence the issue of access to effective judicial and nonjudicial remedies for corporate-related human rights violations;

2) In their work and reports, the WG must abide by the highest human rights standards as per international human rights law and the jurisprudence of UN treaty bodies;

3) The WG should prioritize the implementation of the GPs in state-owned financial institutions;

4) The WG should clarify its procedures to address alleged corporate human rights abuses, be more transparent over its funding sources and expenditures, and establish a clear working plan for the next mandate.

We achieved small progress in the "Norway resolution" text, which made reference to the challenges in the area of effective judicial remedies.[20] The resolution also organized a study on these challenges and instituted them as a new item in the upcoming UN Forum on Business and Human Rights.[21]

Although the resolution refers to the jurisprudence of UN treaty bodies, States failed to include an explicit mention of the Declaration on the Rights of Indigenous

---

[17] See CONECTAS, "NGOs Should Expose the Limitations of Pragmatism," 2 December 2013, http://conectas.org/en/actions/business-and-human-rights/news/8495-ngos-should-expose-the-limitations-of-pragmatism

[18] Cairo Institute for Human Rights Studies (Egypt), Center for Applied Legal Studies (South Africa), Centro de Estudios Legales y Sociales (Argentina), Conectas Direitos Humanos (Brazil), Dejustica (Colombia), FORUM-ASIA, Indian Law Resource Center (USA) and Justiça Global (Brazil).

[19] Open Letter regarding the Draft Resolution on Human Rights and Transnational Corporations and Other Business Enterprises to be Adopted During the 26th Session of the UN Human Rights Council for the Renovation of the Mandate of the Working Group, available http://conectas.org/arquivos/editor/files/Advocacy_letter_WG_business-humanrights_June_2014%20(1).pdf.

[20] A/HRC/26/L.1, Paragraph 6, http://ap.ohchr.org/documents/dpage_e.aspx?si=A/HRC/26/L.1.

[21] A/HRC/26/L.1, Paragraph 10, http://ap.ohchr.org/documents/dpage_e.aspx?si=A/HRC/26/L.1. The reference to access to remedies for victims of business-related human rights abuses is quite contradictory because the issue is included in the agenda of the Forum "in order to foster mutual understanding and greater consensus among different viewpoints" instead of establishing a clear vision of the gaps and the need of further developments.

Peoples or the jurisprudence of the Inter-American Court, both of which would contribute to the WG's adoption of the highest standards of human rights. The resolution also did not improve language on human rights defenders, defining public financial institutions as a priority for GP implementation, or clarifying its working methods.

It was clear for many participating in the June session and also trying to improve the "Norway resolution" that treaty negotiations dominated the agenda. Many stakeholders extensively bargained over the potential existence of two resolutions. In this scenario, states did not seriously evaluate WG's work and its shortcomings, especially regarding its methods of work, which states did not address at all.

II ROLES FOR CIVIL SOCIETY GROUPS

In the opening Chapter of this volume, in discussing the processes of experimental governance, Rodríguez-Garavito highlights that "civil society participation in these processes is an essential source of pressure for compliance with existing standards and cumulative regulatory progress." He also mentions Elliot and Freeman's argument that the coexistence of confronters and engagers benefits the effective protection of human rights. These two arguments inform the following discussion on how civil society can improve its efforts for corporate accountability for human rights violations.

First, human rights organizations should reengage in the monitoring of the UN WG. The treaty process will move in parallel to the work of the WG. Those of us in CSOs need to improve what the WG is doing, such as by bringing to the UN victims' claims and working to fill regulatory gaps. The WG should also develop a tool to document and measure the degree of impact of the GPs on the "real world."

Our call is for a rich and diverse human rights movement dealing with business human rights violations. We foresee five priorities for the coming years.

1 *Documenting violations*

Reports containing well-documented cases of human rights violations by business enterprises are one of the most important tools to bring violations to surface and to call relevant stakeholders to action to end the injustices and impunity. Despite limited resources, there are a growing number of reports addressing human rights violations by businesses. Impressive CSO efforts make possible this growing body of knowledge through their commitment to bringing the public robust and evidence-based information about the impact of business activities on individuals' and communities' enjoyment of human rights.[22]

---

[22]   Some illustrative examples of recent reports prepared by organizations in Brazil are Justiça Global's report on human rights defenders www.global.org.br/wp-content/uploads/2014/05/Na-Linha-de-Frente-III.pdf ; Plataforma Dhesca's report on the environmental damages and human rights

Some organizations, such as the Netherlands-based Centre for Research on Multinational Corporations (SOMO), have issued publications containing methodological guidance for researches aimed at documenting human rights violations committed by business enterprises. According to them, open discussions with the company about the objectives of the research are essential features of this type of research. In the spring of 2014, Conectas, Repórter Brasil, and SOMO organized a workshop in Sao Paulo, Brazil, about methodologies for enhancing research on human rights abuses by corporations. The workshop had Oxfam and Greenpeace as speakers, among others. The seminar brought together more than fifteen organizations working directly or indirectly with business and human rights, ranging from land rights to the regulation of media to children's rights. By organizing this workshop, we probably held the first meeting in Brazil with the specific purpose of sharing experiences and improving the skills of participants to conduct research with the objective of documenting cases of corporate-related human rights abuses.

The seminar allowed participants to share some good and innovative practices. For instance, the collective Movement of Peoples Affected by Vale[23] employs creative advocacy strategies to disseminate information about violations of human rights linked to Vale's activities. By using comic relief (despite the seriousness of the content), the Movement publishes every year the "Vale Report on Unsustainability." The "nonofficial" report, which purportedly has the dual intentions of calling investors' and society's attention to the controversial sustainability practices of the mining company and also of presenting an alternative to the official account. The report even uses the exact same colors and design picked by the company for its own reports.[24] Additionally, members of the Movement buy one share of the company in order to attend the shareholders' annual meetings to make denouncements and to challenge management's opinions and statements to investors.

Some of the main obstacles in the process of documenting violations is the difficulty to prove the causality between corporate action and human rights impact, and to have technical support to produce evidence. One of the most pressing issues is the need for a team of independent experts (e.g., anthropologists, biologists, engineers) to support building the cases. In many countries, some professionals are virtually nonexistent, such as independent chemical engineers to do tests in cases

---

violations associated with the Petrochemical Complex of Rio de Janeiro www.global.org.br/wp-content/uploads/2016/03/platdhesca_o_caso_do_comperj.pdf; Conectas and ICJ's publication on the obstacles to effective judicial remedies in case of human rights violations by businesses in Brazil http://conectas.org/arquivos-site/Brasil%20ElecDist-6(1).pdf; and Brazilian Interdisciplinary AIDS Association's and the Intellectual Property Working Group's case study on transnational pharmaceutical companies operating in Brazil www.enlazandoalternativas.org/IMG/pdf/5-POR.pdf.

23 Vale is a Brazilian-based mining company and one of the largest in the world.
24 International Movement of People Affected by Vale, "The Vale 2012 Unsustainability Report," (2012), http://atingidospelavale.wordpress.com/2012/04/18/relatorio-de-insustentabilidade-da-vale-2012/.

of air pollution and water contamination. Universities have played an important role as knowledge actors in some occasions. Unfortunately, there have been situations in which independent researchers, renowned in their fields and even linked to prestigious institutions, have suffered threats. One emblematic case in Brazil is the legal lawsuit filed by the German company ThyssenKrupp Companhia Siderúrgica do Atlântico (TKCSA) against researchers of the State University of Rio de Janeiro (UERJ) and the Oswaldo Cruz Foundation (Fiocruz) National School of Public Health (ENSP), following complementary studies that linked the company's activities to human rights violations in the west side of Rio de Janeiro.[25]

From the Brazilian experience and from the discussions that took place in the workshop held in Sao Paulo, we think that civil society urgently needs better strategies for disseminating materials and evidence collected through their work. Human rights organizations and groups of affected populations need to learn how to use social media and the press to influence society in general. Human rights organizations should also continue to prioritize advocacy targeting consumers in their overall strategies.

2 *Campaigning*

In terms of campaigning, Oxfam's campaign "Behind the Brands" has become an example of success. The Behind the Brands Scorecard assesses the agricultural sourcing policies of the world's ten largest food and beverage companies. It exclusively focuses on publicly available information that relates to the policies of these companies on their sourcing of agricultural commodities from developing countries. This could serve as an example to other organizations on new ways to disseminate information.

In contrasting Oxfam's use of innovative tools to the more classic human rights campaigning mindset, three issues appear as relevant. First, despite rigorous research underpinning campaigns, the dissemination of the report should not be an end in itself. Activists should aim to put the issue on the agenda and, if possible, to call for action. Second, a social media outreach plan is now mandatory. In the Behind the Brands example, you can track the product you use, find out how the company behind that product scores, and take action by using social media. Third, Oxfam has involved itself in the solution. If the company is open to discussion and change, Oxfam helps them improve their practices. This capacity to recognize small changes, which obviously do not solve all of the identified problems, continues to be a challenge for organizations accustomed to more classical human rights advocacy.

---

[25] The Oswaldo Cruz Foundation National School of Public Health, "Pesquisadores da ENSP são processados pela TKCSA," *ENSP Informe*, 28 October 2010, www.ensp.fiocruz.br/portal-ensp /informe/site/materia/detalhe/27947.

3 Litigation

Litigation against companies has increased all around the world. ICJ's reports on access to justice and human rights abuses involving corporations, which now covers ten different countries, possibly offers the most thorough review of cases of this nature.[26]

However, we perceive that despite quite extensive litigation at the national level in several countries (including in the Global South) the international debate has focused on the possibilities of litigation in the United States, the United Kingdom, and the Netherlands. Proponents have dedicated more effort to understanding the limitations of the Alien Tort Statute (ATS) and the recent jurisprudence of the U.S. Supreme Court, to the detriment of solid analysis of the litigative possibilities in the courts of the countries where violations occur.

In many cases litigation in the country where the violation occurs yields no meaningful results (and defenders know that upfront), but many others require further study on the legal possibilities. We also need to expand the use of extraterritorial jurisdiction in countries other than the United States and the United Kingdom. For example, possibilities of extraterritorial litigation in Brazil need to be explored.[27]

4 New tools for enforcement of the GPs at the national level

We need creative thinking to imagine more effective tools for the implementation and enforcement of the GPs. Maybe creating additional focal points at the national level? Or incorporating GP implementation in states' reports submitted for Universal Periodic Review? Some governments have developed National Action Plans, such as the Netherlands, the United Kingdom, and Italy, but these plans lack strength as they have a very programmatic and nonbinding character.

5 New coalitions

Finally, activists should build new coalitions. Broad coalitions involving "peoples affected by" a certain company, including workers, consumers, victims of evictions

---

[26] The countries are: China, Colombia, the Netherlands, Philippines, Poland, South Africa, India, Brazil, Nigeria, Democratic Republic of Congo. International Commission of Jurists, Access to Justice Reports, http://business-humanrights.org/en/documents/international-commission-of-jurists-access-to-justice-country-reports.

[27] In a study by Conectas and the International Commission of Jurists, elements for extraterritorial responsibility were identified in the Civil Procedures Act. Brazilian courts can appreciate a violation committed abroad if it can be demonstrated that the violating conduct was originated in Brazilian territory, if the violation creates an obligation that must be fulfilled within the country and if the company is domiciled in Brazil. There is a need to deepen this analysis as well as to find or build leading cases with an application of such legal provisions. Conectas and the International Commission of Jurists, "Acesso à Justiça: violações de Direitos Humanos por Empresas – Brasil," (2011), http://conectas.org/arquivos-site/Brasil%20ElecDist-6(1).pdf.

or pollution, etc., have increased in number and their actions have had greater influence. Such coalitions can also include persons in very different countries, as they are tied together by a common element that goes beyond territoriality. For example, the "Affected by Vale" movement has built this type of transnational solidarity to provide some protection to local communities and movements that have to deal more directly with the company. Most often they are the ones suffering the most serious threats and abuses.

We also need to enhance interaction between victims, consumers, and trade unions. Trade unions and workers in general can have privileged access to information and often have an intimate understanding of the company. Of course, they can have different interests than victims, but if they are convinced that the suffering of victims is a battle worth fighting for, these broad coalitions including "insiders" can achieve significant changes.

Ultimately, we need closer collaborations among organizations focusing on different business sectors and rights holders (e.g., extractives, tobacco, protection of children) to more effectively share information and strategies as well as foster a greater sense of solidarity.

FINAL REMARKS

Working on business and human rights poses new challenges to classical human rights work. The conflicts between victims and companies (that in many cases are backed by states) are very uneven. Those of us in CSOs have too much to do and few resources. We also have great difficulty producing evidence. Human rights organizations are still made uncomfortable in many cases by companies' requests for help in improving their performance. In addition, the regulatory framework, at least at the international level, is rapidly changing.

In such a challenging context, it is even more important to call for complementary approaches by civil society and for solidarity among groups. In a moment that requires abandoning distrust and divisions, the recent resolution for the adoption of a treaty creates the risk of divisions between those "in favor" and those "against." We need everyone. We need to take new groups on board if we really want to make substantial improvement in the coming years in ending impunity and enhancing the regulatory framework that governs business conduct.

11

Committing the Crime of Poverty: The Next Phase of the Business and Human Rights Debate

Bonita Meyersfeld[*]

1 INTRODUCTION

The UN Guiding Principles on Business and Human Rights (GPs)[1] and the adoption of the UN Human Rights Council Resolution on the elaboration of a binding instrument,[2] represent the latest stage in the evolution of attempts to regulate multinational corporations (MNCs). The advocates of the GPs propose a rigorous drive toward National Action Plans (NAPs) to implement the GPs; those in favor of a binding treaty veer away from the emphasis on NAPs, emphasizing the nonbinding nature of the GPs. Irrespective of one's view as to the best way to regulate cross border corporate conduct, we are all facing the "what next" question. This chapter posits that the "what next" question requires an analysis of the context of global economic hegemony and its accompanying harm – arguably the greatest violation of our age – structural poverty.

The chapter begins with an analysis of two specific structural flaws in the architecture of the GPs, namely: the context of poverty and the role of global politics in shaping the GPs. These principles must be considered in the development of a treaty if it is to be effective and genuinely fill the identified gap in the GPs. This analysis segues into a discussion of the various categories of players within the business and human rights debate who have been elided or inappropriately conflated. I challenge the current groupings by the UN into the state, business, and affected communities. I propose a revised categorization of relevant actors that

---

[*] The author thanks Tammy-Lynne Bekker for her helpful assistance with editing and reviewing the chapter.
[1] UN Human Rights Council, "Guiding Principles on Business and Human Rights: Implementing the United Nations 'Protect, Respect and Remedy' Framework: Report of the Special Representative of the Secretary-General on the Issue of Human Rights and Transnational Corporations and Other Business Enterprises," John Ruggie, 21 March 2011, A/HRC/17/31.
[2] Human Rights Council, "Elaboration of an internationally legally binding instrument on transnational corporations and other business enterprises with respect to human rights" A/HRC/26/L.22/Rev.1 (25 June 2014) ("resolution for a binding treaty" or "binding treaty resolution").

requires a profoundly uncomfortable review of the harm that the business and human rights regulatory system should be addressing, specifically structural poverty and economic inequality between the Global North and the Global South. Finally, the piece proposes two global adjustments that are necessary in order for any regulatory framework to be successful. These two criteria are (i) regional trade cooperation and (ii) the recalibration of the value of human labor.

2 THE DEFICIENCIES OF THE GPS AND CHALLENGES FOR A TREATY

2.1 *Design Flaw in the Architecture of the Protect, Respect, and Remedy Pillars*

Is there a design flaw in the architecture of the GPs' three-pillar framework? In theory, no; in practice, yes. The GPs are a framework that rests on three pillars, the well-known Protect, Respect, and Remedy triumvirate ("the pillars"). The effectiveness of the framework is dependent on the mutually reinforcing pillars, each operating at maximum strength. The success of the GP framework relies on a coexistence of three factors: a robust state that has the interests of its citizens at heart; a strengthening of corporate compliance with human rights standards; and effective remedial systems. If all three work together, the GPs would indeed produce a remarkable structure for attenuating corporate malfeasance. But, if one of the three pillars fails, does the overall structure stand?

Pillar one, for example, suffers from the reality that host states, in which multinational corporations operate, may not comply with their international human rights obligations to protect their citizens from violations perpetrated by non-state actors. Because of the need for foreign capital, host states in the developing world tend to compete with one another for foreign business. This may be achieved in part by keeping social and environmental regulation weak and labor costs low. This results in the oft discussed governance gaps, where multinational corporations operate outside the jurisdictional reach of their home state, in host states, which are encouraged to keep their corporate laws and regulations flexible. The result is a race to the bottom, where a deceleration of state control of corporations is accompanied by an acceleration of violations of human rights, environmental standards, and good governance practices.[3]

What happens when multinational corporations deliberately target states with high levels of poverty and low regulatory standards precisely to avoid the overhead costs associated with doing business in developed economies? What happens if a corporation operates in a state, which allows for, or is involved in, the commission of human rights violations? Is it justifiable for a corporation to still make a profit? Or,

---

[3] Bonita C. Meyersfeld, "Institutional Investment and the Protection of Human Rights: A Regional Proposal," in *Globalisation and Governance* (ed.), Laurence Boulle (Siber Ink South Africa, 2011), 174.

more likely, what happens when there is an incoherent regulatory system and a multinational corporation exploits that incoherence to maximize its profits, knowing that human rights violations and poverty may follow? And what happens if these scenarios play out to the detriment of the Global South and the advantage of the Global North and emerging economies?

When tested by the reality of global and economic exigencies, the pillars reveal fractures, some of which are hairline and can be fixed; others are structural and undermine the entire framework.[4]

2.2 *Design Flaw in the Consultation Around and Construction of the Pillars*

The GPs, as with all international instruments, are the product of heavily negotiated processes involving varying levels of power and control. Within this highly politicized context, the Global North has been the key driver of the GPs. While the Global South has not been absent, there are, however, two important questions to consider: *who* in the Global South has been engaged; and have they been engaged *to the same extent* as big business and states from the Global North?

On the whole, the Special Representative of the Secretary-General's (SRSG) consultation occurred with powerful and privileged individuals or groups in empowered locations.[5] The individuals who attended the consultations were state agents, law firms, trade unionists, academics, and activists who represented victims. The formally reported consultations all took place in major cities. The consultations (funded mostly by governments and corporations) occurred in Geneva (4), Johannesburg (2), Bangkok (1), London (2), Oslo (1), Brussels (1), New York (4), Bogota (1), Berlin (2), The Hague (1), Copenhagen (1), Boston (3), New Delhi (1), Buenos Aires (1), Salzburg (1), Paris (1), Toronto (1), and Moscow (1). Thirteen of the cities are in the Global North (if one includes Moscow) and five of the cities are in the Global South. The SRSG consulted in eight Western European cities; one African city; two Asian cities; three cities in North America; two cities in Latin America, and one in Eastern Europe.[6]

The African consultation took place in Johannesburg, the financial powerhouse of sub-Saharan Africa and the economic capital of an emerging market force. Johannesburg is the epicenter of South Africa, where the majority of wealth and

---

[4] Bilchitz, "A Chasm Between 'Is' and 'Ought'? A Critique of the Normative Foundations of the SRSG's Framework and the Guiding Principles" in The Human Rights Obligations of Business: A Critical Framework for the Future (eds.), S. Deva and D. Bilchitz (2013) 1, at 5–10. See also Surya Deva, *Regulating Corporate Human Rights Violations – Humanizing Business* (London /New York: Routledge, 2012).

[5] While there were engagements with local and indigenous communities, the details of the GPs were hammered out in boardrooms.

[6] "UN Secretary-General's Special Representative on Business and Human Rights, Consultations, Meetings and Workshops," Business and Human Rights Resource Centre, accessed 3 August 2014, http://business-humanrights.org/en/un-secretary-generals-special-representative-on-business-human-rights/consultations-meetings-workshops.

corporate power remains in the hands of the white minority of the population. This consultation could never claim to be representative of Africa as a whole or of the varying interested parties within the continent.

There are very practical reasons why the SRSG's focus was on the Global North (for example, the proximity to the UN headquarters in Geneva and New York), but it remains a truism that the GPs cannot be claimed to be informed by, or respond to, the full rubric of interests across the globe. This is not a critique of the GPs' accuracy, efficacy or their impetus in advancing the business and human rights debate. However, it is about their appropriateness for full-blown implementation.

The practical omission from *high-level* consultations of people living in poverty; people living in conflict situations; people working in rural areas; and workers themselves, means that the GPs have been informed largely by one set of constituents to the exclusion of others.[7]

This is a key challenge for the Intergovernmental Working Group (IGWG) on a binding instrument (established in terms of the binding instrument resolution).[8] It will be essential to the legitimacy of the treaty process that full consultation is undertaken, not only in New York and Geneva, but in impoverished areas globally.

2.3 The "Be Patient" Mantra

Does the participation deficit impact the viability of implementing the GPs? Yes. In time, the GPs may gain traction but this will not be soon. The GPs pragmatically call for an incremental approach to achieving accountability for corporate human rights violations. But are such remedial steps sufficiently meaningful when compared with the continued problem of economic exploitation? For the most part, the remedial steps imposed on corporations are characterized by voluntarism and corporate social responsibility – corporate accountability relies entirely on regulation by the host state, which often is not able to mitigate the harmful status quo. Whatever the strengths or weaknesses of these steps, they are, ultimately, (i) determined by those with power and, with few exceptions, (ii) come with little evidence of sacrifice or a commitment to change on the part of the empowered.

The "be patient" mantra may be practical but it is one-sided request. Those who must be patient are people living in poverty while those who benefit from delayed reform are those living in comparable wealth. It suits those who have the power to delay reform and it is an indescribable sacrifice for those in poverty to wait.

At the same time, one cannot ignore the politics of pragmatism. The SRSG has shifted the global discussion around business and human rights to an unprecedented

---

7   The ideal of participation by affected populations is at the heart of UN Guiding Principles on extreme poverty and human rights, which demands the participation of people living in poverty in crafting solutions to extreme poverty, see paragraphs 4 and 5 of the Preamble to the UN Guiding Principles on Extreme Poverty and Human Rights, A/HRC/21/3, 2012.

8   Binding Treaty Resolution.

point of engagement. We therefore have two competing, coexisting realities: (i) business (and some states) will not easily reform and they need to be led cautiously to a standard of human rights compliance; and (ii) human rights violations continue to affect communities, whose suffering will continue while multinational corporations slowly become comfortable with the idea of human rights compliance. This delay becomes especially difficult when those crafting the position have not partnered equally with those suffering from the status quo.

The limited participation of affected individuals and communities from the consultation process has had an impact on the content of the GPs as well as the extent to which the victims of human rights violations do and will endorse them. This is indeed a flaw in the construction of the Pillars.

The GPs therefore provide a structure that is compelling in design but relies greatly, perhaps detrimentally, on the variables of robust state and corporate conduct, with no clear consequences for noncompliance. These design flaws are not abstract considerations. They are the daily manifestation of human rights violations, particularly in the Global South.

These structural flaws will not be attenuated without addressing: (i) the inaccurate disaggregation and categorization of the multitude of players relevant to business and human rights; and (ii) the inaccurate diagnosis of the harm that needs to be healed. In the next two sections I address each of these problems.

3 DISAGGREGATING THE PLAYERS

3.1 *The Three Interest Groups*

The business and human rights debate oscillates around three broad interest groups: the state; the corporation; and civil society. This delineation is inaccurate and either excludes, or collapses, several distinct interest groups into this triad of players. This is one of the key weaknesses in the UN response to cross-border corporate conduct, creating the potential to elide important viewpoints. Some examples of this improper categorization are discussed below.

3.2 *Government and Business*

The GPs draw a distinction between the role of the state and that of business. This distinction, however, is often artificial. There are many occasions where the interests of the state (in the form of the government) and big business are aligned. This occurs mainly in two contexts: the illegitimate context of corruption of foreign officials by corporations and, the legitimate context of a government having pro-business policies that may be beneficial to corporations operating in the country but prejudicial to its impoverished citizens. Government and business, in other words, often represent the same interests, even where those interests may risk human rights violations and the perpetuation of poverty.

3.3 *Government and Citizens*

Similarly, a government and its citizens are not always pursuing the same goals and may have divergent interests. The GPs rely on the assumption that state actors will act in the best interests of the people they govern. This is not always the case. Government representatives generally make policy decisions based on the short-term view of the next political cycle. Such short-term political interests may not be consistent with long-term social benefits. The theory of pillars one and two, therefore, depends to some extent on an oft artificial conflation of government and citizen interests. The GPs' reliance on the state to regulate business assumes the fiction that the state will, or can, act in the best interests of its citizens. We see this for example in the South African National Development Plan and the associated large-scale infrastructural development legislation.[9] These plans seek to grow the economy and may well increase South Africa's GDP. The real question, however, is whether this plan is pro-poor and will alleviate the poverty in which the majority of the country lives. Increasing GDP is only in the interests of the people of a country if it reaches them. This is exacerbated by the proliferation of illicit capital flight, with South Africa coming in at number two in the sub-Saharan region for the highest levels of capital flight after Nigeria.[10]

The development and growth plans of governments in the Global South do not always advance the eradication of poverty. It is too simple to suggest that corporations working in such jurisdictions should avoid doing harm when a fundamental component of their operations, with the support of a complicit government, involves the flow of profits out of the country. It is not the norm that MNC profits flow into impoverished communities.[11]

Therefore, government interests are not always distinct from those of business. Similarly, the interests of government do not always include advancing the interests of their citizens, especially those living in poverty.

3.4 *Civil Society and Victims*[12]

The international debate has also collapsed several distinct players under the heading of "civil society." Civil society is not the same as affected communities and

---

[9] "Infrastructure Development Act, 2014," and "National Development Plan, 2030," accessed 3 August 2014, http://www.gov.za/issues/national-development-plan/.

[10] Dev Kar and Devon Cartwright-Smith, "Illicit Financial Flows from Africa: Hidden Resource for Development, a Working Paper of Global Financial Integrity, a Program of the Center for International Policy (CIP)" 1 (2010).

[11] Deva, *Regulating Corporate Human Rights Violations* (2012).

[12] I recognize the difficulty in using the term "victim," which has connotations of weakness and dispossession. I use the term respectfully and without subscribing to the notion of victimhood.

affected communities are not the same as workers. Each has a distinct contribution, which should inform the development of a global business and human rights regime, and each has differing (albeit overlapping) interests.

The label "civil society," includes a range of actors with vastly differing interests and contributions. NGOs from the Global North have more funding to address human rights violations but less proximity to the violations themselves. Global South NGOs tend to come from cities and are serviced by individuals with sufficient power and privilege to exercise the rhetoric of outrage against the abuse of power. The "victims," however, remain largely outside this realm of this form of advocacy.

The victims, who have the most knowledge about, and experience of, corporate-related human rights violations, are seldom core to the business and human rights discussion at the UN level. Their input is not central to the development of the policies intended to remediate the problems such peoples experience. So-called grassroots NGOs or community movements have limited resources and the imperative of daily survival mean that they cannot pursue the same level of engagement as NGOs, government and business. Unless there is a deliberate mandate and funding for the engagement of impoverished and affected communities, the international discourse – be it around the implementation of the GPs or the development of a treaty – will be wanting.

3.5 *Workers and Affected Communities*

Finally, workers and affected communities are not the same. They often coexist but workers experience a range of human rights violations that relate to their direct engagement with the corporate player. Affected communities have different experiences, which are often indirectly linked to corporate activity. There is also a multitude of types of affected communities, including: the community that springs up around a mine, consisting of workers' families and social networks; the community in one part of a country that sends its members to mines and factories to work in another part of the country; the community that supports agricultural workers; the community that supports factory workers; and the community that comprises home-workers. Within these categories there is further disaggregation based on gender, age, bodily ability, sexual orientation, religion, tribal affiliation, class and health, all yielding different imperatives.

In contrast, business has been broken down into several distinct categories, such as extractives, agriculture, financial services, retail, production, and construction. The GP consultation process, however, has not undertaken this nuanced examination in respect of victims of human rights violations.

The proper categorization of affected groups may ensure a more inclusive process and more responsive policies in relation to corporate-related human rights violations. In order to advance global corporate accountability, policymakers must develop a much more nuanced understanding of the distinct players. It is important for two reasons: first, we will not get the solution right without the *equal* input of those at the heart of the violation; second, we risk the solution belonging to some, and not to all. The solution as it currently exists is crafted from a perspective of a few who claim to know the perspective of all.

4 WHAT IS THE HARM?

The harm that needs to be addressed is not the Bhopal gas leak or Niger Delta devastation. These are examples or *symptoms* of the harm that needs to be addressed by global regulation. We have to acknowledge that the majority of tragic human rights violations occur regularly and largely in the Global South as a result of projects designed to secure the flow of profits to the Global North.

The GPs do not address or attenuate this problem. The problem forces us to question the very global structures in which the GPs were developed. This is the structure of Global North versus Global South (with BRICS and emerging econo-mies combining characteristics of both, i.e., that they are both the recipients of human rights violations and the perpetrators of human rights violations in other developing or least developed economies). The harm is that global corporate profit relies on, and often exacerbates, poverty in the Global South. And yet poverty is not identified as a human rights violation as such under international law. The current international law regime identifies certain socio-economic rights as human rights; however, an accumulation of the violations of the rights to water, to health, to housing or justice, – we call this "poverty." Yet poverty is not considered a human rights violation or a breach of international law.

But poverty is not an accident. Poverty is structural and continues *not* because of deficiencies in the people living in poverty but because of global trade and economic regimes, political and government policies, and an entrenched inequality which is well documented by developmental specialists.[13] If we accept that poverty is a structure,[14] then we can identify winners and losers in this normative framework. The loser is the Global South, battling continued poverty, thereby making such states prime targets for corporations looking for low overhead costs, lax regulations, and high levels of impoverished people who are compelled to work for indigent wages (i.e., nonliving wages).

It is also impossible to ignore the colonial gloss that continues to inform international law. For example, the prime focus of international criminal law has been African heads of state. In all these cases African leaders are responsible

---

[13] Amartya Sen, *Development as Freedom* (Oxford University Press, 1999); "The Rigged Rules of Global Trade," Oxfam International, accessed 3 August 2014, www.oxfam.org/en/campaigns/trade/rigge d_rules. and "Pricing Farmers Out of Cotton: The costs of World Bank reforms in Mali," *Oxfam Briefing Paper* (2007), accessed 3 August 2014, www.oxfam.org/sites/www.oxfam.org/files/pfooc.pdf.

[14] Oxfam, "The Rigged Rules of Global Trade."

for unspeakable human rights violations. The issue is not that such leaders are prosecuted. The issue is who is *not* prosecuted. The international criminal justice system is largely silent about the array of human rights violations and violators that emanate from the Global North. For example, Charles Taylor was targeted for his involvement in fueling the Sierra Leone conflict and financing the rebel factions. However, the individuals and corporations who bought the timber or diamonds, providing the funds for the war, escaped liability. The millions of dollars sent outside Liberia and Sierra Leone, often housed in banks in the Global North, remain out of reach of the citizens of these countries. And as the global loan and aid machine begins to grind into effect, Liberia will depend on aid and loans (often with unfair repayment conditions) while its natural resource wealth remains outside the country.

This one-sided approach to international criminal justice, fuels the narrative of Africa as dangerous and delinquent, with leaders who cannot be trusted with human rights standards. The architects of poverty, former colonial countries, and aid and loan agencies, sit as judges of African states and insulate their own corporate foot soldiers from any liability, either for committing human rights violations or for benefiting from and exacerbating structural poverty.

The GPs are embedded in this doctrinal preference that has created a reality in which the Global North benefits from the trade and economic status quo, a status quo they have no interest in changing; but a status quo that must shift if we are serious about mitigating corporate-linked human rights violations.

5 WHAT NEXT? PRECONDITIONS TO ADVANCING HUMAN RIGHTS PROTECTION?

Following the 2014 UN Human Rights Council's adoption of the Ecuador / South African sponsored resolution to work toward a binding treaty, the business and human rights debate has become more obviously polarized. There is no need to take an "either/or" approach to a treaty or GPs. Both options are simultaneously viable and flawed solutions. The GPs may infiltrate state and corporate conduct, achieving some level of consciousness and change. A treaty steps away from voluntarism and toward formal legal obligations for human rights violations. However, it is also true that the governance gaps in the globalized marketplace will remain and that the GPs are not designed to attenuate this. It is also true that a treaty will be a long-term solution but one that may provide a watered-down set of harms for which corporations may be held liable.

The polarization is not about the content of each approach; it is about power. The strongest economic powers in the Global North aggressively reject a treaty; those supporting the treaty on the whole hail from the Global South. Advanced plans to implement the GPs are from the Global North, with the European Commission and OECD favoring the GPs.

What does this polarization represent? It represents a rift that is about something larger: the increasing rejection of the status quo of economic hegemony. The UN system set about crafting a global solution, penned by the Global North. Even with the best intentions, the UN would always have difficulty claiming that a solution crafted by the Global North would be a global solution. The long, languishing dialogue around business and human rights has not included *as partners* the mothers of miners, the children who pick fruit, or the informal trader in inner cities across the world. Truly, the business and human rights debate and the GPs are neither global nor authoritative because they represent the views of those with power.

Therefore, there are two preconditions to any solution to the business and human rights problem, be it the GPs or a treaty: (i) strong regional alliances; and (ii) the recalibration of the value of human labor.

5.1 Regional Alliance

Developing economies ought to act in regional solidarity when imposing human rights compliance standards on outside corporations.[15] A regulatory body operated by a set of united developing states, could exercise a range of protective functions requiring human rights compliance by *both* states and corporations (possibly with adjudicative functions). The Corporate Responsibility Coalition (CORE Coalition) proposal, for example, encapsulates this notion of a cross-border regulatory body with an advisory and policy-making mandate accompanied by a dispute resolution mechanism.[16]

Imagine the same kind of body for an entire region, or group of regions, which regulates the role of corporate actors to achieve enhanced trade and human rights standards. A collaborative regional approach will help to reverse the pattern of state polarization in many developing regions. This pattern is one which has seen a cycle of static comparative advantage, where states loosen their labor protection system and ownership requirements of their natural resources in order to woo investors away from neighboring states with comparatively stronger regulatory frameworks. Powerful political collaboration can create a strong de facto system which, if well balanced, can both incentivize foreign investment and effectively constrain the extent to which investors can operate in a manner that compromises the region's human and natural resources.

The Southern African Development Community (SADC) offers a useful case in point. SADC members are rich in natural resources. However, members have not leveraged this shared strength to create human rights compliance requirements for foreign investors and MNCs. SADC is actually mandated to "promote sustainable and equitable economic growth and socio-economic development that will

---

15   Meyersfeld, "Institutional Investment," p. 201.
16   Jennifer A. Zerk, "Filling the Gap: A New Body to Investigate, Sanction and Provide Remedies for Abuses Committed by UK Companies Abroad" A report prepared for the Corporate Responsibility (CORE) Coalition (2008).

ensure poverty alleviation with the ultimate objective of its eradication [. . .] through regional integration."[17] This mandate is linked to the objective of promoting "self-sustaining development on the basis of collective self-reliance, and the interdependence of Member States"[18] acting in accordance with "human rights, democracy and the rule of law."[19]

Clearly, SADC member states have an obligation to eradicate poverty, pursue economic development through cooperation and collaboration, and protect human rights. This mandate of cohesive development and human rights protection provides the structure under which SADC must carry out its activities. These activities also include investment by and in SADC member states.[20] The SADC Treaty is very specific in this regard, identifying "trade, industry, finance, investment, and mining" as areas in which member states must cooperate.[21]

SADC's mandate to develop the region arguably requires the creation of a regulatory framework that protects the region's natural and human resources from improper exploitation. Individual states (who compete with each other and, in doing so, may allow reduced human rights compliance to secure foreign investment), through a regional body, could create standardized investment requirements which would mitigate the race to the bottom phenomenon. The regional raising of standards will create a chain of control that enhances human rights compliance by otherwise exploitative MNCs.

Such a body could operate in much the same way as large stock exchanges and apply an equivalent of the stock exchanges' listing requirement. The Johannesburg Stock Exchange, for example, requires listed companies "to show that it applies a core set of principles" relating, inter alia, to "environmental, social and economic sustainability, with good corporate governance underpinning each."[22] The Investment Committee of the OECD similarly has recognized and focused on reporting to ensure compliance with human rights standards in corporations' sphere of influence.[23] Regional bodies have a ready-made comparator to pursue regional regulation.

5.2 *The Power of Contractual Negotiations and Recalibrating the Value of Human Commodity*

Reform also requires the recalibration of the financial value attributed to different forms of work. Labor, management, and ownership are categories of work that are valued differently in the global marketplace. The latter two are seen to be far more economically valuable than the first. This type of value system is ripe for change.

---

[17] Treaty of the Southern African Development Community, Art 5(1)(a).
[18] SADC Treaty, art 5(1)(d).   [19] SADC Treaty, art 4(c).
[20] SADC Treaty, art 2(2)(a)(i) and 14(1)(m).   [21] SADC Treaty, art 21(3)(c).
[22] Johannesburg Stock Exchange SRI Index, Background and Selection Criteria, JSE and EIRIS, 2007–9, pp. 2–3.
[23] 2003 Annual Report on the OECD Guidelines for Multinational Enterprises, pp. 21–22.

The mining industry provides a useful example to explain this disparity. There are five entities required for the extractive process. Without anyone of these players mining is not possible. The players are: (i) the government: as custodian or regulators of the minerals in the ground, the government legitimizes extraction; (ii) financiers: the cost of mining requires the commitment of financial institutions, without which large-scale extraction could not occur; (iii) the mining company: mining companies have the expertise and project management experience indispensable to large-scale extraction; (iv) miners: no matter the extent of mechanization, mining projects will always need human beings to go underground. Without the individual miner, large-scale extractive mining is not feasible. Finally, mining projects need (v) the mine-affected communities, including both the sending community from where workers hail and the affected community that services the mine and its workers.

Although the mining project needs each entity's input equally, the output each receives differs vastly. This unequal sharing of the profits from the mining project is due, in part, to factors such as the surplus or deficiency of skills, labor, and education. However, it is also due to the inheritance of a particular historic moment, over 200 years ago, when the value of an individual was based on their race or gender. The work of white men has been, and continues to be, valued more than the work of others, even where the contribution of all is equally valuable.

When it comes to negotiating the contractual terms that ascribe value to human work, we should be injecting notions of danger, life expectancy, and difficulty of work together with principles of skills scarcity and education, which currently dominate the determination of human capital's value.

How does one ameliorate this imbalance in the value of work? Mining again provides a useful portal of analysis. The negotiation between mines and people living in poverty occurs in a context of information asymmetry and the exigencies of poverty. For example, South African mining law requires mines to adopt a social and labor plan in order to obtain a mining license.[24] In negotiations with mine affected communities and government, mining corporations must detail the way in which the mining project will improve human lives on a long-term basis through housing, education, sanitation, and other such initiatives. South African law, however, also allows the practice of mining companies to suspend operations for over eighteen months for so-called "care and maintenance."[25] Corporations have used the "care and maintenance" suspension to raise more capital when they encounter unexpected impediments to the extractive process. This temporary closure undermines the promise of poverty alleviation as migrant workers return home, without pay, for years. When a company negotiates with a community, they will not disclose the

---

[24]   Mineral and Petroleum Resource Development Act (MPRDA), 2004.
[25]   Republic of South Africa, Mineral and Petroleum Resources Development Act, 2002, www.dmr.gov
      .za/publications/summary/109-mineral-and-petroleum-resources-development-act-2002/225-minera
      land-petroleum-resources-development-actmprda.html.

possibility of a "care and maintenance" long-term closure during the life of the mine. Such negotiations are vastly different from negotiations between a mining company and a bank, for example, in large part due to the asymmetry of information.

Governments need to engage in regional exchanges and implement strategies to ameliorate this information asymmetry and unbalanced bargaining leverage. With stronger negotiating bases, the extraordinary value of human labor can better come to the fore. This, in turn, would be a step toward meaningful poverty alleviation and, with that, the reduction in corporate-linked human rights violations.

How can governments and communities achieve this? If communities who experience mining can represent and negotiate on behalf of communities yet to be affected, this could enhance information symmetry and equality of arms in the negotiation around mining. Governments, civil society and corporations should *facilitate* this engagement but the engagement should be from one community to another. This enhances information, equalizes negotiation and could lead to a far more stable – and equal – corporate project.

These suggestions are not without their faults and unintended consequences. However, they do highlight the structural inequality and myopic acceptance of a very harmful status quo: where the leaders of the Global South continue to be scuppered by conflict and the workers of the Global South continue to be valued at a radically reduced rate.

6 CONCLUSION

The UN system, as it pursues reform, should ask itself honestly whether it includes persons living in poverty as agents of change or as subjects of change. If the former, a different type of process and nature of discussion must begin. If the latter, we must resign ourselves to a deeply fractured and potentially unsuccessful battle to mitigate the problem of corporate-related human rights violations. We must also ask why we speak so little about the global trade regime, which institutes subsidy policies and trade barriers that perpetuate and entrench poverty. The topic is central to the business and human rights debate and without a rich and honest assessment of the harm caused by trade, the business and human rights discussion will remain just that: a discussion.

Conclusions: Whither the Business and Human Rights Field?

An Ecosystemic View

César Rodríguez-Garavito

After two decades of prolific academic production and intense policy debates, business and human rights (BHR) exhibits the traits of a differentiated field of scholarship and practice. A growing number of academics identify as members of the field and explicitly engage with each other, as this and other recent books bear witness.[1] Specialized journals, courses, centers, and textbooks – unmistakable signs of a research field – provide reference points for such a scholarly community.[2]

On the practice side, institutional structures and spaces have emerged that regularly bring together practitioners in the field. Transnational advocacy networks (TANs) have evolved and consolidated, from the Treaty Campaign and ESCR-Net's Working Group on Corporate Accountability, to the International Corporate Accountability Roundtable, and the Conectas-Dejusticia Observatory of the UN Working Group. Through online communications and regular personal meetings, they carry out the various strategies that TANs pursue in other issue areas.[3] They engage in information politics (by exchanging information about BHR cases, campaigns, and regulatory developments), symbolic politics (by invoking symbolically powerful cases, stories or characters to advance the cause of corporate accountability), leverage politics (by calling upon influential states and corporations to endorse actions or regulations against human rights abuses) and accountability politics (by holding states and corporations to their duties and responsibilities to protect and respect human rights). The field also includes an increasing number of domestic and international officials that staff new BHR offices in institutions such as Ombudsman's offices and OECD national contact points, as well as consultancy firms specialized in providing monitoring and

---

[1]   See, for instance, Jena Martin and Karen E. Bravo (eds.), *The Business and Human Rights Landscape* (Cambridge: Cambridge University Press, 2015).

[2]   See, for instance, the *Business and Human Rights Journal* and Dorothée Bauman-Pauly and Justine Nolan (eds.), *Business and Human Rights: From Principles to Practice* (New York: Routledge, 2016).

[3]   Margaret Keck and Kathryn Sikkink, *Activists Beyond Borders* (Ithaca: Cornell University Press, 1998).

certification services to corporations in order to determine whether the latter comply with regulatory standards such as the UN Guiding Principles (GPs).[4]

Contributors to this book engage with some of the core debates within the field. Given that they dialogue with each other and expose the commonalities and differences among them, and given that the debate itself is the purpose of this volume, I will not seek to extract general conclusions in this chapter. Instead, I will shift the vantage point on the discussion. While previous chapters largely adopt an internal point of view of the field – that of those who participate in it as norm makers, advocates, engaged scholars, and others – this chapter takes on an external point of view, that of observers interested in a sociological understanding of the field.[5]

From this perspective, I take a step back and ask: What do debates in this volume tell us about BHR as a field? And what future directions might increase the likelihood that BHR will contribute to improving the protection of human rights on the ground in the context of corporate activity?

I briefly address these questions in three steps. First, I characterize the BHR field in terms of the conceptual, normative, and political stakes and positions that are at play in it. I propose to view BHR as an emerging field whose analytical and practical boundaries are still being actively contested, with different actors offering contrasting frames to understand and act upon practical developments such as the implementation of the GPs and the negotiation of a binding treaty. Second, I posit that debates on BHR can be usefully viewed as an instance of broader discussions about the ongoing transformation of human rights at large. I highlight how BHR instantiates opportunities and challenges common to other spheres of human rights theory and practice. I close by proposing an ecosystemic conception of the field that may help it advance in the direction of constructive engagement with other fields and have greater impact on the actual protection of human rights.

THE CONTESTED CONTOURS OF THE FIELD

A distinctive trait of emerging or transitional fields is the active contestation of its boundaries. In the absence of dominant paradigms, such fields are marked by open debates between proponents of competing paradigms.[6] As theorists of boundary work have posited, social actors and analysts propose competing frames that embody different demarcations among social actors and understandings of the field.[7]

---

[4] For an analysis of the different actors in the BHR on the civil society side, including TANs and consultancies, see (my) Chapter 1.

[5] For the analytical distinction between internal and external points of view (with regard to the legal field), see Herbert Hart, *The Concept of Law* (Oxford: Oxford University Press, 1961). For a sociological understanding of fields, see Pierre Bourdieu, "The Force of Law: Toward a Sociology of the Juridical Field," *The Hastings Law Journal* 38 (1987), 805–53.

[6] Thomas Khun, *The Structure of Scientific Revolutions* (Chicago: Chicago University Press, 1962).

[7] Mark Pachucki, Sabrina Pendergrass, and Michelle Lamont, "Boundary Processes: Recent Theoretical Developments and New Contributions," *Poetics* 35 (2007).

Contestation relates both to external and internal boundaries. As Jochnik's Chapter cogently shows, other social justice approaches to corporate accountability were already firmly in place before the contemporary rise of BHR. The abolitionist, anticolonial, union, alternative development, and environmental movements, among others, struggled for corporate accountability long before the international human rights movement systematically took on the private sector. As recent entrants, human rights actors and analysts are in the process of demarcating the frontiers of their approach, as well as negotiating their relationship with neighboring fields. I will focus on external borders in the next section. As we shall see, while some approaches to BHR favor specialization within the field and clearer boundaries vis-a-vis other takes on corporate accountability, others are inclined to develop synergistic, ecosystemic approaches based on porous boundaries.

Here I am mainly concerned with contestation over internal borders, that is, with the type of boundary work that is evident in ongoing debates within the field. I distinguish between three types of debates: conceptual, normative, and strategic.

Conceptual Maps of the Field

A number of contributions to BHR, including chapters in Part One of this book, focus on *framing and reframing the conceptual boundaries* of the field. From different analytical angles, Ruggie, Deva, Melish, Backer, Vargas, and Rodríguez-Garavito question the binary frame (voluntary vs. binding standards) that has oftentimes been used to characterize disagreements within BHR, including those about the GPs. Although they come to different conclusions and propose different alternative framings, they all call for a more nuanced understanding of the conceptual issues at play.

Rather than rehashing the discussion among those frames, for the purposes of this chapter, I single out two analytical variables that cut across many of those frames. Distinguishing between these variables yields a more fine-grained view of the range of framing positions being discussed in the field. Some of the misunderstandings and occasional acrimony among participants in the BHR debate stem from the conflation of two analytically different variables. The first one is indeed the level of the "binding-ness" of regulatory standards. Contrasting views on voluntary vs. binding approaches (as well as hybrids between them) continue to animate the debate, as shown by participant observation of sessions of the UN's Forum on BHR and the civil society People's Forum on BHR over the years.[8] Diagnoses of the reasons behind this contrast vary widely: proposals focusing on a binding treaty, for instance, could be partially inspired by frustration with the lack of efficacy of voluntary standards,[9] by the need to reinforce the expressive content and impact of international rules,[10] by the

---

[8]   For empirical evidence about this discussion, see my background chapter.
[9]   See Deva, Chapter 3 in this volume.   [10]   See Melish, Chapter 4 in this volume

TABLE 1 *Types of BHR Regulations*

	Binding	Non-Binding
Integrated	UN Norms	UN Declaration
Polycentric	UNCRPD-like treaty	UN Guiding Principles; Multistakeholder initiatives

inertia of traditional legal doctrines and approaches,[11] by conceptual misunderstandings,[12] or by a combination of all of the above. Regardless of the reasons, the fact remains that the level of bindingness is a recurrent issue in discussions around BHR regulatory proposals, a variable to reckon with in mapping out the field.

Another recurrent variable is the level of centralization of BHR regulatory schemes. Some proposals place the emphasis on an integrated regulatory instrument, from a UN declaration to a treaty clarifying state or business entities' duties with regard to human rights.[13] Others fundamentally doubt the feasibility and usefulness of integrated frameworks in light of a multipolar and fragmented international legal regime, and suggest reinforcing the polycentric nature of the field.[14]

The two aforementioned variables are conceptually and practically distinct. This can be better appreciated if the different combinations of the two variables are mapped out (see Table 1). The resulting typology illuminates some of the positions in the debate.[15]

Regulatory centralization is compatible with different levels of "bindingness." While some actors in the field emphasize the need for a top-down, binding comprehensive treaty on BHR, others sponsor a nonbinding UN Declaration. Interestingly, although by design the GPs are polycentric,[16] at times their staunchest defenders seem to view them not just as a focal point, but as *the* focal point in BHR, thus approaching the integrated view and limiting experimentation in the field. Polycentric approaches may be combined with different views on the advisability and feasibility of binding standards. While the myriad multistakeholder initiatives in specific economic sectors embody a voluntary, decentralized approach, some

---

[11] See Ruggie, Chapter 2 in this volume.   [12] See Backer, Chapter 5 in this volume.

[13] For a defense of the role of the GPs as a focal point in the field, see Ruggie, Chapter 2, in this volume. For a proposal for a UN Declaration on BHR, see Deva, Chapter 3. For an overview of potential forms and content of an integrated binding instrument, see Olivier de Schutter, "Towards a New Treaty on Business and Human Rights," *Business and Human Rights Journal* 1 (2016).

[14] See Backer, Chapter 5, in this volume.

[15] I use the term "typology" in the Weberian sense to capture the contrast between different values of the two variables. In line with Weber's concept of ideal types, I use the extreme values of the variables (binding/nonbinding, integrated/polycentric) in order to clarify the conceptual contrast between them. As with all ideal types, the contrast between the different positions at play can be less stark in practice, and hybrid approaches are common. On ideal types, see Gianfranco Poggi, *Weber: A Short Introduction* (London: Polity, 2006), 24.

[16] See Ruggie, Chapter 2, in this book.

proposals for a BHR treaty take cues from the model of the UN Convention on the Rights of People with Disabilities, with its combination of broad binding standards and polycentric participatory implementation and assessment mechanisms.[17]

As in any typology, in practice, intermediate and hybrid locations are possible, and indeed common. The GPs themselves can be best understood as a form of nonbinding regulation that sits between integrated and polycentric approaches. While expressly polycentric, they were designed to be one of the "focal points" in the field by fomenting normative convergence toward a regulatory floor. In contrast to top-down integrated schemes, the GPs' integrative force is supposed to work from the bottom up: state, corporate, and civil society regulatory and political pressures are expected to reinforce each other and gradually ratchet up standards.

This broader map of positions helps understand why some regulatory proposals, such as a binding treaty, are criticized from very different angles. For instance, while Ruggie's objections to a focus on the treaty process are anchored in a polycentric nonbinding approach, others like Jochnik and Mehra object to a focus on any single strategy, and instead advocate a combination of all four forms of regulatory proposals, "always in all ways."

Again, these are not the only relevant variables in the debate; nor is the above typology the only possible way to frame the conceptual and analytical positions at play. As noted, framing and reframing efforts are typical of emerging fields such as BHR, and indeed contributors to this volume formulate a wide range of alternative frames. In Chapter 1, for instance, I hone in on the level of empowered participation by rights-holders and their representatives as a crucial variable to take into consideration in designing and evaluating regulations on state and corporate duties regarding human rights.

In order to contribute to the advancement of the field, alternative framings should not only be conceptually defensible, but also hold up to empirical scrutiny. This is an important analytical pending task for BHR. Thus far, the central place of law and legal thinking in the field has meant that normative classifications and generalizations, in which variables and conclusions tend to be derived from normative *fiat*, have been all too common. This brings us to a second set of issues, on normative and strategic alternatives, that cuts across discussions in the field.

Normative and Strategic Debates: Between Pragmatism and Principlism

A second layer of debates hinges on the principles and strategies that should orient efforts to ensure corporate accountability with regard to human rights. An interesting trait of the field is that these two types of debates have been lumped together, probably as a result of the influential "principled pragmatism" synthesis that John Ruggie, the former UN Secretary-General's Special Representative on

---

[17]   See Melish, Chapter 4, in this volume.

Business and Human Rights (SRSG) offered as his approach to his mandate. Principled pragmatism, he wrote, entails "an unflinching commitment to the principle of strengthening the promotion and protection of human rights as it relates to business, coupled with a pragmatic attachment to what works best in creating change where it matters most – in the daily lives of people."[18]

Different BHR actors have lauded and derided principled pragmatism in equally forceful terms.[19] For the purposes of this chapter, I am not concerned with engaging with this specific synthesis, but to deconstruct it into its constitutive parts and analyze the various possible combinations of these parts, so as to better understand and map out the diverse views in the field.

Normative considerations relate to the *principled goals* driving the work of actors in the field. Empirical research on the evolution of the field – including participant observation in key venues of the field and a systematic review of governmental, intergovernmental, and academic publications – reveals two main principles at play.[20] The dominant one, of course, is the effective enforcement of human rights on the ground. Although their conception of human rights and the extent to which they actually make it the priority in practice vary widely, virtually all actors in the field claim it as their guiding goal. The other principled goal that comes through clearly, especially in TANs' statements and actions, is the reduction of power asymmetries between states and corporations, on the one hand, and affected communities, rights-holders, and their representatives, on the other.[21]

Strategic considerations relate to the *practical means* through which enhanced protection of human rights and the reduction of power inequalities may be achieved. The richness and diversity of proposed mechanisms to advance these goals resist simple classification. However, it is worth highlighting a strategic debate that, although common to other fields, has been particularly visible in BHR: the debate between consensus-based and contestation-based approaches to regulatory and social change. While the GPs have been criticized for erring on the side of consensus to the point of allegedly constituting a "lowest common denominator,"[22]

---

[18] Interim Report of the Special Representative of the Secretary General on the Issue of Human Rights and Transnational Corporations and Other Business Enterprises, E/CN.4/2006/97, 2006, para. 81.

[19] For an early critique, see Misereor and Global Policy Forum, "Problematic Pragmatism: The Ruggie Report: Background, Analysis and Perspectives," available at www.wdev.eu/downloads/martens strohscheidt.pdf; for a largely sympathetic review of the evolution of the former SRGG's principled pragmatism, see Larry Catá Backer, "From Institutional Misalignments to Socially Sustainable Governance: The Guiding Principles for the Implementation of the United Nations Protect, Respect and Remedy and the Construction of Inter-Systemic Global Governance," *Pac. McGeorge Global Bus. & Dev. L.J.* 25 (2012), 69

[20] See Chapter 1 for the description of sources and methods.

[21] See Chapters 11, 7, 9, 10, and 1 by Meyersfield, Jochnik, Bickford, Kweitel, and Rodríguez-Garavito in this volume.

[22] See Deva, Chapter 3, in this volume. See also Surya Deva, "Treating Human Rights Lightly: A Critique of the Consensus Rhetoric and the Language Employed by the Guiding Principles," in Surya Deva and David Bilchitz (eds.), *Human Rights Obligations of Business Beyond the Corporate Responsibility to Respect?* (Cambridge: Cambridge University Press, 2013)

initiatives such as the campaign for a binding treaty have in turn been criticized for allegedly ignoring the political reality of consensus-based processes of norm making at the UN level.[23]

Some of the most pointed debates on BHR involve actors embracing different approaches to principled and pragmatic considerations. I distinguish between four approaches. The first one is *principlism*, that is, an overriding concern with normative goals coupled with scarce attention to pragmatic concerns such as political feasibility, trade-offs, and timing. As noted, examples of this *fiat iustitia et pereas mundus* view are not rare in the BHR field, partly because of the continued dominance of law-based reasoning and strategies, to the point that defending law-based means to attain substantive goals at times seems to become an end in itself.

The second approach is *pragmatism* tout court, that is, a dominant preoccupation with issues of feasibility in light of actual political opportunities for change, to the detriment of efforts to expand those opportunities in the direction of greater protection of human rights and reduction of power inequalities. As I noted in Chapter 1, although the GPs were designed as a consensual, pragmatic regulatory floor upon which normative improvements would be gradually achieved, in practice some of its implementation mechanisms (notably the UN Working Group on BHR) embraced an overwhelmingly pragmatic approach during its first five years of operation.

Most views in the field are hybrids between principlism and pragmatism, although with contrasting emphases. Whether one approach or the other is the noun or the adjective in the sentence makes an important difference in theory and practice. As noted, the former SGSR's approach is a qualified form of pragmatism in two relevant ways. In terms of goals, it is qualified by the principle of effectively promoting and protecting human rights in practice. In terms of means, it is inspired by a belief in consensus building as the approach that works best in producing change in the context of contemporary global governance. The trade-offs involved in these options help explain both the GPs' achievements and limitations. Attention to consensus, for instance, underlies the GP's gains in becoming a useful focal point in BHR, as well as its swift uptake in corporate and state circles. It also underlies the GP's regulatory under-inclusiveness (in that it does not recognize all of the core international human rights treaties as sources of duties and obligations)[24] and slower uptake and influence among CSOs.

Although not explicitly articulated as such, pragmatic principlism comes through in many contributions to debates in the field, both in this book and elsewhere. Like principled pragmatists, actors embracing this approach are simultaneously mindful of normative and practical considerations. But they are equally concerned with pushing the boundaries of what is pragmatically feasible, if necessary, through nonconsensual, adversarial means such as litigation and campaigning.

---

[23] See Ruggie, Chapter 2, in this volume. See also John Ruggie, *Just Business: Multinational Corporations and Human Rights* (New York: Norton, 2013).

[24] On this point, see Chapters 1 and 3 by Deva and Rodríguez-Garavito, respectively.

To my mind, rather than an issue to be settled by means of theoretical elaboration, the relative merits of principled pragmatism and pragmatic principlism is an open empirical question, one that may yield different answers at different moments and with regard to different debates in the field. What is sure is that the parameter for adjudicating between the two approaches is the one that they both embrace: whether or not, in practice, they contribute to upholding the rights of individuals and communities affected by corporate activities.

2 BHR AND THE HUMAN RIGHTS FIELD: BOUNDARIES, TRANSFORMATIONS, AND CHALLENGES

Conceptual, strategic, and normative disagreements are not unique to BHR. Seen from the outside, from the viewpoint of a sociological observer, debates within BHR bear striking resemblances to some of the core discussions about the human rights field at large. Indeed, due to its relative youth and remarkable dynamism, the BHR arena exhibits with particular clarity some of the transformations, challenges, and dilemmas of contemporary human rights.

Active contestation and revision of basic tenets, boundaries, and paradigms is not exclusive to BHR. As I have argued elsewhere, a sense of transition and uncertainty pervades human rights circles these days.[25] A new wave of scholarship debates foundational issues about the human rights movement,[26] and wonders whether we have now entered its "end times."[27] Leading NGOs and activists sense that the ground is shifting under their feet. In the words of the program director of WITNESS, a leading online human rights advocacy organization active in corporate accountability coalitions, "mountains of new information and rapid changes are coming at us from different directions at dizzying speed."[28]

The sense of transition stems from the convergence of three structural transformations that are pulling the human rights field in different directions. First, the rise of emerging powers (such as the BRICS countries – Brazil, Russia, India, China, and South Africa) and the relative decline of Europe and the United States point to a multipolar world order. Together with the above-mentioned explosion of soft-law and hard-law international standards, this trend results in a legal and political arena that is both broader and more fragmented. In this new context, states and NGOs in the Global North no longer have exclusive control over the creation and implementation of human rights standards, as new actors (from transnational social movements to transnational corporations to Global South

---

[25] César Rodríguez-Garavito, "The Future of Human Rights: From Gatekeeping to Symbiosis," *SUR International Journal of Human Rights* 20 (2015). This section is partially drawn from this article.

[26] Costas Douzinas and Conor Gearty (eds.), *The Meaning of Rights: The Philosophy and Social Theory of Human Rights* (Cambridge: Cambridge University Press, 2014).

[27] Stephen Hopgood, *The Endtimes of Human Rights* (Ithaca: Cornell University Press, 2013).

[28] Interview with Sam Gregory, Marrakesh, April 2014.

states and NGOs) emerge as influential voices. As a result, processes leading to comprehensive global agreements, such as human rights treaties and declarations, have become more challenging and protracted, as shown by negotiations on binding international norms on climate change and BHR.

Second, the range of actors and legal and political strategies has expanded considerably. Time-honored strategies such as naming and shaming recalcitrant states into compliance with human rights are being complemented with new strategies for transnational advocacy that involve a host of actors and targets of activism, including social movements, online media outlets, transnational corporations, intergovernmental organizations, universities, and virtual activism networks. Importantly, with the rise of BHR, national and transnational corporations have become recognizable actors in the field as TANs' targets, participants at UN venues such as the WG Forums, members of multistakeholder initiatives, and even objects of direct international law regulation.[29]

Third, information and communication technologies present new challenges and opportunities for human rights. As shown by corporate accountability campaigns coordinated through online platforms such as Avaaz and Change.org, tools such as social networks, video documentaries, digital reporting, online learning, and long-distance education have the potential to accelerate political change, reduce the informational disadvantages suffered by marginalized groups, and bring together national, regional, and global groups capable of having a direct impact on the protection of rights.[30]

The resulting uncertainty is not entirely comfortable for the human rights community, which has courageously confronted dictatorships, corporate abuse, socioeconomic injustice, ethnocide, and environmental degradation for decades. Being left with more questions than answers is disconcerting for NGOs that have come to be expected to provide clear-cut legal solutions to complex moral and political dilemmas.

Yet there are reasons for embracing the resulting challenges for human rights scholarship and practice. Transitions – between strategic models, intellectual paradigms, governance structures, technologies, or all of the above – represent moments of creativity and innovation in social fields. In human rights circles, this raises an important opportunity to reconsider some of the core assumptions of the field: who counts as a member of the human rights movement, what the disciplinary bases of human rights knowledge should be, which strategies can be most efficacious in a multipolar and multimedia world. Important tensions and asymmetries – South vs. North, elite vs. grassroots, national vs. global – are being openly discussed with

---

[29]　Philip Alston, "The 'Not-a-Cat Syndrome,'": Can the International Human Rights Regime Accommodate Non-State Actors?" in Philip Alston (ed.), *Non-State Actors and Human Rights* (Oxford, Oxford University Press, 2005), 3–36.

[30]　Ethan Zuckerman, *Rewire: Digital Cosmopolitans in the Age of Connection* (New York: Norton, 2013).

a view to overcoming such divisions and strengthening the collective capacity of the movement.

I discuss these challenges in detail elsewhere.[31] In line with the goal of this chapter, I will focus on how those challenges affect the boundaries of BHR and the human rights field in general, and how different actors in such fields are negotiating, shaping, and reshaping those boundaries.

Reshaping Boundaries, Accommodating Diversity

For both participants and observers of human rights practice, the most visible trait of the field is its sheer diversity, which has exploded under pressure from the above-mentioned transformations. New types of actors, strategies, networks, targets, and standards coexist with well-established ones. This patent plurality belies empirically unsound, monolithic views of the field as coalescing around a single set of approaches across its various internal frontiers (elite/grassroots, South/North, global/local, legal/nonlegal expertise, etc.).

Such diversity is evident, for instance, among civil society organizations (CSOs) in human rights circles. As Amartya Sen has argued, rather than a set of strategies or tools, the unifying theme in human rights work is a commitment to a form of moral reasoning that centers on the dignity of every human being and the importance of the basic freedoms that are necessary for a dignified life.[32] Different types of CSOs and networks, equally committed to that normative goal, deploy a wide array of tools and tactics and strategies. Rather than a strategic weakness or a fact to be obscured by unwarranted generalizations, this diversity holds out the prospect for effectively improving the protection of human rights in different contexts, including business activities.

Bickford and Jochnik have documented this diversity as it relates to BHR.[33] CSOs in the field include, among others, (1) national and international professional NGOs of different sizes and ages working on a range of human rights issues (from Northern-based organizations such as Amnesty International and HRW to the Legal Resources Institute, Dejusticia, and Conectas in the Global South), (2) international networks and movement builders (from ESCR-Net to ICAR to FIDH), (3) social movement organizations such as the Alianza Social Continental (the Americas' Continental Social Alliance), and (4) organizations not typically associated with the human rights field that increasingly experiment with human right frames and tools, such as Greenpeace and Rainforest Action Network.

---

[31] Rodríguez-Garavito, "The Future of Human Rights," previously cited.

[32] Amartya Sen, "Human Rights and the Limits of the Law." *Cardozo Law Review* 27(6) 2006, 2913–2927.

[33] See their chapters in this volume, as well as Chris Jochnik and Louis Bickford, "The Role of Civil Society in Business and Human Rights," in Dorothée Bauman-Pauly and Justine Nolan (eds.), *Business and Human Rights: From Principles to Practice* (New York: Routledge, 2016), 181–193.

The repertoire of CSO strategies is equally plural. In addition to law-based strategies such as litigation or international norm-making, human rights CSOs engage in advocacy for corporate accountability that seeks to influence their corporate targets through "market campaigns" aimed at putting financial pressure on corporations through shaming campaigns that create reputational risks for companies dependent on their brand image; engagement with investors, lenders, or shareholders geared to get the target corporation to address human rights concerns and violations; and coordination of global and local campaigns to simultaneously leverage pressure points at different nodes of global supply chains.[34]

Jochnik and Bickford rightly note that CSOs modes of engagement include not only adversarial tactics, but also negotiation and even joint work with corporations willing to collaborate on improving their human rights practices and commitments. Although controversial in human rights advocacy circles, especially in national contexts marked by a history of mutual suspicion and antagonism between CSOs and corporate actors, a number of NGOs incorporate this mode of engagement into their toolbox. Thus, as Kweitel and I argue in our chapters in this volume, the field includes both "confronters" and "engagers," and indeed many CSOs are hybrid types, as they move between advocacy and collaboration in different campaigns or different stages during a given campaign.

This is evident also with regard to CSO engagement vis-à-vis the norm-making processes examined in this book, such as those revolving around GPs and a possible binding treaty. While some human rights CSOs have decided to put most of their weight behind one of those processes, others simultaneously engage with both – shifting, for instance, between participating in domestic discussions on national actions plans to implement the GPs and critically engaging with the WG, to actively contributing to coalitions working toward an international binding instrument.

Toward a BHR Ecosystem

In light of the explosion of actors, strategies, and issues, a pressing question in human rights in general and BHR in particular is how to address the opportunities and challenges associated with the new landscape. I have distinguished two approaches that are evident in human rights practice: gatekeeping and symbiosis.[35] The first one seeks to manage diversity by narrowing it down, that is, by prioritizing a set of issues, actors, and strategies over others. This entails guarding the internal and external boundaries of the field through theoretical and practical gatekeeping efforts. For example, in some academic and advocacy circles there are continued efforts to build a wall between "core" human rights and other rights, such as social and economic

---

[34] Ibid., pp. 187–188.

[35] César Rodríguez-Garavito, "Human Rights: Gated community or Ecosystem?" *openGlobalRights* 23 July 2014, available at www.opendemocracy.net/openglobalrights-blog/c%C3%A9sar-rodr%C3% ADguezgaravito/human-rights-gated-community-or-ecosystem.

rights.[36] This happens despite the fact that social movements, NGOs, courts, international treaties, and contemporary theories of justice effectively tore down this fence during the last two decades. Similar gatekeeping exercises are evident in BHR, where a disproportionate amount of time and energy is spent on guarding the boundaries between regulatory approaches such as the GPs and a binding treaty.

Similar to what occurs in cities, gatekeeping efforts multiply in times of uncertainty and insecurity such as that which the human rights field is experiencing. The human rights neighborhood is changing: the gatekeepers and traditional guards (Northern governments and NGOs) no longer have the same power as before in an increasingly multipolar world. Trespassing has become the norm as new actors (from e-activists to local NGOs) circumvent the gates by directly networking with each other across borders and contesting the very borders of the field (North vs. South, elite vs. grassroots, legal vs. nonlegal).

From an empirical point of view, gatekeeping is at odds with the abovementioned transformations in the geopolitical, social, and technological context in which human rights work takes place. Gatekeeping implies that there is a group of actors that set the priorities, and therefore, act as gatekeepers who determine the international agenda of human rights. If this approach sounds familiar, it is because it describes the predominant way in which the international human rights agenda has traditionally been set, with disproportionate influence from governments and CSOs in Washington, Brussels, Geneva, or London.[37] Yet, looking forward, it is increasingly out of pace with a less uneven international order, a fragmented governance system, and a human rights movement that is much more diverse and decentralized than in past decades.

The centrifugal pressure in the field of human rights is intensified by ICTs and the rise of "network societies."[38] Priority setting is a fundamental task in forms of organization characterized by hierarchical structures and centralized decision-making. But they become less relevant and feasible in the network-like structures that key actors in the field have increasingly adopted, from intergovernmental governance bodies to transnational social movements and multinational corporations.

As noted, the cumulative effect of these transformations has led to an explosion of actors who use the language and the values of human rights, but have broken down the fences of the gated community. Among them are grassroots groups, online

---

[36] Aryeh Neier, "Misunderstanding Our Mission," *openGlobalRights* 23 July 2013, available at www .opendemocracy.net/openglobalrights/aryeh-neier/misunderstanding-our-mission; Emilie Hafner-Burton, "Beyond the Law: Towards More Effective Strategies for Protecting Human Rights," *openGlobalRights* 6 May 2014, available at www.opendemocracy.net/openglobalrights-blog/emilie-hafnerburton/beyond-law-%E2%80%93-towards-more-effective-strategies-for-protect.

[37] Clifford Bob, *The International Struggle for Human Rights* (Philadelphia: University of Pennsylvania Press, 2010); Charli Carpenter, *"Lost" Causes: Agenda Vetting in Global Issue Networks and the Shaping of Human Security* (Ithaca: Cornell University Press, 2014).

[38] Manuel Castells, *The Rise of the Network Society* (New York: Blackwell, 2009).

activists, religious organizations, think tanks, artists' collectives, scientific associations, filmmakers, and many other individuals and organizations around the world. They are mobilizing for human rights and corporate accountability not just through traditional legal advocacy tactics, but also through new ones like online campaigns that have put effective pressure on states and corporate actors to comply with human rights. This is what has happened in some of the most recent successful cases, such as the 2013 campaign against sweatshop labor in the Bangladesh apparel industry, which involved the transnational labor movement, national and international NGOs, and virtual activist networks like Avaaz.

In light of this, I have argued that instead of reinforcing the traditional boundaries of the field, human rights theory and practice must expand, so as to open spaces for new actors, themes, and strategies that have emerged in the last two decades. To capture and maximize this diversity, I have suggested elsewhere that the field should be understood as an ecosystem, rather than as a unified movement or institutional architecture.[39] As in every ecosystem, the emphasis would need to be on the highly disparate contributions of its members, and the relationships and connections between them.

From just looking around, we can see examples of this ecosystem in motion. With regard to the diversity of *actors*, current BHR campaigns involve not only (and often, not predominantly) professional NGOs and specialized international agencies, but also many others. The Oxfam-led 2013 "Behind the Brands" campaign is a case in point. Targeting the ten largest food and beverage multinational companies, it involved NGO allies, over 700,000 activists and consumers signing online petitions, investors, shareholders, celebrities, and a host of other actors.

Importantly, campaign actors included organizations and individuals that do not primarily identify with a human rights approach, but rather with alternative frames like global justice or environmental justice. This is an illustration of an ecosystemic view of *frames*, in which human rights actors brought to bear their perspective and toolkit on a broader conversation and collaboration, instead of rigidly imposing them on complementary approaches.

A similar approach is required with regard to the expanding range of *issues* that BHR is taking up. In addition to the treatment of workers and women in the supply chain, the Behind the Brands campaign successfully included issues of land rights and land grabbing in the context of food and beverage supply chains.

An ecosystemic approach is needed also with regard to the *strategies* in the field. In dealing with their corporate targets, the coalition behind the campaign included confronters and engagers. Oxfam itself resorted to a mix of confrontation and collaboration. It put pressure on companies by revealing their failings and human

---

39   César Rodríguez-Garavito, "Towards a Human Rights Ecosystem," Doutje Lettinga and Lars van Troost (eds.), *Debating the Endtimes of Human Rights: Activism and Institutions in a Neo-Westphalian World* (The Hague: Amnesty International 2014)

rights abuses through reports and interactive scorecards on performance with regard to human rights, and it effectively pressured investors and shareholders to in turn put pressure on the companies. At the same time, it engaged and collaborated with corporations willing to commit to designing policies and programs aimed at ending and preventing violations. Oxfam is now monitoring implementation of such policies and programs, and offering guidance to NGOs and corporations on implementation.

Finally, promising corporate accountability efforts creatively leverage and combine different *regulatory tools*. In addition to invoking relevant national regulations, the campaign demands were explicitly aligned with the GPs, and emphasized due diligence and disclosure.

Nurturing collaborations within the field and with neighboring fields is easier said than done. For global professional human rights organizations, this implies a difficult challenge: transitioning from the vertical and highly autonomous *modus operandi* that has allowed them to make key contributions to the emergence of the field, to a more horizontal model that would allow them to work with networks of diverse actors. For domestic organizations, adjusting to the new ecosystem entails pursuing strategies that allow them to link up with each other and using the new leverage points created by increased multipolarity, as well as opening themselves up to nonlegal professionals, social movements, and online activists.

In sum, the strength and effectiveness of the BHR will depend on whether it can operate as a diverse ecosystem. In a more complex and interdependent world, the field's challenges and questions should be informed by biology as much as by law and politics. And its actors would do well to spend less time on gatekeeping and more time on symbiosis.

Index